Kipling and the Sea

PRAISE FOR *KIPLING ABROAD*

'[Kipling] was one of the great travel writers . . . But despite his wonderful fluency, quality inevitably suffers with volume, making a selection such as this particularly valuable. This excellent selection shows us once again, if we were in any doubt, that this man really could write.'

Jad Adams, *Guardian*

'This perfect bedside book collects the most descriptive and revealing of Kipling's travel writing, never before published in a single volume. Kipling comes across as an engaging travel companion – thoughtful, curious, acute – and a writer perfectly able to evoke and crystallise the sights, sounds and spirit of a place.'

Clover Stroud, *The Telegraph*

'Andrew Lycett has had the good idea of making a collection of Kipling's travel writing . . . [he] has compiled a very enjoyable anthology. There is scarcely a single piece that isn't worth reading. Kipling's keen observation and gift for illuminating phrase are everywhere apparent and book will be welcomed by aficionados.'

Allan Massie, *Literary Review*

'Kipling's biographer Andrew Lycett presents a useful anthology of the author's travel writings, drawing on letters and journalism as well as on Kipling's published books and poems.'

London Review Bookshop

RUDYARD KIPLING

Kipling
and the Sea

*Voyages and Discoveries from
North Atlantic to South Pacific*

Introduced and Edited by
Andrew Lycett

I.B. TAURIS
LONDON · NEW YORK

Published in 2014 by I.B.Tauris & Co Ltd
6 Salem Road, London W2 4BU
175 Fifth Avenue, New York NY 10010
www.ibtauris.com

Distributed in the United States and Canada
Exclusively by Palgrave Macmillan
175 Fifth Avenue, New York NY 10010

ISBN: 978 1 78076 273 9

A full CIP record for this book is available from the British Library
A full CIP record is available from the Library of Congress

Library of Congress Catalog Card Number: available

Typeset by JCS Publishing Services Ltd., www.jcs-publishing.co.uk
Printed and bound in Sweden by ScandBook AB

CONTENTS

ACKNOWLEDGEMENTS

My two most valuable resources were the three-volume *Cambridge Edition of the Poems of Rudyard Kipling*, edited by Professor Thomas Pinney (Cambridge: Cambridge University Press, 2013) and the *New Reader's Guide to the Works of Rudyard Kipling*, edited by John Radcliffe et al. under the auspices of the Kipling Society and published online at www.kipling.org.uk/rg_index.htm.

My thanks to Tom Pinney, John Radcliffe, David Richards, John Walker and Commander Alastair Wilson for their assistance.

INTRODUCTION
POSEIDON'S LAW

KIPLING IS RIGHTLY ACCLAIMED for his love of the land and his admiration for soldiers, but there is a strong case to be made that his real passion was the sea and his quintessential hero the sailor. The reason, as suggested in his jovial poem 'Poseidon's Law', was that the sea was the ultimate (because most fickle and most dangerous) natural force, and its subjection a true test of a man's courage and resolve. Thus the sailor in those verses makes a pact with Poseidon, who tells him:

> Let Zeus adjudge your landward kin, whose votive meal and salt
> At easy-cheated altars win oblivion for the fault,
> But ye the unhoodwinked waves shall test – the immediate gulfs
>   condemn –
> Unless ye owe the Fates a jest, be slow to jest with them.

This poem appears in *Traffics and Discoveries*, a collection of stories published in 1904, when Kipling was at his most enthusiastic about the sea. At that point it had already been a forty-year affair. Kipling's first experience of the wide blue deep was of 'far-going' Arab dhows and sudden winds blowing up from the warm Indian Ocean close to where he was born in Bombay in 1865. In his autobiography *Something of Myself* he recalls his evening walks 'by the sea in the shadow of palm-groves which, I think, were called the Mahim Woods. When the wind blew the great nuts would tumble, and we fled – my ayah, and my sister in her perambulator – to the safety of the open.'

At the age of two, and again when he was six, Kipling made the long journey back from India to Suez, and then – because the Canal had not yet been built – up overland to Alexandria, and back to Britain. In his autobiography he remembered 'a ship with an immense semi-circle blocking all vision on each side of her' and thought she must have been the old paddlesteamer *Ripon*.

He did not return to India for many years after that, because he was left with so-called foster parents at a 'house of desolation' in Southsea, a suburb of the naval port of Portsmouth. There were some compensations. He enjoyed exploring the naval aspects of his new home. He was encouraged by Captain Holloway, a former coastguard who was by far the more agreeable of his foster parents. The captain used to regale young Rudyard with stories of his exploits at the Battle of Navarino, a sea battle against the Turks in the Greek War of Independence in 1827. He would accompany Rudyard on walks to the naval dockyards, where the young lad would feast his eyes on the sight of so many ships, including Admiral Nelson's flagship at Trafalgar, HMS *Victory*. The young Kipling once saw a ship which had been on one of the great voyages of exploration to the Arctic. Occasional verses such as 'The Carolina', composed when he was ten, show promise of great things to come and give a sense that, before he really had anything to do with the army or the land, he was being inculcated into an appreciation of the sea – and of its crucial role in history and in exploration.

These were not dominant themes during the next phase of his life – his schooling at the United Services College in Devon. Despite its all-inclusive name, it was very much a training establishment for the army and the imperial civil service. Kipling was, however, exposed to the bleak seascapes and the crashing of the waves on the Atlantic shore.

After returning to India in 1882, he began to appreciate something of the nature of sea travel as a global enterprise, part of a burgeoning tourist trade. Although, on his voyage out to Bombay, he was moping about, having left his girlfriend Flo Garrard behind, he was also taking in details, later used in his poem 'The Exiles' Line', of how the P&O Line acted as a universal transporter, enabling the business of empire.

> The Exiles' Line brings out the exiles' line
> And ships them homeward when their work is done.

There was another hiatus in Kipling's involvement with the sea during his 'seven years' hard' as a journalist in India. He experienced something of the great force of the ocean on his journey back to Britain again in 1889, when he took (and wrote about) the eastward route across the Pacific and then, after traversing the North American continent, across the Atlantic.

He found it hard to come to terms with the niceties of living in *fin-de-siècle* London. He tried to capitalise on his reputation as a chronicler of the military life in his poems, the *Barrack-Room Ballads,* but the sea had begun to tug at him. To complement his soldierly stuff he also produced seafaring ballads such as 'The Ballad of the *Bolivar*' and 'The Ballad of the *Clampherdown*'. After a visit to his old school in Devon in 1890, he wrote of the terrible power of the sea in his poem 'The Gift of the Sea', in which a mother mourns her dead husband, lost to the sea, as well as her dead baby. And there was also 'The Finest Story in the World', his remarkable account of a bank clerk who has flashes of his experiences in past lives as a seaman, both as a Viking adventurer on a voyage to America, and as a Greek galley slave.

However, Kipling came to dislike London so much that he had a minor nervous breakdown. So, succumbing to the 'go fever' he had attributed to his hero Dick Heldar in his recent novel *The Light That Failed*, he quit London on a mad voyage to visit his literary hero Robert Louis Stevenson in Samoa.

En route to Cape Town he met a naval officer, Commander (later Captain) Edward Bayly, who was travelling to take up command of a cruiser, HMS *Mohawk*, at the main South African base of Simonstown. The two men became good friends, and Bayly was to play a significant role later in the decade by introducing Kipling to the intricacies of imperial naval politics. At this stage Kipling was more interested in completing a poem called 'The Long Trail', which hailed not the miseries but the delights of travel on the ocean wave. Another taster:

And it's 'All clear aft' on the old trail, our own trail, the out trail,
We're backing down on the Long Trail – the trail that is always new.

At Simonstown Kipling was introduced to the camaraderie of the officers' mess, which, as he was clubbable, made a lasting impression. He particularly relished a naval yarn about a young naval officer who, on taking command of a new ship, had mistakenly and clearly ignorantly barked out an order the 'topmast wants staying forward'. These words only had to be mentioned in the mess for the whole place to erupt into guffaws. Kipling recalled the atmosphere fondly and made the neophyte officer the model for 'Bai-Jove-Judson', hero of 'Judson and the Empire', a light tale about imperial pretensions in southern waters, published in *Many Inventions* in 1893.

After the romanticism of 'The Long Trail', his interest in the sea now started to become more practical, as became apparent on the next stage of his journey, to Australia on board the Shaw Savill Line's SS *Doric*. Kipling did not mind the stormy voyage because he had found a new hero, the dour Scots ship's engineer, whose exploits he trumpeted in his magnificent poem 'McAndrew's Hymn'. Here was a man to rival the engineers and administrators whom Kipling had so much admired in India. Here was someone whose unsung exploits ensured that the empire ran smoothly. Kipling would give him his just metrical deserts. The engineer wishes for a man like Robbie Burns to sing his mechanical orchestra's – that is, his ship's engine's – 'song of steam':

> They're all awa! True beat, full power, the clangin' chorus goes
> Clear to the tunnel where they sit, my purrin' dynamoes.

Kipling never reached Samoa. Organised shipping lines did not run beyond Auckland. So he turned back to England, taking the opportunity to visit his parents in Lahore on the way. While he was there he was summoned to hasten back to London, following the death of his American publishing friend, Walcott Balestier. He soon found himself married to Walcott's sister Caroline and crossing the Atlantic to live in her hometown of Brattleboro', Vermont.

Once again he was not living by the sea, but from time to time he went to the Atlantic coast, north of Boston, and specifically to the port of Gloucester, out of which his local physician, Dr James Conlan, had once worked on the cod fishing boats that plied the Grand Banks, south-east of Newfoundland. Kipling pumped him for information, which he used in his short novel *Captains Courageous*. There is a nice description in *Something of Myself* of their nautical quests on the Massachusetts shore.

While living in the United States, Kipling felt homesick, partly for England, but also for India and the whole idea of empire that he had come to cherish. He dealt with his nostalgia for India in stories such as *The Jungle Book*, but his yearning for the British Empire was more complicated. As he thought more deeply about it, he concluded that the sea was an essential element.

So, while in Vermont, he started a new series of poems about the sea and its importance in British history. Some were generic, such as 'The Merchantmen' and 'The Liner She's a Lady'. When he wanted to rail against the greed of American publishers, he used an extended metaphor about the three-decker ship. Then there was 'The *Mary Gloster*', a wonderful ballad looking into the mind of a dying man who had built up a shipping company – a poem well worth setting beside 'McAndrew's Hymn'. There were also poems about subsidiary aspects of the sea, such as 'The Anchor Song', 'The Coastwise Lights' and 'The Deep-Sea Cables', which celebrated the laying of cables under the ocean, allowing greater communication across the empire:

> Hush! Men talk to-day o'er the waste of the ultimate slime,
> And a new Word runs between: whispering, 'Let us be one!'

Several of these poems were collected in his appropriately named *The Seven Seas* in 1896. That also was the year when Kipling decided to return with his family to live in England. He took time to settle down and it was not until 1902, after he had visited South Africa several times, that he finally found the home he wanted at Bateman's in Sussex.

During the intervening period Kipling lost no opportunity to expand his knowledge of the sea, particularly of the Royal Navy. While living for a short while in Torquay, he visited the training ship HMS *Britannia*, and the following year he accepted an invitation to attend the sea-trials of a destroyer which had been designed and built by the Thornycroft company. He also linked up again with Captain Bayly, his old friend from the voyage to South Africa, who invited him to spend some time on board HMS *Pelorus*, the new 20-knot cruiser of which Bayly had recently taken command. Kipling joined the ship on manoeuvres for about a fortnight and he repeated this for a shorter time the following year.

Kipling wrote a series of newspaper articles about these experiences (collected in *A Fleet in Being*). He also gave fictional form to *Pelorus*, one of a number of breezy tales about naval life, featuring a petty officer called Pyecroft. These started in the *Windsor Magazine* in December 1902 and were mostly collected in 1904 in *Traffics and Discoveries*, where the poem 'Poseidon's Law' runs alongside the story 'The Bonds of Discipline'. These are not my favourite pieces of Kipling's output – they seem to mimic Mulvaney without the authenticity. However, they have been compared to the work of C.S. Forester.

In the early years of the twentieth century Kipling maintained his nautical theme, in poems such as 'The Harp Song of the Dane Women', in which he returned to a favourite idea – about the cruelty of the sea which robbed families of loved ones. He also began to stress the need for Britain to keep up its naval defences – as in 'The Dykes'. He could not resist taking a historical perspective to seafaring: for example, in 'King Henry VII and the Shipwrights' (published in *Rewards and Fairies* in 1910) and in verses such as 'The Pirates in England' and 'With Drake in the Tropics' for C.R.L. Fletcher's *A School History of England* in 1911.

This was all part of a protracted propaganda exercise. Over the previous few years, Kipling had become increasingly vocal in support of campaigns to boost Britain's defences, particularly naval defences, as the threat from Germany became more apparent. Initially, Kipling was a friend of the First Sea Lord, Admiral Sir John Fisher, but he fell out with him over the matter of the modernisation of the British fleet. Kipling refused to support the admiral's campaign for a new Dreadnought style of battleship, backing instead Fisher's implacable and much more conservative opponent, Admiral Lord Charles Beresford, who argued that the construction of these modern capital ships would leave the Royal Navy too thinly stretched.

On 21 October 1908, the anniversary of Nelson's victory at the Battle of Trafalgar, Kipling gave a talk on 'The Spirit of the Navy' at the Trafalgar Dinner of the Royal Naval Club in London. In this he argued forcefully,

Isn't the morale of a Service a thousandfold more important than its material? Can't we scratch up a fleet of *Impossibles* or *Undockables* in a few years for a few millions; but hasn't it taken thirty generations to develop the spirit of the Navy? And is anything except that spirit going to save the nation in the dark days ahead of us?

His admiration for that service was evident from the fact that his son John initially hoped to serve in the Royal Navy, until his poor eyesight pushed him into an army career.

With the start of the First World War, Kipling took up where he had left off – with a naval story, 'Sea Constables', which was a virulent attack on the neutral nations, particularly the United States, which were staying out of the conflict. Among his few compensations around the time of John's death at Loos in September 1915 were his sorties with various units of the home waters fleet for a series of articles for the *Daily Telegraph*. These were collected in a book, *The Fringes of the Fleet*, which was later expanded into *Sea Warfare*, to include material about submarines and the Battle of Jutland.

Several of these pieces were accompanied by poems such as 'Farewell and Adieu', about the submarines he boarded in Harwich (although in the poem he had to pretend this was in Greenwich). Elgar set four of these songs to music, but Kipling was unhappy with the result and banned performances.

One of his most poignant pieces of writing about the sea was his poem 'My Boy Jack', which is not, as has been widely suggested, about the death of his son John. Rather, its nautical setting gives it the air of a more universal lament for those who lost their lives at sea. The Jack in the verses was probably 'Jack' Cornwell, a young sailor who was awarded a posthumous Victoria Cross for his bravery at the Battle of Jutland.

After the war, Kipling kept up his written output about the sea, in stories such as 'A Naval Mutiny' and 'A Sea Dog'. Following a subdued period, he continued to travel and sail widely – over the Mediterranean to Algiers and across the Atlantic to the West Indies and Brazil (where he went, in the words of an earlier poem in the *Just So Stories*, 'Rolling Down to Rio'). In Bermuda he was appalled by his encounters with Americans from cruise liners, a form of craft that he obliquely satirised in his late (1933) mini-play *The Pleasure Cruise*, which railed once again against the dangers of relaxing Britain's defences. This did not stop him enjoying the company of dedicated amateur seamen such as Peter Stanley, a doctor who had married into the Park/Taufflieb family Kipling had known since his time in Vermont. Stanley sailed *Trenora*, a massive ocean-going yacht whose design was based on a gin palace owned by the industrialist Sir Bernard Docker.

In his last decade or so Kipling was much feted in the official world of shipping. In an address to the Chamber of Shipping of the United Kingdom in February 1925, he aired deeply felt views about the importance of maritime transport in the British economy. In June 1927 he himself became an honorary Master Mariner and, that December, he wrote the epitaph for the war memorial commemorating members of the merchant navy.

Now he mixed with admirals and chairmen of shipping companies rather than mere sailors. Two of his new friends were Sir Donald Currie, head of the Union Castle Line, and Sir Percy Bates, who ran Cunard. Bates endeared himself to Kipling when he presented him with a replica of the alphabet necklace from the *Just So Stories*, which contained an amusing catalogue of shipping companies in its poem beginning 'China-going P.&O.'s'.

Kipling advised Bates on names for the new Cunard liner, *Queen Mary* (and built a small working model for children to sail on his pond outside Bateman's). In return, he sought his friend's professional comments on his story 'The Manner of Men', subtitled 'A Romance of the Middle Sea', about the voyage across the Mediterranean in which St Paul was shipwrecked on Malta.

Another friend was Lord Stanhope, Civil Lord of the Admiralty, to whom Kipling suggested that the proposed new National Nautical Naval Museum at Greenwich should adopt the simpler name of the National Maritime Museum. Later when Stanhope was first chairman of the trustees of the museum, Kipling donated part of his collection of nautical books to the institution.

One of Kipling's last poems, written in 1935, the year before his death, was 'The King and the Sea', a paean to his friend King George V, emphasising the latter's love of the sea. Around the same time, he told a visitor of his two unrealised ambitions in life: one had been to be an archaeologist and the other, fittingly, to build or buy a 400-ton brig and sail her around the world. This was a task which in a sense was accomplished posthumously by his extraordinary output of poetry and prose.

KIPLING AND THE SEA

Kipling was fond of nautical metaphors; he found them useful to describe his writing. One of his most memorable was in his memoir *Something of Myself*, where he wrote about his early ambitions to write a 'three-decker', one of the three-volume novels which were widespread in mid-nineteenth-century England.

> I dreamed for many years of building a veritable three-decker out of chosen and longstored timber – teak, green-heart, and ten-year-old oak knees – each curve melting deliciously into the next that the sea might nowhere meet resistance or weakness; the whole suggesting motion even when, her great sails for the moment furled, she lay in some needed haven – a vessel ballasted on ingots of pure research and knowledge, roomy, fitted with delicate cabinet-work below-decks, painted, carved, gilt and wreathed the length of her, from her blazing stern-galleries outlined by bronzy palm-trunks, to her rampant figure-head – an East Indiaman worthy to lie alongside *The Cloister and the Hearth*.

The market changed, but Kipling retained the idea that books were like vessels and publishers like ships' captains. This was the conceit in the two forewords which he wrote to editions of his works published in the United States by his friend Frank N. Doubleday and then, later, by Frank's son Nelson. In 1897, Kipling sent a foreword to the Outward Bound edition of his writings to Frank Doubleday, who was then working at Charles Scribner's Sons. Almost forty years later, after Doubleday had set up his own eponymous publishing company and passed it on to his son, Kipling sent the latter a new 'bill of instructions' to serve as the foreword to *A Kipling Pageant*, a selection of his prose and verse, in 1935.

As well as the nautical metaphor, Kipling also liked to summon up a sense of the Orient in his language. So it was no surprise when he addressed Frank Doubleday as the captain (*nakhoda*) of a *buggalow*, a type of dhow, carrying his literary fare or cargo to new ports or markets. Always keen to use his time in the East to literary advantage, he called Doubleday 'effendi', an honorific meaning 'master', in this case playing on the publisher's initials. By the time the younger Nelson Doubleday was in charge, Kipling was happy to describe the publishing business as a steamship, which 'has no sail but only engines which jig up and down, and must needs be anointed with oils as though they were dancing-girls. (In the old days, a sailing-ship was as a beloved wife, whereon, with a rope's end, one wrought miracles.)' Here is the first of those letters to Frank Doubleday.

A LETTER OR BILL OF INSTRUCTION

To the Nakhoda or Skipper
of the Venture
A Letter or Bill of Instruction
from the Owner
1897

In the Name of God, the Compassionate,
the Merciful!

THIS, O *NAKHODA*, IS a new voyage, nothing at all like those which you have already taken to Aden or Muscat, or even to Macassar and the islands where we can count upon the monsoons. Therefore consider the matter carefully. I have given you a new compass, with new rigging, masts, sails, and other gear suitable to the *buggalow*, and these cannot be picked up for the asking at Sewree or on Sion Bunder. The cargo is all in new mats, stowed like by like, to be reached more easily; and I have painted her before and behind, and I have put a new plank deck in place of the old bamboo one, and the tiller-ropes are new as well. This is at my risk, and the returns must be prepared with zeal and a single heart. Many men of the seas have told me lies, secretly selling anchors and cables and ascribing the loss to the waves, sharks, and seafairies. That was long ago, O *Nakhoda*, and now I do not believe all the stories that come up from the beaches.

The road is West and by South from England, where she will not touch, for the cargo is all for the Western ports, and these, if Allah please, you will find upon the other side of the sea. It is cold water, heavy with fog, and ships go up and down in their hundreds bellowing. Avoid these, for they are of iron and suddenly divide wooden vessels. None the less I have carried many cargoes across, and in lighter craft than the *buggalow*.

The men of those ports – I have lived among them, and Allah, whose name be exalted, has augmented my understanding – come down to trade early in the day, and their hours are longer than we use in the East. Do not, then, sleep in the forenoon or sling a hammock under the stern-awnings; neither unroll the sleeping-mats at sundown.

On Bhao Malung we pray before the voyage; at the Jakaria Musjid we give thanks when the voyage is over, but during the voyage we must trade.

In trading it is to be remembered that there be many who can immediately discern the bad from the good. Do not seek to overwhelm such men with market-talk, or else we two are shamed. Say nothing: let them choose; and throw a sail over certain bales of lesser worth.

Yet there be others who, stamping on the deck and talking loud, infallibly choose the worst. To these it is lawful to sell beads, brass rods, and coarse cloths, since it is written: 'The blind pay for him who hath eyes.'

And there is a third muster, very cunning in the outside of things and full of words as the foresail of wind. Take these to the lower hold and show them that I do not altogether sell toys or looking-glasses.

Remember, too, that many of the cloths are double- and treble-figured, giving a new pattern in a shift of light. Some are best seen in full sun, others under a lamp, and a few are only good to be used in dark places where they were made. The women should know this.

When, however, the little children come down to the beaches hide away that which is uncomely; let down the gangplank with the railing on either hand; and spare nothing of the painted clay figures, the talking apes, the dancing bears, the coloured lights, or the sweetmeats to give them pleasure. Thus they will first plague their parents to buy, and later – for a child's memory is very long – will bring down their own babes when we return. But have a care that they do not wander unchecked through all the holds or sully themselves in the bilges.

But the chief part of our business lies with men who are wearied at the end of the day. It is for the sake of these men that I have laded the *buggalow*. Seek these, O *Nakhoda*, before all others – at the end of the day, as I have said, and in whatever dress (I have put many dresses aboard) may make them look up. Then, little by little, entice them away from their houses and their occupations till they come aboard the *buggalow*. And whether they descend into the run and read the private marks I have put upon the bales, or whether they lie upon the deck in the moonlight pricing the small-arms and krises; whether they stare a little and go overside again; or whether they take passage in the *buggalow* for a far voyage, you are the servant of these men, O *Nakhoda*, and the *buggalow* is theirs so long as they please. For though I am only a trader with no ware upon which there is not an open price, I do not forget how, when I was wearied at the end of the day, certain great captains sold me for a little silver that which I could not now find in any market. Pay, then, that debt to these men who are my brothers. (They will not bring their womenfolk aboard, so the talk may be trimmed with a slack-sheet.)

The chances of the sea are many and come on all. If ye spy any struggling in broken water or on hen-coops that roll over and over, do not consider the voyage, but go to him, and, with the tackle I have put aboard for such use, work as Allah allows to his comfort. I have myself been many times extricated from calamity by ships whose very names and *Nakhodas* were unknown to me.

Answer questions as to the sun, moon, and stars openly, according to the custom of the sea; for we find our way thereon only by the Lights of God the refuge of terminations which are common to all. It is not needed to show strangers our charts, for these be of man's making, and each must prick his own for himself.

Do not press her overmuch in a following wind, nor think that one good slant will serve without change to land. And I have met long-lasting calms.

I know that all chance-found wreckage is the free gift of Allah to him who finds it, but still I say let not my *buggalow* be first in this work. It is not auspicious to use stray-gathered gear; and who knows but in the very next port may wait the lawful owner and an open shame?

For the rest, her place in port is sideways to the quay, with all hatches clear; and your place, O *Nakhoda*, is upon her after-deck by the gangway, to receive those coming aboard, to make my salaams to friends who remember me when I traded there, to open out the bales, to tempt new men to buy, to give no credit, and to keep a strict account of all.

On the black water it must be as it is ordained, but in my estimation she is well found. Get ready now, and take her out when the wind serves, remembering this one thing sure in all uncertainty; as it is written:–

O true believer, his destiny none can escape: And safe are we against all that is not predestined!

[Written 1897, collected in *Two Forewords*, which was published privately in 1935, and in Sussex and Burwash editions of Kipling's work of 1938 and 1941, respectively.]

�֍ ✖ ✖

Kipling addressed five basic themes in his poetry about the sea. It is worth giving a couple of examples of each, before adopting a more chronological approach to the rest of his output.

One theme was his sense of the power and unpredictability of the ocean. He was alert to its magnificence, as well as to its capacity to wreak havoc in people's lives.

POSEIDON'S LAW

W<small>HEN THE ROBUST AND</small> Brass-bound Man commissioned first for Sea
His fragile raft, Poseidon laughed, and 'Mariner', said he,
'Behold, a Law immutable I lay on thee and thine,
That never shall ye act or tell a falsehood at my shrine.

'Let Zeus adjudge your landward kin whose votive meal and salt
At easy-cheated altars win oblivion for the fault,
But you the unhoodwinked wave shall test – the immediate gulf
condemn –
Except ye owe the Fates a jest, be slow to jest with them.

Ye shall not clear by Greekly speech, nor cozen from your path
The twinkling shoal, the leeward beach, or Hadria's white-lipped
wrath;
Nor tempt with painted cloth for wood my fraud-avenging hosts;
Nor make at all, or all make good, your bulwarks and your boasts.

Now and henceforward serve unshod, through wet and wakeful
shifts,
A present and oppressive God, but take, to aid, my gifts –
The wide and windward-opening eye, the large and lavish hand,
The soul that cannot tell a lie – except upon the land!'

In dromond and in catafract – wet, wakeful, windward-eyed –
He kept Poseidon's Law intact (his ship and freight beside),
But, once discharged the dromond's hold, the bireme beached
once more,
Splendaciously mendacious rolled the Brass-bound Man ashore.
. . .

The thranite now and thalamite are pressures low and high,
And where three hundred blades bit white the twin-propellers ply.
The God that hailed, the keel that sailed are changed beyond
recall,
But the robust and Brass-bound Man he is not changed at all!

From Punt returned, from Phormio's Fleet, from Javan and Gadire,
He strongly occupies the seat about the tavern fire,
And, moist with much Falernian or smoked Massilian juice,
Revenges there the Brass-bound Man his long-enforced truce!

[First published in *Traffics and Discoveries* (London: Macmillan; New York:
Doubleday, Page, 1904).]

✠　✠　✠

THE GIFT OF THE SEA

THE DEAD CHILD LAY in the shroud,
   And the widow watched beside;
And her mother slept, and the Channel swept
   The gale in the teeth of the tide.

But the mother laughed at all.
   'I have lost my man in the sea,
And the child is dead. Be still,' she said,
   'What more can ye do to me?'
The widow watched the dead,
   And the candle guttered low,
And she tried to sing the Passing Song
   That bids the poor soul go.

And 'Mary take you now,' she sang,
   'That lay against my heart.'
And 'Mary smooth your crib to-night,'
   But she could not say 'Depart.'

Then came a cry from the sea,
   But the sea-rime blinded the glass,
And 'Heard ye nothing, mother?' she said,
   ''Tis the child that waits to pass.'

And the nodding mother sighed:
   ''Tis a lambing ewe in the whin,
For why should the christened soul cry out
   That never knew of sin?'

'O feet I have held in my hand,
   O hands at my heart to catch,
How should they know the road to go,
   And how should they lift the latch?'

They laid a sheet to the door,
   With the little quilt atop,
That it might not hurt from the cold or the dirt,
   But the crying would not stop.

The widow lifted the latch
　And strained her eyes to see,
And opened the door on the bitter shore
　To let the soul go free.

There was neither glimmer nor ghost,
　There was neither spirit nor spark,
And 'Heard ye nothing, mother?' she said,
　''Tis crying for me in the dark.'

And the nodding mother sighed:
　''Tis sorrow makes ye dull;
Have ye yet to learn the cry of the tern,
　Or the wail of the wind-blown gull?'

'The terns are blown inland,
　The grey gull follows the plough.
'Twas never a bird, the voice I heard,
　O mother, I hear it now!'

'Lie still, dear lamb, lie still;
　The child is passed from harm,
'Tis the ache in your breast that broke your rest,
　And the feel of an empty arm.'

She put her mother aside,
　'In Mary's name let be!
For the peace of my soul I must go,' she said,
　And she went to the calling sea.

In the heel of the wind-bit pier,
　Where the twisted weed was piled,
She came to the life she had missed by an hour,
　For she came to a little child.

She laid it into her breast,
　And back to her mother she came,
But it would not feed and it would not heed,
　Though she gave it her own child's name.

And the dead child dripped on her breast,
    And her own in the shroud lay stark;
And 'God forgive us, mother,' she said,
    'We let it die in the dark!'

[First published in the *English Illustrated Magazine* on 17 August 1890 and also in the *New York Tribune*, collected in *Barrack-Room Ballads and Other Verses* (London: Methuen, 1892). The American edition of this book, entitled *Ballads and Barrack-Room Ballads* (New York: Macmillan and Company, 1892), was published a week before the British one.]

❈ ❈ ❈

Kipling was always very conscious of the crucial role that the sea had played in the history of the British, an island race.

THE COASTWISE LIGHTS

OUR BROWS ARE BOUND with spindrift and the weed is on our
    knees;
Our loins are battered 'neath us by the swinging, smoking seas.
From reef and rock and skerry – over headland, ness, and voe –
The Coastwise Lights of England watch the ships of England go!

Through the endless summer evenings, on the lineless, level floors;
Through the yelling Channel tempest when the siren hoots and
    roars –
By day the dipping house-flag and by night the rocket's trail –
As the sheep that graze behind us so we know them where they
    hail.

We bridge across the dark and bid the helmsman have a care,
The flash that wheeling inland wakes his sleeping wife to prayer;
From our vexed eyries, head to gale, we bind in burning chains
The lover from the sea-rim drawn – his love in English lanes.

We greet the clippers wing-and-wing that race the Southern wool;
We warn the crawling cargo-tanks of Bremen, Leith, and Hull;

To each and all our equal lamp at peril of the sea –
The white wall-sided war-ships or the whalers of Dundee!

Come up, come in from Eastward, from the guardports of the
    Morn!
Beat up, beat in from Southerly, O gipsies of the Horn!
Swift shuttles of an Empire's loom that weave us, main to main,
The Coastwise Lights of England give you welcome back again!

Go, get you gone up-Channel with the sea-crust on your plates;
Go, get you into London with the burden of your freights!
Haste, for they talk of Empire there, and say, if any seek,
The Lights of England sent you and by silence shall ye speak!

[First published in the *English Illustrated Magazine*, May 1893, as one of the six sub-sectional poems to 'A Song of the English'. It was then collected in *The Seven Seas* (London: Methuen; New York: Appleton, 1896).

   'The Seven Seas' referred to the North Atlantic, South Atlantic, North Pacific, South Pacific, the Arctic, the Indian Ocean and the Mediterranean Sea. 'It's an unscientific system but it covers all the seas with which our Empire and Army are concerned.' (Letter from Kipling to Captain G.A. Robinson, 29 August 1917.)]

✠ ✠ ✠

BIG STEAMERS

'OH, WHERE ARE YOU going to, all you Big Steamers,
    With England's own coal, up and down the salt seas?'
'We are going to fetch you your bread and your butter,
    Your beef, pork, and mutton, eggs, apples, and cheese.'

'And where will you fetch it from, all you Big Steamers,
    And where shall I write you when you are away?'
'We fetch it from Melbourne, Quebec, and Vancouver.
    Address us at Hobart, Hong-Kong, and Bombay.'

'But if anything happened to all you Big Steamers,
    And suppose you were wrecked up and down the salt sea?'

'Why, you'd have no coffee or bacon for breakfast,
    And you'd have no muffins or toast for your tea.'

'Then I'll pray for fine weather for all you Big Steamers,
    For little blue billows and breezes so soft.'
'Oh, billows and breezes don't bother Big Steamers:
    We're iron below and steel-rigging aloft.'

'Then I'll build a new lighthouse for all you Big Steamers,
    With plenty wise pilots to pilot you through.'
'Oh, the Channel's as bright as a ball-room already,
    And pilots are thicker than pilchards at Looe.'

'Then what can I do for you, all you Big Steamers,
    Oh, what can I do for your comfort and good?'
'Send out your big warships to watch your big waters,
    That no one may stop us from bringing you food.'

'For the bread that you eat and the biscuits you nibble,
    The sweets that you suck and the joints that you carve,
They are brought to you daily by All Us Big Steamers,
    And if any one hinders our coming you'll starve!'

[First published in *A [School] History of England* (Oxford: Clarendon Press, 1911).]

✠　✠　✠

Kipling had a fine journalist's eye for the varieties of ocean-going craft.

THE LINER SHE'S A LADY

THE LINER SHE'S A lady, an' she never looks nor 'eeds –
The Man-o'-War's 'er 'usband, an' 'e gives 'er all she needs;
But, oh, the little cargo-boats, that sail the wet seas roun',
They're just the same as you an' me a-plyin' up an' down!
    Plyin' up an' down, Jenny, 'angin' round the Yard,

All the way by Fratton tram down to Portsmouth 'Ard;
Anythin' for business, an' we're growin' old –
Plyin' up an' down, Jenny, waitin' in the cold!

The Liner she's a lady by the paint upon 'er face,
An' if she meets an accident they count it sore disgrace.
The Man-o'-War's 'er 'usband, and 'e's always 'andy by,
But, oh, the little cargo-boats, they've got to load or die!

The Liner she's a lady, and 'er route is cut an' dried;
The Man-o'-War's 'er 'usband, an' 'e always keeps beside;
But, oh, the little cargo-boats that 'aven't any man,
They've got to do their business first, and make the most they can!

The Liner she's a lady, and if a war should come,
The Man-o'-War's 'er 'usband, and 'e'd bid 'er stay at home,
But, oh, the little cargo-boats that fill with every tide!
'E'd 'ave to go up an' fight for them, for they are England's pride.

The Liner she's a lady, but if she wasn't made,
There still would be the cargo-boats for 'ome an' foreign trade.
The Man-o'-War's 'er 'usband, but if we wasn't 'ere,
'E wouldn't have to fight at all for 'ome an' friends so dear.

'Ome an' friends so dear, Jenny, 'angin' round the Yard,
All the way by Fratton tram down to Portsmouth 'Ard;
Anythin' for business, an' we're growin' old –
'Ome an' friends so dear, Jenny, waitin' in the cold!

[First published in the *Pall Mall Gazette*, 13 June 1895, collected in *The Seven Seas* (1896).]

✖ ✖ ✖

THE JUNK AND THE DHOW

ONCE A PAIR OF savages found a stranded tree.
    (One-piecee stick-pidgin – two piecee man.
Straddle-um-paddle-um-push-um off to sea.

That way Foleign Debbil-boat began.)
But before, and before, and ever so long before
    Any shape of sailing-craft was known,
The Junk and Dhow had a stern and a bow,
    And a mast and a sail of their own – ahoy! alone!
    As they crashed across the Oceans on their own!

Once there was a pirate-ship, being blown ashore –
    (Plitty soon pilum up, s'posee no can tack.
Seven-piecee stlong man pullum sta'boa'd oar.
    That way bling her head alound and sail-o back.)
But before, and before, an ever so long before
    Grand Commander Noah took the wheel,
The Junk and the Dhow, though they look like anyhow,
    Had rudders reaching deep below their keel – ahoy! akeel!
    As they laid the Eastern Seas beneath their keel!

Once there was galliot yawing in a tide.
    (Too much foolee side-slip. How can stop?
Man catchee tea box lid – lasha longaside.
    That way make her plenty glip and sail first-chop.)
But before and before, and ever so long before
    And such contrivances were used,
The whole Confucian sea-board had standardized the lee-board.
    And hauled it up or dropped it as they choosed – or chose –
        or chused!
    According to the weather, when they cruised!

Once there was a caravel in a beam-sea roll –
    (Ca'go shiftee – alla dliftee – no can livee long.
S'posum' nail-o boa'd acloss – makee ploper hol'?
    That way ca'go sittum still, an' ship mo' stlong.)
But before, and before, and ever so long before
    Any square-rigged vessel hove in sight,
The Canton deep-sea craft carried bulkheads fore and aft,
    And took good care to keep 'em water-tight-atite-atite!
    From Amboyna to the Great Australian Bight!

Once there was a sailor-man singing just this way –
    (Too muchee yowl-o, sickum best flend!

Singee all-same pullee lope – haul and belay!
    Hully up and coilum down an'– bite off end!)
But before, and before, and ever so long before
    Any sort of chanty crossed our lips,
The Junk and the Dhow, though they look like anyhow,
      Were the Mother and the Father of all Ships – ahoy! – a'ships
      And of half the new inventions in our Ships!
      From Tarifa to Formosa in our Ships!
        From Socotra to Sel*an*khor of the windlass and the anchor,
      And the Navigators Compass in our Ships – ahoy! – our
        Ships!
(O, hully up and coilum down and – bite – off – end!)

[First published with the story 'An Unqualified Pilot' in *Land and Sea Tales for Scouts and Guides* (London: Macmillan, 1923).]

✠   ✠   ✠

He also had a well-developed sense of the characters associated with the sea, as was evident in two great ballads from the mid-1890s.

MCANDREW'S HYMN

Lord, Thou hast made this world below the shadow of a dream,
An', taught by time, I tak' it so – exceptin' always Steam.
From coupler-flange to spindle-guide I see Thy Hand, O God –
Predestination in the stride o' yon connectin'-rod.
John Calvin might ha' forged the same – enorrmous, certain, slow –
Ay, wrought it in the furnace-flame – *my* 'Institutio'.
I cannot get my sleep to-night; old bones are hard to please;
I'll stand the middle watch up here – alone wi' God an' these
My engines, after ninety days o' race an' rack an' strain
Through all the seas of all Thy world, slam-bangin' home again.
Slam-bang too much – they knock a wee – the crosshead-gibs are
    loose;
But thirty thousand mile o' sea has gied them fair excuse. . . .
Fine, clear an' dark – a full-draught breeze, wi' Ushant out o' sight,

An' Ferguson relievin' Hay. Old girl, ye'll walk to-night!
His wife's at Plymouth. . . . Seventy – One – Two – Three since he
    began –
Three turns for Mistress Ferguson . . . and who's to blame the man?
There's none at any port for me, by drivin' fast or slow,
Since Elsie Campbell went to Thee, Lord, thirty years ago.
(The year the *Sarah Sands* was burned. Oh roads we used to tread,
Fra' Maryhill to Pollokshaws – fra' Govan to Parkhead!)
Not but they're ceevil on the Board. Ye'll hear Sir Kenneth say:
'Good-morrn, McAndrew! Back again? An' how's your bilge
    to-day?'
Miscallin' technicalities but handin' me my chair
To drink Madeira wi' three Earls – the auld Fleet Engineer,
That started as a boiler-whelp – when steam and he were low.
I mind the time we used to serve a broken pipe wi' tow.
Ten pound was all the pressure then – Eh! Eh! – a man wad drive;
An' here, our workin' gauges give one hunder fifty-five!
We're creepin' on wi' each new rig – less weight an' larger power:
There'll be the loco-boiler next an' thirty knots an hour!
Thirty an' more. What I ha' seen since ocean-steam began
Leaves me no doot for the machine: but what about the man?
The man that counts, wi' all his runs, one million mile o' sea:
Four time the span from earth to moon. . . . How far, O Lord, from
    Thee?
That wast beside him night an' day. Ye mind my first typhoon?
It scoughed the skipper on his way to jock wi' the saloon.
Three feet were on the stokehold-floor – just slappin' to an' fro –
An' cast me on a furnace-door. I have the marks to show.
Marks! I ha' marks o' more than burns – deep in my soul an' black,
An' times like this, when things go smooth, my wickudness comes
    back.
The sins o' four and forty years, all up an' down the seas,
Clack an' repeat like valves half-fed. . . . Forgie's our trespasses.
Nights when I'd come on deck to mark, wi' envy in my gaze,
The couples kittlin' in the dark between the funnel stays;
Years when I raked the ports wi' pride to fill my cup o' wrong –
Judge not, O Lord, my steps aside at Gay Street in Hong-Kong!
Blot out the wastrel hours of mine in sin when I abode –
Jane Harrigan's an' Number Nine, The Reddick an' Grant Road!
An' waur than all – my crownin' sin – rank blasphemy an' wild.

I was not four and twenty then – Ye wadna judge a child?
I'd seen the Tropics first that run – new fruit, new smells, new air –
How could I tell – blind-fou wi' sun – the Deil was lurkin' there?
By day like playhouse-scenes the shore slid past our sleepy eyes;
By night those soft, lasceevious stars leered from those velvet
   skies,
In port (we used no cargo-steam) I'd daunder down the streets –
An ijjit grinnin' in a dream – for shells an' parrakeets,
An' walkin'-sticks o' carved bamboo an' blowfish stuffed an' dried –
Fillin' my bunk wi' rubbishry the Chief put overside.
Till, off Sambawa Head, Ye mind, I heard a land-breeze ca',
Milk-warm wi' breath o' spice an' bloom: 'McAndrew, come awa'!'
Firm, clear an' low – no haste, no hate – the ghostly whisper went,
Just statin' eevidential facts beyon' all argument:
'Your mither's God's a graspin' deil, the shadow o' yoursel',
Got out o' books by meenisters clean daft on Heaven an' Hell.
They mak' Him in the Broomielaw, o' Glasgie cold an' dirt,
A jealous, pridefu' fetich, lad, that's only strong to hurt,
Ye'll not go back to Him again an' kiss His red-hot rod,
But come wi' Us' (Now, who were *They*?) 'an' know the Leevin'
   God,
That does not kipper souls for sport or break a life in jest,
But swells the ripenin' cocoanuts an' ripes the woman's breast.'
An' there it stopped: cut off: no more; that quiet, certain voice –
For me, six months o' twenty-four, to leave or take at choice.
'Twas on me like a thunderclap – it racked me through an'
   through –
Temptation past the show o' speech, unnameable an' new –
The Sin against the Holy Ghost? . . . An' under all, our screw.

That storm blew by but left behind her anchor-shiftin' swell,
Thou knowest all my heart an' mind, Thou knowest, Lord, I fell.
Third on the *Mary Gloster* then, and first that night in Hell!
Yet was Thy hand beneath my head, about my feet Thy care –
Fra' Deli clear to Torres Strait, the trial o' despair,
But when we touched the Barrier Reef Thy answer to my prayer!
We dared not run that sea by night but lay an' held our fire,
An' I was drowsin' on the hatch – sick – sick wi' doubt an' tire:
'*Better the sight of eyes that see than wanderin' o' desire!*'
Ye mind that word? Clear as our gongs – again, an' once again,

When rippin' down through coral-trash ran out our moorin'-chain;
An' by Thy Grace I had the Light to see my duty plain.
Light on the engine-room – no more – bright as our carbons burn.
I've lost it since a thousand times, but never past return.

. . .

Obsairve. Per annum we'll have here two thousand souls aboard –
Think not I dare to justify myself before the Lord,
But – average fifteen hunder souls safe-borne fra' port to port –
I *am* o' service to my kind. Ye wadna blame the thought?
Maybe they steam from grace to wrath – to sin by folly led, –
It isna mine to judge their path – their lives are on my head.
Mine at the last – when all is done it all comes back to me,
The fault that leaves six thousand ton a log upon the sea.
We'll tak' one stretch – three weeks an' odd by any road ye steer –
Fra' Cape Town east to Wellington – ye need an engineer.
Fail there – ye've time to weld your shaft – ay, eat it, ere ye're spoke;
Or make Kerguelen under sail – three jiggers burned wi' smoke!
An' home again, the Rio run: it's no child's play to go
Steamin' to bell for fourteen days o' snow an' floe an' blow –
The bergs like kelpies overside that girn an' turn an' shift
Whaur, grindin' like the Mills o' God, goes by the big South drift.
(Hail, snow an' ice that praise the Lord: I've met them at their work,
An' wished we had anither route or they anither kirk.)
Yon's strain, hard strain, o' head an' hand, for though Thy Power
    brings
All skill to naught, Ye'll understand a man must think o' things.
Then, at the last, we'll get to port an' hoist their baggage clear –
The passengers, wi' gloves an' canes – an' this is what I'll hear:
'Well, thank ye for a pleasant voyage. The tender's comin' now.'
While I go testin' follower-bolts an' watch the skipper bow.
They've words for every one but me – shake hands wi' half the
    crew,
Except the dour Scots engineer, the man they never knew.
An' yet I like the wark for all we've dam' few pickin's here –
No pension, an' the most we earn's four hunder pound a year.
Better myself abroad? Maybe. *I'd* sooner starve than sail
Wi' such as call a snifter-rod *ross* . . . French for nightingale.
Commeesion on my stores? Some do; but I can not afford

To lie like stewards wi' patty-pans – I'm older than the Board.
A bonus on the coal I save? Ou ay, the Scots are close,
But when I grudge the strength Ye gave I'll grudge their food to
    those.
(There's bricks that I might recommend – an' clink the fire-bars
    cruel.
No! Welsh – Wangarti at the worst – an' damn all patent fuel!)
Inventions? Ye must stay in port to mak' a patent pay.
My Deeferential Valve-Gear taught me how that business lay,
I blame no chaps wi' clearer head for aught they make or sell.
I found that I could not invent an' look to these – as well.
So, wrestled wi' Apollyon – Nah! – fretted like a bairn –
But burned the workin'-plans last run wi' all I hoped to earn.
Ye know how hard an Idol dies, an' what that meant to me –
E'en tak' it for a sacrifice acceptable to Thee. . . .
Below there! Oiler! What's your wark? Ye find it runnin' hard?
Ye needn't swill the cap wi' oil – this isn't the Cunard!
Ye thought? Ye are not paid to think. Go, sweat that off again!
Tck! Tck! It's deeficult to sweer nor tak' The Name in vain!
Men, ay an' women, call me stern. Wi' these to oversee
Ye'll note I've little time to burn on social repartee.
The bairns see what their elders miss; they'll hunt me to an' fro,
Till for the sake of – well, a kiss – I tak' 'em down below.
That minds me of our Viscount loon – Sir Kenneth's kin – the chap
Wi' Russia leather tennis-shoon an' spar-decked yachtin'-cap.
I showed him round last week, o'er all – an' at the last says he:
'Mister McAndrew, don't you think steam spoils romance at sea?'
Damned ijjit! I'd been doon that morn to see what ailed the throws,
Manholin', on my back – the cranks three inches off my nose.
Romance! Those first-class passengers they like it very well,
Printed an' bound in little books; but why don't poets tell?
I'm sick of all their quirks an' turns – the loves an' doves they
    dream –
Lord, send a man like Robbie Burns to sing the Song o' Steam!
To match wi' Scotia's noblest speech yon orchestra sublime
Whaurto – uplifted like the Just – the tail-rods mark the time.
The crank-throws give the double-bass, the feed-pump sobs an'
    heaves,
An' now the main eccentrics start their quarrel on the sheaves:
Her time, her own appointed time, the rocking link-head bides,

Till – hear that note? – the rod's return whings glimmerin' through
  the guides.
They're all awa'! True beat, full power, the clangin' chorus goes
Clear to the tunnel where they sit, my purrin' dynamos.
Interdependence absolute, foreseen, ordained, decreed,
To work, Ye'll note, at any tilt an' every rate o' speed.
Fra' skylight-lift to furnace-bars, backed, bolted, braced an' stayed,
An' singin' like the Mornin' Stars for joy that they are made;
While, out o' touch o' vanity, the sweatin' thrust-block says:
'Not unto us the praise, or man – not unto us the praise!'
Now, a' together, hear them lift their lesson – theirs an' mine:
'Law, Orrder, Duty an' Restraint, Obedience, Discipline!'
Mill, forge an' try-pit taught them that when roarin' they arose,
An' whiles I wonder if a soul was gied them wi' the blows.
Oh for a man to weld it then, in one trip-hammer strain,
Till even first-class passengers could tell the meanin' plain!
But no one cares except mysel' that serve an' understand
My seven thousand horse-power here. Eh, Lord! They're grand –
  they're grand!
Uplift am I? When first in store the new-made beasties stood,
Were Ye cast down that breathed the Word declarin' all things good?
Not so! O' that warld-liftin' joy no after-fall could vex,
Ye've left a glimmer still to cheer the Man – the Arrtifex!
That holds, in spite o' knock and scale, o' friction, waste an' slip,
An' by that light – now, mark my word – we'll build the Perfect
  Ship.
I'll never last to judge her lines or take her curve – not I.
But I ha' lived an' I ha' worked. 'Be thanks to Thee, Most High!
An' I ha' done what I ha' done – judge Thou if ill or well –
Always Thy Grace preventin' me. . . . Losh! Yon's the 'Stand by' bell.
Pilot so soon? His flare it is. The mornin'-watch is set.
Well, God be thanked, as I was sayin', I'm no Pelagian yet.
Now I'll tak' on. . . . '*Morrn, Ferguson. Man, have ye ever thought
What your good leddy costs in coal? . . . I'll burn 'em down to port.*

[First published in December 1894, in *Scribner's Magazine*, and collected in
The Seven Seas (1896).

   Some versions of the poem have the title as 'M'Andrew's Hymn'.
However, it is 'McAndrew's Hymn' in *The Definitive Edition of Kipling's
Verse* (New York: Doubleday, 1940).]

✠ ✠ ✠

THE *MARY GLOSTER*

I'VE PAID FOR YOUR sickest fancies; I've humoured your crackedest
   whim –
Dick, it's your daddy, dying; you've got to listen to him!
Good for a fortnight, am I? The doctor told you? He lied.
I shall go under by morning, and – Put that nurse outside.
'Never seen death yet, Dickie? Well, now is your time to learn,
And you'll wish you held my record before it comes to your turn.
Not counting the Line and the Foundry, the yards and the village,
   too,
I've made myself and a million; but I'm damned if I made you.
Master at two-and-twenty, and married at twenty-three –
Ten thousand men on the pay-roll, and forty freighters at sea!
Fifty years between 'em, and every year of it fight,
And now I'm Sir Anthony Gloster, dying, a baronite:
For I lunched with his Royal 'Ighness – what was it the papers
   a-had?
'Not least of our merchant-princes.' Dickie, that's me, your dad!
I didn't begin with askings. *I* took my job and I stuck;
And I took the chances they wouldn't, an' now they're calling it
   luck.
Lord, what boats I've handled – rotten and leaky and old!
Ran 'em, or – opened the bilge-cock, precisely as I was told.
Grub that 'ud bind you crazy, and crews that 'ud turn you grey,
And a big fat lump of insurance to cover the risk on the way.
The others they dursn't do it; they said they valued their life
(They've served me since as skippers). *I* went, and I took my wife.
Over the world I drove 'em, married at twenty-three,
And your mother saving the money and making a man of me.
I was content to be master, but she said there was better behind;
She took the chances I wouldn't, and I followed your mother
   blind.
She egged me to borrow the money, an' she helped me to clear the
   loan,
When we bought half shares in a cheap 'un and hoisted a flag of
   our own.

Patching and coaling on credit, and living the Lord knew how,
We started the Red Ox freighters – we've eight-and-thirty now.
And those were the days of clippers, and the freights were
    clipper-freights,
And we knew we were making our fortune, but she died in
    Macassar Straits –
By the Little Paternosters, as you come to the Union Bank –
And we dropped her in fourteen fathom; I pricked it off where she
    sank.
Owners we were, full owners, and the boat was christened for her,
And she died in the *Mary Gloster*. My heart, how young we were!
So I went on a spree round Java and well-nigh ran her ashore,
But your mother came and warned me and I wouldn't liquor no
    more:
Strict I stuck to my business, afraid to stop or I'd think,
Saving the money (she warned me), and letting the other men
    drink.
And I met M'Cullough in London (I'd turned five 'undred then),
And 'tween us we started the Foundry – three forges and twenty
    men:
Cheap repairs for the cheap 'uns. It paid, and the business grew,
For I bought me a steam-lathe patent, and that was a gold mine
    too.
'Cheaper to build 'em than buy 'em,' I said, but M'Cullough he
    shied,
And we wasted a year in talking before we moved to the Clyde.
And the Lines were all beginning, and we all of us started fair,
Building our engines like houses and staying the boilers square.
But M'Cullough 'e wanted cabins with marble and maple and all,
And Brussels an' Utrecht velvet, and baths and a Social Hall,
And pipes for closets all over, and cutting the frames too light,
But M'Cullough he died in the Sixties, and – Well, I'm dying
    to-night. . . .
I knew – *I* knew what was coming, when we bid on the *Byfleet's*
    keel –
They piddled and piffled with iron: I'd given my orders for steel!
Steel and the first expansions. It paid, I tell you, it paid,
When we came with our nine-knot freighters and collared the
    long-run trade!
And they asked me how I did it, and I gave 'em the Scripture text,

'You keep your light so shining a little in front o' the next!'
They copied all they could follow, but they couldn't copy my
    mind,
And I left 'em sweating and stealing a year and a half behind.
Then came the armour-contracts, but that was M'Cullough's side;
He was always best in the Foundry, but better, perhaps, he died.
I went through his private papers; the notes was plainer than
    print;
And I'm no fool to finish if a man'll give me a hint.
(I remember his widow was angry.) So I saw what the drawings
    meant,
And I started the six-inch rollers, and it paid me sixty per cent –
Sixty per cent *with* failures, and more than twice we could do,
And a quarter-million to credit, and I saved it all for you!
I thought – it doesn't matter – you seemed to favour your ma,
But you're nearer forty than thirty, and I know the kind you are.
Harrer an' Trinity College! I ought to ha' sent you to sea –
But I stood you an education, an' what have you done for me?
The things I knew was proper you wouldn't thank me to give,
And the things I knew was rotten you said was the way to live.
For you muddled with books and pictures, an' china an' etchin's
    an' fans,
And your rooms at college was beastly – more like a whore's than
    a man's –
Till you married that thin-flanked woman, as white and as stale as
    a bone,
An' she gave you your social nonsense; but where's that kid o'
    your own?
I've seen your carriages blocking the half o' the Cromwell Road,
But never the doctor's brougham to help the missus unload.
(So there isn't even a grandchild, an' the Gloster family's done.)
Not like your mother, she isn't. *She* carried her freight each run.
But they died, the pore little beggars! At sea she had 'em – they
    died.
Only you, an' you stood it; you haven't stood much beside.
Weak, a liar, and idle, and mean as a collier's whelp
Nosing for scraps in the galley. No help – my son was no help!
So he gets three 'undred thousand, in trust and the interest paid.
I wouldn't give it you, Dickie – you see, I made it in trade.
You're saved from soiling your fingers, and if you have no child,

It all comes back to the business. Gad, won't your wife be wild!
'Calls and calls in her carriage, her 'andkerchief up to 'er eye:
'Daddy! dear daddy's dyin'!' and doing her best to cry.
Grateful? Oh, yes, I'm grateful, but keep her away from here.
Your mother 'ud never ha' stood 'er, and, anyhow, women are
    queer. . . .
There's women will say I've married a second time. Not quite!
But give pore Aggie a hundred, and tell her your lawyers'll fight.
She was the best o' the boiling – you'll meet her before it ends;
I'm in for a row with the mother – I'll leave you settle my friends:
For a man he must go with a woman, which women don't
    understand –
Or the sort that say they can see it they aren't the marrying brand.
But I wanted to speak o' your mother that's Lady Gloster still –
I'm going to up and see her, without it's hurting the will.
Here! Take your hand off the bell-pull. Five thousand's waiting for
    you,
If you'll only listen a minute, and do as I bid you do.
They'll try to prove me crazy, and, if you bungle, they can;
And I've only you to trust to! (O God, why ain't he a man?)
There's some waste money on marbles, the same as M'Cullough
    tried –
Marbles and mausoleums – but I call that sinful pride.
There's some ship bodies for burial – we've carried 'em, soldered
    and packed;
Down in their wills they wrote it, and nobody called *them* cracked.
But me – I've too much money, and people might. . . . All my fault:
It come o' hoping for grandsons and buying that Wokin' vault.
I'm sick o' the 'ole dam' business; I'm going back where I came.
Dick, you're the son o' my body, and you'll take charge o' the
    same!
I want to lie by your mother, ten thousand mile away,
And they'll want to send me to Woking; and that's where you'll
    earn your pay.
I've thought it out on the quiet, the same as it ought to be done –
Quiet, and decent, and proper – an' here's your orders, my son.
You know the Line? You don't, though. You write to the Board,
    and tell
Your father's death has upset you an' you're goin' to cruise for a
    spell,

An' you'd like the *Mary Gloster* – I've held her ready for this –
They'll put her in working order and you'll take her out as she is.
Yes, it was money idle when I patched her and put her aside
(Thank God, I can pay for my fancies!) – the boat where your
  mother died,
By the Little Paternosters, as you come to the Union Bank,
We dropped her – I think I told you – and I pricked it off where
  she sank –
['Tiny she looked on the grating – that oily, treacly sea –]
'Hundred and eighteen East, remember, and South just three.
Easy bearings to carry – three South – three to the dot;
But I gave M'Andrew a copy in case of dying – or not.
And so you'll write to M'Andrew, he's Chief of the Maori Line;
They'll give him leave, if you ask 'em and say it's business o' mine.
I built three boats for the Maoris, an' very well pleased they were,
An' I've known Mac since the Fifties, and Mac knew me – and her.
After the first stroke warned me I sent him the money to keep
Against the time you'd claim it, committin' your dad to the deep;
For you are the son o' my body, and Mac was my oldest friend,
I've never asked 'im to dinner, but he'll see it out to the end.
Stiff-necked Glasgow beggar, I've heard he's prayed for my soul,
But he couldn't lie if you paid him, and he'd starve before he stole!
He'll take the *Mary* in ballast – you'll find her a lively ship;
And you'll take Sir Anthony Gloster, that goes on 'is wedding-trip,
Lashed in our old deck-cabin with all three port-holes wide,
The kick o' the screw beneath him and the round blue seas
  outside!
Sir Anthony Gloster's carriage – our 'ouse-flag flyin' free –
Ten thousand men on the pay-roll and forty freighters at sea!
He made himself and a million, but this world is a fleetin' show,
And he'll go to the wife of 'is bosom the same as he ought to go –
By the heel of the Paternosters – there isn't a chance to mistake –
And Mac'll pay you the money as soon as the bubbles break!
Five thousand for six weeks' cruising, the staunchest freighter
  afloat,
And Mac he'll give you your bonus the minute I'm out o' the boat!
He'll take you round to Macassar, and you'll come back alone;
He knows what I want o' the *Mary*. . . . I'll do what I please with
  my own.
Your mother 'ud call it wasteful, but I've seven-and-thirty more;

I'll come in my private carriage and bid it wait at the door. . . .
For my son 'e was never a credit: 'e muddled with books and art,
And 'e lived on Sir Anthony's money and 'e broke Sir Anthony's
    heart.
There isn't even a grandchild, and the Gloster family's done –
The only one you left me, O mother, the only one!
Harrer and Trinity College – me slavin' early an' late –
An' he thinks I'm dying crazy, and you're in Macassar Strait!
Flesh o' my flesh, my dearie, for ever an' ever amen,
That first stroke come for a warning; I ought to ha' gone to you
    then,
But – cheap repairs for a cheap 'un – the doctors said I'd do:
Mary, why didn't *you* warn me? I've allus heeded to you,
Excep' – I know – about women; but you are a spirit now;
An', wife, they was only women, and I was a man. That's how.
An' a man 'e must go with a woman, as you could not understand;
But I never talked 'em secrets. I paid 'em out o' hand.
Thank Gawd, I can pay for my fancies! Now what's five thousand
    to me,
For a berth off the Paternosters in the haven where I would be?
I believe in the Resurrection, if I read my Bible plain,
But I wouldn't trust 'em at Wokin'; we're safer at sea again.
For the heart it shall go with the treasure – go down to the sea in
    ships.
I'm sick of the hired women – I'll kiss my girl on her lips!
I'll be content with my fountain, I'll drink from my own well,
And the wife of my youth shall charm me – an' the rest can go to
    Hell!
(Dickie, *he* will, that's certain.) I'll lie in our standin'-bed,
An' Mac'll take her in ballast – an' she trims best by the head. . . .
Down by the head an' sinkin', her fires are drawn and cold,
And the water's splashin' hollow on the skin of the empty hold –
Churning an' choking and chuckling, quiet and scummy and dark –
Full to her lower hatches and risin' steady. Hark!
That was the after-bulkhead. . . . She's flooded from stem to
    stern. . . .
Never seen death yet, Dickie? . . . Well, now is your time to learn!

[First published in *The Seven Seas* (1896).]

■ ■ ■

Finally, Kipling could always be relied upon to say something original and worthwhile about the Royal Navy.

'TIN FISH'

THE SHIPS DESTROY US above
And ensnare us beneath.
We arise, we lie down, and we move
In the belly of Death.

The ships have a thousand eyes
To mark where we come . . .
But the mirth of a seaport dies
When our blow gets home.

[First published in the *Daily Telegraph*, 27 November 1915, then collected in *The Fringes of the Fleet* (London: Macmillan; New York: Doubleday, 1915), and then, with other naval stories, in *Sea Warfare* (London: Macmillan, 1916).]

■ ■ ■

MINE SWEEPERS

DAWN OFF THE FORELAND – the young flood making
    Jumbled and short and steep –
Black in the hollows and bright where it's breaking –
    Awkward water to sweep.
    'Mines reported in the fairway,
    Warn all traffic and detain.
'Sent up *Unity, Cralibel, Assyrian, Stormcock,* and *Golden Gain.*'

Noon off the Foreland – the first ebb making
    Lumpy and strong in the bight.
Boom after boom, and the golf-hut shaking
    And the jackdaws wild with fright!
      'Mines located in the fairway,
      Boats now working up the chain,
Sweepers – *Unity, Claribel, Assyrian, Stormcock,* and *Golden Gain.'*

Dusk off the Foreland – the last light going
    And the traffic crowding through,
And five damned trawlers with their syreens blowing
    Heading the whole review!
      'Sweep completed in the fairway.
      No more mines remain.
'Sent back *Unity, Claribel, Assyrian, Stormcock,* and *Golden Gain.'*

[First published in *The Times,* 21 June 1915, then collected in *Sea Warfare* (1916).]

✠ ✠ ✠

Adopting a chronological approach, we find that Kipling's first encounters with the sea were in Bombay – the town where he was born – in his travels back to England and in the English Channel off Southsea in Hampshire, where his parents placed him in what he called a 'house of desolation'.

SOMETHING OF MYSELF

THEN THOSE DAYS OF strong light and darkness passed, and there was a time in a ship with an immense semi-circle blocking all vision on each side of her. (She must have been the old paddlewheel P.&O. *Ripon.*) There was a train across a desert (the Suez Canal was not yet opened) and a halt in it, and a small girl wrapped in a shawl on the seat opposite me, whose face stands out still. There was next a dark land, and a darker room full of cold, in one wall of which a white woman made naked fire, and I cried aloud with dread, for I had never before seen a grate.

Then came a new small house smelling of aridity and emptiness, and a parting in the dawn with Father and Mother, who said that I must learn quickly to read and write so that they might send me letters and books.

I lived in that house for close on six years. It belonged to a woman who took in children whose parents were in India. She was married to an old Navy Captain, who had been a midshipman at Navarino, and had afterwards been entangled in a harpoon-line while whale-fishing, and dragged down till he miraculously freed himself. But the line had scarred his ankle for life – a dry, black scar, which I used to look at with horrified interest.

The house itself stood in the extreme suburbs of Southsea, next to a Portsmouth unchanged in most particulars since Trafalgar – the Portsmouth of Sir Walter Besant's *By Celia's Arbour*. The timber for a Navy that was only experimenting with iron-clads such as the *Inflexible* lay in great booms in the Harbour. The little training-brigs kept their walks opposite Southsea Castle, and Portsmouth Hard was as it had always been. Outside these things lay the desolation of Hayling Island, Lumps Fort, and the isolated hamlet of Milton. I would go for long walks with the Captain, and once he took me to see a ship called the *Alert* (or *Discovery*) returned from Arctic explorations, her decks filled with old sledges and lumber, and her spare rudder being cut up for souvenirs. A sailor gave me a piece, but I lost it. Then the old Captain died, and I was sorry, for he was the only person in that house as far as I can remember who ever threw me a kind word.

[First published as *Something of Myself* (London: Macmillan, 1937).]

✖ ✖ ✖

After his early career as a journalist in India in the 1880s, Kipling travelled back to England in an easterly direction, via Southeast Asia, Japan and the United States – an experience recalled in various pieces in *From Sea to Sea*.

FROM SEA TO SEA

A further consideration of Japan. The inland sea, and good cookery. The mystery of passports and consulates, and certain other matters.

'Rome! Rome! Wasn't that the place where I got the good cigars?'
— *Memoirs of a Traveller.*

ALAS FOR THE INCOMPLETENESS of the written word! There was so much more that I meant to tell you about Nagasaki and the funeral procession that I found in her streets. You ought to have read about the wailing women in white who followed the dead man shut up in a wooden sedan chair that rocked on the shoulders of the bearers, while the bronze-hued Buddhist priest tramped on ahead, and the little boys ran alongside.

I had prepared in my mind moral reflections, purviews of political situations, and a complete essay on the future of Japan. Now I have forgotten everything except O-Toyo in the tea-garden.

From Nagasaki we – the P. and O. Steamer – are going to Kobé by way of the Inland Sea. That is to say, we have for the last twenty hours been steaming through a huge lake, studded as far as the eye can reach with islands of every size, from four miles long and two wide to little cocked-hat hummocks no bigger than a decent hayrick. Messrs. Cook and Son charge about one hundred rupees extra for the run through this part of the world, but they do not know how to farm the beauties of nature. Under any skies the islands – purple, amber, grey, green, and black – are worth five times the money asked. I have been sitting for the last half-hour among a knot of whooping tourists, wondering how I could give you a notion of them. The tourists, of course, are indescribable. They say, 'Oh my!' at thirty-second intervals, and at the end of five minutes call one to another: 'Sa-ay, don't you think it's vurry much the same all along?' Then they play cricket with a broomstick till an unusually fair prospect makes them stop and shout 'Oh my!' again. If there were a few more oaks and pines on the islands, the run would be three hundred miles of Naini Tal lake. But we are not near Naini Tal; for as the big ship drives down the alleys of water, I can see the heads of the breakers flying ten feet up the side of the echoing cliffs, albeit the sea is dead-still.

Now we have come to a stretch so densely populated with islands that all looks solid ground. We are running through broken water thrown up by the race of the tide round an outlying reef, and apparently are going to hit an acre of solid rock. Somebody on the bridge saves us, and we head out for another island, and so on, and so on, till the eye wearies of watching the nose of the ship swinging right and left, and the finite human soul, which, after all, cannot repeat 'Oh my!' through a chilly evening, goes below. When you come to Japan – it can be done comfortably in three months, or even ten weeks – sail through this marvellous sea, and see how quickly wonder sinks to interest, and interest to apathy. We brought oysters with us from Nagasaki. I am much more interested in their appearance at dinner to-night than in the shag-backed starfish of an islet that has just slidden by like a ghost upon the silver-grey waters, awakening under the touch of the ripe moon. Yes, it is a sea of mystery and romance, and the white sails of the junks are silver in the moonlight. But if the steward curries those oysters instead of serving them on the shell, all the veiled beauties of cliff and water-carven rock will not console me. To-day being the seventeenth of April, I am sitting in an ulster under a thick rug, with fingers so cold I can barely hold the pen. This emboldens me to ask how your thermantidotes are working. A mixture of steatite and kerosene is very good for creaking cranks, I believe, and if the coolie falls asleep, and you wake up in Hades, try not to lose your temper. I go to my oysters.

Shows how I came to America before my time and was much shaken in body and soul.

> 'Then spoke der Captain Stossenheim
> Who had theories of God,
> "Oh, Breitmann, this is judgment on
> Der ways dot you have trod.
> You only lifs to enjoy yourself
> While you yourself agree
> Dot self-development requires
> Der religious Idee."'
>
> – *C.G. Leland.*

This is America. They call her the *City of Peking*, and she belongs to the Pacific Mail Company, but for all practical purposes she is the United States. We are divided between missionaries and generals – generals who were at Vicksburg and Shiloh, and German by birth, but more American than the Americans, who in confidence tell you that they are not generals at all, but only brevet majors of militia corps. The missionaries are perhaps the queerest portion of the cargo. Did you ever hear an English minister lecture for half an hour on the freight-traffic receipts and general working of, let us say, the Midland? The Professor has been sitting at the feet of a keen-eyed, close-bearded, swarthy man who expounded unto him kindred mysteries with a fluency and precision that a city leader-writer might have envied. 'Who's your financial friend with the figures at his fingers' ends?' I asked. 'Missionary – Presbyterian Mission to the Japs,' said the Professor. I laid my hand upon my mouth and was dumb.

As a counterpoise to the missionaries, we carry men from Manila – lean Scotchmen who gamble once a month in the Manila State lottery and occasionally turn up trumps. One, at least, drew a ten-thousand-dollar prize last December and is away to make merry in the New World. Everybody on the staff of an American steamer this side the Continent seems to gamble steadily in that lottery, and the talk of the smoking-room runs almost entirely on prizes won by accident or lost through a moment's delay. The tickets are sold more or less openly at Yokahama and Hong-Kong, and the drawings – losers and winners both agree here – are above reproach.

We have resigned ourselves to the infinite monotony of a twenty days' voyage. The Pacific Mail advertises falsely. Only under the most favorable circumstances of wind and steam can their under-engined boats cover the distance in fifteen days. Our *City of Peking*, for instance, had been jogging along at a gentle ten knots an hour, a pace out of all proportion to her bulk. 'When we get a wind,' says the Captain, 'we shall do better.' She is a four-master and can carry any amount of canvas. It is not safe to run steamers across this void under the poles of Atlantic liners. The monotony of the sea is paralysing. We have passed the wreck of a little sealing-schooner lying bottom up and covered with gulls. She weltered by in the chill dawn, unlovely as the corpse of a man, and the wild birds piped thinly at us as they steered her across the surges. The pulse of the Pacific is no little thing even in the quieter moods of the sea. It set our bows swinging and nosing and ducking ere we were a day clear of Yokohama, and yet there was never swell nor crested wave in sight. 'We ride very high,' said the Captain, 'and she's a dry boat. She has a knack of crawling over things somehow; but we shan't need to put her to the test this journey.'

The Captain was mistaken. For four days we have endured the sullen displeasure of the North Pacific, winding up with a night of discomfort. It began with a grey sea, flying clouds, and a head-wind that smote fifty knots off the day's run. Then rose from the southeast a beam sea warranted by no wind that was abroad upon the waters in our neighbourhood, and we wallowed in the trough of it for sixteen mortal hours. In the stillness of the harbour, when the newspaper man is lunching in her saloon and the steam-launch is crawling round her sides, a ship of pride is a 'stately liner.' Out in the open, one rugged shoulder of a sea between you and the horizon, she becomes 'the old hooker,' a 'lively boat,' and other things of small import, for this is necessary to propitiate the Ocean. 'There's a storm to the southeast of us,' explained the Captain. 'That's what's kicking up this sea.'

The *City of Peking* did not belie her reputation. She crawled over the seas in liveliest wise, never shipping a bucket till – she was forced to. Then she took it green over the bows to the vast edification of, at least, one passenger who had never seen the scuppers full before.

Later in the day the fun began. 'Oh, she's a daisy at rolling,' murmured the chief steward, flung starfish-wise on a table among his glassware. 'She's rolling some,' said a black apparition new risen from the stoke-hold. 'Is she going to roll any more?' demanded the ladies grouped in what ought to have been the ladies' saloon, but, according to American custom, was labelled 'Social Hall.'

Passed in the twilight the chief officer – a dripping, bearded face. 'Shall I mark out the bull-board?' said he, and lurched aft, followed by the tongue of a wave. 'She'll roll her guards under to-night,' said a man from Louisiana, where their river-steamers do not understand the meaning of bulwarks. We dined to a dashing accompaniment of crockery, the bounds of emancipated beer-bottles livelier than their own corks, and the clamour of the ship's gong broken loose and calling to meals on its own account.

After dinner the real rolling began. She did roll 'guards under,' as the Louisiana man had prophesied. At thirty-minute intervals to the second arrived one big sea, when the electric lamps died down to nothing, and the screw raved and the blows of the sea made the decks quiver. On those occasions we moved from our chairs, not gently, but discourteously. At other times we were merely holding on with both hands.

It was then that I studied Fear – Terror bound in black silk and fighting hard with herself. For reasons which will be thoroughly understood, there was a tendency among the passengers to herd together and to address inquiries to every officer who happened to stagger through the saloon. No one was in the least alarmed, – oh dear, no! – but all were keenly anxious for information. This anxiety redoubled after a more than usually vicious roll. Terror was a large, handsome, and cultured lady who knew the precise value of human life, the inwardness of *Robert Elsmere*, the latest poetry – everything in fact that a clever woman should know. When the rolling was near its worst, she began to talk swiftly. I do not for a moment believe that she knew what she was talking about. The rolling increased. She buckled down to the task of making conversation. By the heave of the labouring bust, the restless working of the fingers on the tablecloth, and the uncontrollable eyes that turned always to the companion stairhead, I was able to judge the extremity of her fear. Yet her words were frivolous and commonplace enough; they poured forth unceasingly, punctuated with little laughs and giggles, as a woman's speech should be. Presently, a member of her group suggested going to bed. No, she wanted to sit up; she wanted to go on talking, and as long as she could get a soul to sit with her she had her desire. When for sheer lack of company she was forced to get to her cabin, she left reluctantly, looking back to the well-lighted saloon over her shoulder. The contrast between the flowing triviality of her speech and the strained intentness of eye and hand was a quaint thing to behold. I know now how Fear should be painted.

No one slept very heavily that night. Both arms were needed to grip the berth, while the trunks below wound the carpet-slips into knots and battered the framing of the cabins. Once it seemed to me that the whole of the labouring fabric that cased our trumpery fortunes stood on end and in this undignified posture hopped a mighty hop. Twice I know I shot out of my berth to join the adventurous trunks on the floor. A hundred times the crash of the wave on the ship's side was followed by the roar of the water, as it swept the decks and raved round the deckhouses. In a lull I heard the flying feet of a man, a shout, and a far-away chorus of lost spirits singing somebody's requiem.

[Kipling's articles, which appeared in *The Pioneer* (Allahabad) from April 1889 to April 1890, were first collected in *From Sea to Sea* (New York: Doubleday McClure, 1899; London: Macmillan, 1900). This particular article appeared on 23 November 1889.]

❊ ❊ ❊

Kipling's experience of the sea during the voyages which brought him from Calcutta to London in 1889 sparked an interest in nautical matters which had not been apparent while he was in India. Certainly during his first years back in London he wrote several strong poems with nautical themes.

THE BALLAD OF THE *CLAMPHERDOWN*

IT WAS OUR WAR-SHIP *Clampherdown*
  Would sweep the Channel clean,
Wherefore she kept her hatches close
When the merry Channel chops arose,
  To save the bleached marine.

She had one bow-gun of a hundred ton
  And a great stern-gun beside.
They dipped their noses deep in the sea,
They racked their stays and stanchions free
  In the wash of the wind-whipped tide.

It was our war-ship *Clampherdown*,
  Fell in with a cruiser light
That carried the dainty Hotchkiss gun
And a pair of heels wherewith to run
  From the grip of a close-fought fight.

She opened fire at seven miles –
  As ye shoot at a bobbing cork –

And once she fired and twice she fired,
Till the bow-gun dropped like a lily tired
   That lolls upon the stalk.

'Captain, the bow-gun melts apace,
   The deck-beams break below,
'Twere well to rest for an hour or twain,
And botch the shattered plates again.'
   And he answered, 'Make it so.'

She opened fire within the mile –
   As ye shoot at the flying duck –
And the great stern-gun shot fair and true,
With the heave of the ship, to the stainless blue,
   And the great stern-turret stuck.

'Captain, the turret fills with steam,
   The feed-pipes burst below –
You can hear the hiss of the helpless ram,
You can hear the twisted runners jam.'
   And he answered, 'Turn and go!'

It was our war-ship *Clampherdown*,
   And grimly did she roll;
Swung round to take the cruiser's fire
As the White Whale faces the Thresher's ire
   When they war by the frozen Pole.

'Captain, the shells are falling fast,
   And faster still fall we;
And it is not meet for English stock
To bide in the heart of an eight-day clock
   The death they cannot see.'

'Lie down, lie down, my bold A.B.,
   We drift upon her beam;
We dare not ram, for she can run;
And dare ye fire another gun,
   And die in the peeling steam?'

It was our war-ship *Clampherdown*
   That carried an armour-belt;
But fifty feet at stern and bow
Lay bare as the paunch of the purser's sow,
   To the hail of the *Nordenfeldt*.

'Captain, they hack us through and through;
   The chilled steel bolts are swift!
We have emptied our bunkers in open sea,
Their shrapnel bursts where our coal should be.'
   And he answered, 'Let her drift.'

It was our war-ship *Clampherdown*,
   Swung round upon the tide,
Her two dumb guns glared south and north,
And the blood and the bubbling steam ran forth,
   And she ground the cruiser's side.

'Captain, they cry, the fight is done,
   They bid you send your sword.'
And he answered, 'Grapple her stern and bow.
They have asked for the steel. They shall have it now;
   Out cutlasses and board!'

It was our war-ship *Clampherdown*
   Spewed up four hundred men;
And the scalded stokers yelped delight,
As they rolled in the waist and heard the fight,
   Stamp o'er their steel-walled pen.

They cleared the cruiser end to end,
   From conning-tower to hold.
They fought as they fought in Nelson's fleet;
They were stripped to the waist, they were bare to the feet,
   As it was in the days of old.

It was the sinking *Clampherdown*
   Heaved up her battered side –
And carried a million pounds in steel,
To the cod and the corpse-fed conger-eel,
   And the scour of the Channel tide.

It was the crew of the *Clampherdown*
  Stood out to sweep the sea,
On a cruiser won from an ancient foe,
As it was in the days of long ago,
  And as it still shall be!

[First published in the *St James's Gazette*, 25 March 1890, and then collected
in *Barrack-Room Ballads and Other Verses* (1892).]

✖ ✖ ✖

THE RHYME OF THE THREE CAPTAINS

*This ballad appears to refer to one of the exploits of the notorious Paul
Jones, the American pirate. It is founded on fact.*

. . . AT THE CLOSE of a winter day,
Their anchors down, by London town, the Three Great Captains lay;
And one was Admiral of the North from Solway Firth to Skye,
And one was Lord of the Wessex coast and all the lands thereby,
And one was Master of the Thames from Limehouse to Blackwall,
And he was Captain of the Fleet – the bravest of them all.
Their good guns guarded their great gray sides that were thirty
  foot in the sheer,
When there came a certain trading-brig with news of a privateer.
Her rigging was rough with the clotted drift that drives in a
  Northern breeze,
Her sides were clogged with the lazy weed that spawns in the
  Eastern seas.
Light she rode in the rude tide-rip, to left and right she rolled,
And the skipper sat on the scuttle-butt and stared at an empty hold.
'I ha' paid Port dues for your Law,' quoth he, 'and where is the
  Law ye boast
If I sail unscathed from a heathen port to be robbed on a Christian
  coast?
Ye have smoked the hives of the Laccadives as we burn the lice in
  a bunk,
We tack not now to a Gallang prow or a plunging Pei-ho junk;
I had no fear but the seas were clear as far as a sail might fare

Till I met with a lime-washed Yankee brig that rode off Finisterre.
There were canvas blinds to his bow-gun ports to screen the
    weight he bore,
And the signals ran for a merchantman from Sandy Hook to the
    Nore.
He would not fly the Rovers' flag – the bloody or the black,
But now he floated the Gridiron and now he flaunted the Jack.
He spoke of the Law as he crimped my crew – he swore it was
    only a loan;
But when I would ask for my own again, he swore it was none of
    my own.
He has taken my little parrakeets that nest beneath the Line,
He has stripped my rails of the shaddock-frails and the green
    unripened pine;
He has taken my bale of dammer and spice I won beyond the seas,
He has taken my grinning heathen gods – and what should he
    want o' these?
My foremast would not mend his boom, my deckhouse patch his
    boats;
He has whittled the two, this Yank Yahoo, to peddle for shoe-peg
    oats.
I could not fight for the failing light and a rough beam-sea beside,
But I hulled him once for a clumsy crimp and twice because he lied.
Had I had guns (as I had goods) to work my Christian harm,
I had run him up from his quarter-deck to trade with his own
    yard-arm;
I had nailed his ears to my capstan-head, and ripped them off with
    a saw,
And soused them in the bilgewater, and served them to him raw;
I had flung him blind in a rudderless boat to rot in the rocking dark,
I had towed him aft of his own craft, a bait for his brother shark;
I had lapped him round with cocoa husk, and drenched him with
    the oil,
And lashed him fast to his own mast to blaze above my spoil;
I had stripped his hide for my hammock-side, and tasselled his
    beard i' the mesh,
And spitted his crew on the live bamboo that grows through the
    gangrened flesh;
I had hove him down by the mangroves brown, where the mud-
    reef sucks and draws,

Moored by the heel to his own keel to wait for the land-crab's claws!
He is lazar within and lime without, ye can nose him far enow,
For he carries the taint of a musky ship – the reek of the slaver's
    dhow!'
The skipper looked at the tiering guns and the bulwarks tall and
    cold,
And the Captains Three full courteously peered down at the
    gutted hold,
And the Captains Three called courteously from deck to
    scuttle-butt:–
'Good Sir, we ha' dealt with that merchantman or ever your teeth
    were cut.
Your words be words of a lawless race, and the Law it standeth
    thus:
He comes of a race that have never a Law, and he never has
    boarded us.
We ha' sold him canvas and rope and spar – we know that his
    price is fair,
And we know that he weeps for the lack of a Law as he rides off
    Finisterre.
And since he is damned for a gallows-thief by you and better than
    you,
We hold it meet that the English fleet should know that we hold
    him true.'
The skipper called to the tall taffrail:– 'And what is that to me?
Did ever you hear of a Yankee brig that rifled a Seventy-three?
Do I loom so large from your quarter-deck that I lift like a ship o'
    the Line?
He has learned to run from a shotted gun and harry such craft as
    mine.
There is never a Law on the Cocos Keys to hold a white man in,
But we do not steal the niggers' meal, for that is a nigger's sin.
Must he have his Law as a quid to chaw, or laid in brass on his
    wheel?
Does he steal with tears when he buccaneers? 'Fore Gad, then,
    why does he steal?'
The skipper bit on a deep-sea word, and the word it was not sweet,
For he could see the Captains Three had signalled to the Fleet.
But three and two, in white and blue, the whimpering flags began:–
'We have heard a tale of a – foreign sail, but he is a merchantman.'

The skipper peered beneath his palm and swore by the Great Horn
    Spoon:–
''Fore Gad, the Chaplain of the Fleet would bless my picaroon!'
By two and three the flags blew free to lash the laughing air:–
'We have sold our spars to the merchantman – we know that his
    price is fair.'
The skipper winked his Western eye, and swore by a China storm:–
'They ha' rigged him a Joseph's jury-coat to keep his honour warm.'
The halliards twanged against the tops, the bunting bellied broad,
The skipper spat in the empty hold and mourned for a wasted cord.
Masthead – masthead, the signal sped by the line o' the British craft;
The skipper called to his Lascar crew, and put her about and
    laughed:–
'It's mainsail haul, my bully boys all – we'll out to the seas again –
Ere they set us to paint their pirate saint, or scrub at his
    grapnel-chain.
It's fore-sheet free, with her head to the sea, and the swing of the
    unbought brine –
We'll make no sport in an English court till we come as a ship o'
    the Line:
Till we come as a ship o' the Line, my lads, of thirty foot in the
    sheer,
Lifting again from the outer main with news of a privateer;
Flying his pluck at our mizzen-truck for weft of Admiralty,
Heaving his head for our dipsey-lead in sign that we keep the sea.
Then fore-sheet home as she lifts to the foam – we stand on the
    outward tack,
We are paid in the coin of the white man's trade – the bezant is
    hard, ay, and black.
The frigate-bird shall carry my word to the Kling and the
    Orang-Laut
How a man may sail from a heathen coast to be robbed in a
    Christian port;
How a man may be robbed in Christian port while Three Great
    Captains there
Shall dip their flag to a slaver's rag – to show that his trade is fair!'

[First published in *The Athenæum*, 6 December 1890, and then collected in
Barrack-Room Ballads and Other Verses (1892).]

✠ ✠ ✠

THE BALLAD OF THE *BOLIVAR*

SEVEN MEN FROM ALL the world, back to Docks again,
Rolling down the Ratcliffe Road drunk and raising Cain:
Give the girls another drink 'fore we sign away –
We that took the 'Bolivar' out across the Bay!

We put out from Sunderland loaded down with rails;
We put back to Sunderland 'cause our cargo shifted;
We put out from Sunderland – met the winter gales –
Seven days and seven nights to the Start we drifted.

Racketing her rivets loose, smoke-stack white as snow,
All the coals adrift adeck, half the rails below,
Leaking like a lobster-pot, steering like a dray –
Out we took the *Bolivar*, out across the Bay!

One by one the Lights came up, winked and let us by;
Mile by mile we waddled on, coal and fo'c'sle short;
Met a blow that laid us down, heard a bulkhead fly;
Left the Wolf behind us with a two-foot list to port.

Trailing like a wounded duck, working out her soul;
Clanging like a smithy-shop after every roll;
Just a funnel and a mast lurching through the spray –
So we threshed the *Bolivar* out across the Bay!

'Felt her hog and felt her sag, betted when she'd break;
'Wondered every time she raced if she'd stand the shock;
'Heard the seas like drunken men pounding at her strake;
'Hoped the Lord 'ud keep his thumb on the plummer-block.

Banged against the iron decks, bilges choked with coal;
Flayed and frozen foot and hand, sick of heart and soul;
'Last we prayed she'd buck herself into judgment Day –
Hi! we cursed the *Bolivar* knocking round the Bay!

O her nose flung up to sky, groaning to be still –
Up and down and back we went, never time for breath;
Then the money paid at Lloyd's caught her by the heel,
And the stars ran round and round dancin' at our death.

Aching for an hour's sleep, dozing off between;
'Heard the rotten rivets draw when she took it green;
'Watched the compass chase its tail like a cat at play –
That was on the *Bolivar*, south across the Bay.

Once we saw between the squalls, lyin' head to swell –
Mad with work and weariness, wishin' they was we –
Some damned Liner's lights go by like a long hotel;
'Cheered her from the *Bolivar* swampin' in the sea.

Then a grayback cleared us out, then the skipper laughed;
'Boys, the wheel has gone to Hell – rig the winches aft!
Yoke the kicking rudder-head – get her under way!'
So we steered her, pulley-haul, out across the Bay!

Just a pack o' rotten plates puttied up with tar,
In we came, an' time enough, 'cross Bilbao Bar.
Overloaded, undermanned, meant to founder, we
Euchred God Almighty's storm, bluffed the Eternal Sea!

Seven men from all the world, back to town again,
Rollin' down the Ratcliffe Road drunk and raising Cain:
Seven men from out of Hell. Ain't the owners gay,
'Cause we took the 'Bolivar' safe across the Bay?

[First published in the *St James's Gazette*, 29 January 1892, and then collected in *Barrack-Room Ballads and Other Verses* (1892).]

✠ ✠ ✠

Kipling found London restrictive, however, and he tried to escape to South Africa and Australia. He also hoped to visit his great literary hero Robert Louis Stevenson in Samoa. En route to South Africa he met a naval officer, Commander E.H. Bayly, who, when

they landed, introduced him to the officers' mess in Simonstown and stimulated his interest in writing more specifically about the Royal Navy. As a result of his time in South Africa, Kipling wrote his first story with a naval theme, 'Judson and the Empire'.

SOMETHING OF MYSELF

MY NEED WAS TO get clean away and re-sort myself. Cruises were then unknown; but my dependence was Cook. For the great J.M. himself – the man with the iron mouth and domed brow – had been one of my Father's guests at Lahore when he was trying to induce the Indian Government to let him take over the annual pilgrimage to Mecca as a business proposition. Had he succeeded some lives, and perhaps a war or two, might have been saved. His home offices took friendly interest in my plans and steamer connections.

I sailed first to Cape Town in a gigantic three-thousand-ton liner called *The Moor*, not knowing I was in the hands of Fate. Aboard her, I met a Navy Captain going to a new Command at Simon's Town. At Madeira he desired to lay in wine for his two-year commission. I assisted him through a variegated day and fluctuating evening, which laid the foundations of life-long friendship.

Cape Town in '91 was a sleepy, unkempt little place, where the stoeps of some of the older Dutch houses still jutted over the pavement. Occasional cows strolled up the main streets, which were full of coloured people of the sort that my ayah had pointed out to me were curly-haired (*hubshees*) who slept in such posture as made it easy for the devils to enter their bodies. But there were also many Malays who were Muslims of a sort and had their own Mosques, and whose flamboyantly-attired women sold flowers on the kerb, and took in washing. The dry, spiced smell of the land and the smack of the clean sunshine were health-restoring. My Navy Captain introduced me to the Naval society of Simon's Town, where the south-easter blows five days a week, and the Admiral of the Cape Station lived in splendour, with at least a brace of live turtles harnessed to the end of a little wooden jetty, swimming about till due to be taken up for turtle soup. The Navy Club there and the tales of the junior officers delighted me beyond words. There I witnessed one of the most comprehensive 'rags' I had ever seen. It rose out of a polite suggestion to a newly-appointed Lieutenant-Commander that the fore-topmast of his tiny gunboat 'wanted staying forward.' It went on till all the furniture was completely rearranged all over the room. (How was I to guess that in a few years I should know Simon's Town like the inside of my own pocket, and should give much of my life and love to the glorious land around it?)

We parted, my Captain and I, after a farewell picnic, among white, blowing sand where natives were blasting and where, of a sudden, a wrathful baboon came down the rock-face and halted waistdeep in a bed of arum-lilies. 'We'll meet again,' said my Captain, 'and if ever you want a cruise, let me know.'

A day or so before my departure for Australia, I lunched at an Adderley Street restaurant next to three men. One of them, I was told, was Cecil Rhodes, who had made the staple of our passengers' talk on *The Moor* coming out. It never occurred to me to speak to him; and I have often wondered why. . . .

Her name was *The Doric*. She was almost empty, and she spent twenty-four consecutive days and nights trying, all but successfully, to fill her boats at one roll and empty them down the saloon skylight the next. Sea and sky were equally grey and naked on that weary run to Melbourne. Then I found myself in a new land with new smells and among people who insisted a little too much that they also were new. But there are no such things as new people in this very old world.

[First published as *Something of Myself* (1937).]

✠ ✠ ✠

JUDSON AND THE EMPIRE

Gloriana! The Don may attack us
Whenever his stomach be fain;
He must reach us before he can rack us . . .
And where are the galleons of Spain?

– Dobson.

ONE OF THE MANY beauties of a democracy is its almost superhuman skill in developing troubles with other countries and finding its honour abraded in the process. A true democracy has a large contempt for all other lands that are governed by Kings and Queens and Emperors; and knows little and thinks less of their internal affairs. All it regards is its own dignity, which is its King, Queen, and Knave. So, sooner or later, its international differences end in the common people, who have no dignity, shouting the common abuse of the street, which also has no dignity, across the seas in order to vindicate their new dignity. The consequences may or may not be war; but the chances do not favour peace.

One advantage in living in a civilised land which is really governed lies in the fact that all the Kings and Queens and Emperors of the Continent are closely related by blood or marriage; are, in fact, one large family. A wise head among them knows that what appears to be a studied insult may be no more than some man's indigestion or woman's indisposition, to be treated as such, and explained by quiet talk. Again, a popular demonstration, headed by King and Court, may mean nothing more than that so-and-so's people are out of hand for the minute. When a horse falls to kicking in a hunt-crowd at a gate, the rider does not dismount, but puts his open hand behind him, and the others draw aside. It is so with the rulers of men. In the old days they cured their own and their people's bad temper with fire and slaughter; but now that the fire is so long of range and the slaughter so large, they do other things; and few among their people guess how much they owe of mere life and money to what the slang of the minute calls 'puppets' and 'luxuries.'

Once upon a time there was a little Power, the half-bankrupt wreck of a once great empire, that lost its temper with England, the whipping-boy of all the world, and behaved, as every one said, most scandalously. But it is not generally known that that Power fought a pitched battle with England and won a glorious victory. The trouble began with the people. Their own misfortunes had been many, and for private rage it is always refreshing to find a vent in public swearing. Their national vanity had been deeply injured, and they thought of their ancient glories and the days when their fleets had first rounded the Cape of Storms, and their own newspapers called upon Camoens and urged them to extravagances. It was the gross, smooth, sleek, lying England that was checking their career of colonial expansion. They assumed at once that their ruler was in league with England, so they cried with great heat that they would forthwith become a Republic and colonially expand themselves as a free people should. This made plain, the people threw stones at the English Consuls and spat at English ladies, and cut off drunken sailors of Our fleet in their ports and hammered them with oars, and made things very unpleasant for tourists at their customs, and threatened awful deaths to the consumptive invalids of Madeira, while the junior officers of the army drank fruit-extracts and entered into most blood-curdling conspiracies against their monarch; all with the object of being a Republic. Now the history of the South American Republics shows that it is not good that Southern Europeans should be also Republicans. They glide too quickly into military despotism; and the propping of men against walls and shooting them in detachments can be arranged much more economically and with less effect on the death-rate by a hide-bound monarchy. Still the performances of the Power as represented by its people were extremely inconvenient. It was the kicking horse in the crowd, and probably the rider explained that he could not check it. So the people enjoyed all the glory of war with none of the risks, and the tourists who were stoned in their travels returned stolidly to England and told the *Times* that the police arrangements of foreign towns were defective.

This, then, was the state of affairs north the Line. South it was more strained, for there the Powers were at direct issue: England, unable to go back because of the pressure of adventurous children behind her, and the actions of far-away adventurers who would not come to heel, but offering to buy out her rival; and the other Power, lacking men or money, stiff in the conviction that three hundred years of slave-holding and intermingling with the nearest natives gave an inalienable right to hold slaves and issue half-castes to all eternity. They had built no roads. Their towns were rotting under their hands; they had no trade worth the freight of a crazy steamer; and their sovereignty ran almost one musket-shot inland when things were peaceful. For these very reasons they raged all the more, and the things that they said and wrote about the manners and customs of the English would have driven a younger nation to the guns with a long red bill for wounded honour.

It was then that Fate sent down in a twin-screw shallow-draft gunboat, of some 270 tons displacement, designed for the defence of rivers, Lieutenant Harrison Edward Judson, to be known for the future as Bai-Jove-Judson. His type of craft looked exactly like a flat-iron with a match stuck up in the middle; it drew five feet of water or less; carried a four-inch gun forward, which was trained by the ship; and, on account of its persistent rolling, was, to live in, three degrees worse than a torpedo-boat. When Judson was appointed to take charge of the thing on her little trip of six or seven thousand miles southward, his first remark as he went to look her over in dock was, 'Bai Jove, that topmast wants staying forward!' The topmast was a stick about as thick as a clothesprop; but the flat-iron was Judson's first command, and he would not have exchanged his position for second post on the *Anson* or the *Howe*. He navigated her, under convoy, tenderly and lovingly to the Cape (the story of the topmast came with him), and he was so absurdly in love with his wallowing wash-tub when he reported himself, that the Admiral of the station thought it would be a pity to kill a new man on her, and allowed Judson to continue in his unenvied rule.

The Admiral visited her once in Simon's Bay, and she was bad, even for a flat-iron gunboat, strictly designed for river and harbour defence. She sweated clammy drops of dew between decks in spite of a preparation of powdered cork that was sprinkled over her inside paint. She rolled in the long Cape swell like a buoy; her foc's'le was a dog-kennel; Judson's cabin was practically under the water-line; not one of her dead-lights could ever be opened; and her compasses, thanks to the influence of the four-inch gun, were a curiosity even among Admiralty compasses. But Bai-Jove-Judson was radiant and enthusiastic. He had even contrived to fill Mr. Davies, the second-class engine-room artificer, who was his chief engineer, with the glow of his passion. The Admiral, who remembered his own first command, when pride forbade him to slack off a single rope on a dewy night, and he had racked his rigging to pieces in consequence, looked at the flat-iron keenly. Her fenders were done all over with white sennit, which was truly, white; her big gun was varnished with a better composition than the Admiralty allowed; the spare sights were cased as carefully as the chronometers; the chocks for spare spars, two of them, were made of four-inch Burma teak carved with dragons' heads (that was one result of Bai-Jove-Judson's experiences with the naval brigade in the Burmese war), the bow-anchor was varnished instead of being painted, and there were charts other than the Admiralty scale supplied. The Admiral was well pleased, for he loved a ship's husband – a man who had a little money of his own and was willing to spend it on his command. Judson looked at him hopefully. He was only a Junior Navigating Lieutenant under eight years' standing. He might be kept in Simon's Bay for six months, and his ship at sea was his delight. The dream of his heart was to enliven her dismal official gray with a line of gold-leaf and, perhaps, a little scroll-work at her blunt barge-like bows.

'There's nothing like a first command, is there?' said the Admiral, reading his thoughts. 'You seem to have rather queer compasses though. Better get them adjusted.'

'It's no use, sir,' said Judson. 'The gun would throw out the Pole itself. But – but I've got the hang of most of the weaknesses.'

'Will you be good enough to lay that gun over thirty degrees, please?' The gun was put over. Round and round and round went the needle merrily, and the Admiral whistled.

'You must have kept close to your convoy?'

'Saw her twice between here and Madeira, sir,' said Judson with a flush, for he resented the slur on his steamship. 'She's – she's a little out of hand now, but she will settle down after a while.'

The Admiral went over the side, according to the rules of the Service, but the Staff-Captain must have told the other men of the squadron in Simon's Bay, for they one and all made light of the flat-iron for many days. 'What can you shake out of her, Judson?' said the Lieutenant of the *Mongoose*, a real white-painted ram-bow gunboat with quick-firing guns, as he came into the upper verandah of the little Naval Club overlooking the dockyard one hot afternoon. It is in that Club, as the captains come and go, that you hear all the gossip of all the Seven Seas.

'Ten point four,' said Bai-Jove-Judson.

'Ah! That was on her trial trip. She's too much by the head now. I told you staying that topmast would throw her out.'

'You leave my top-hamper alone,' said Judson, for the joke was beginning to pall on him.

'Oh, my soul! Listen to him. Juddy's top-hamper. Keate, have you heard of the flat-iron's top-hamper? You're to leave it alone. Commodore Judson's feelings are hurt.'

Keate was the Torpedo Lieutenant of the big *Vortigern*, and he despised small things. 'His top-hamper,' said he slowly. 'Oh, ah yes, of course. Juddy, there's a shoal of mullet in the bay, and I think they're foul of your screws. Better go down, or they'll carry away something.'

'I don't let things carry away as a rule. You see I've no Torpedo Lieutenant aboard, thank God.'

Keate within the past week had so managed to bungle the slinging-in of a small torpedo-boat on the *Vortigern*, that the boat had broken the crutches on which she rested, and was herself being repaired in the dockyard under the Club windows.

'One for you, Keate. Never mind, Juddy, you're hereby appointed dockyard-tender for the next three years, and if you're very good and there's no sea on, you shall take me round the harbour. Waitabeechee, Commodore. What'll you take? Vanderhum for the "Cook and the captain bold, And the mate o' the *Nancy* brig, And the bo'sun tight" [Juddy, put that cue down or I'll put you under arrest for insulting the lieutenant of a real ship] "And the midshipmite, And the crew of the captain's gig."'

By this time Judson had pinned him in a corner, and was prodding him with the half-butt. The Admiral's Secretary entered, and saw the scuffle from the door.

'Ouch! Juddy, I apologise. Take that – er – topmast of yours away! Here's the man with the bow-string. I wish I were a Staff-Captain instead of a bloody lootenant. Sperril sleeps below every night. That's what makes Sperril tumble home from the waist upwards. Sperril, I defy you to touch me. I'm under orders for Zanzibar. Probably I shall annex it!'

'Judson, the Admiral wants to see you!' said the Staff-Captain, disregarding the scoffer of the *Mongoose*.

'I told you you'd be a dockyard-tender yet, Juddy. A side of fresh beef to-morrow and three dozen snapper on ice. On ice, you understand, Juddy?'

Bai-Jove-Judson and the Staff-Captain went out together.

'Now, what does the old man want with Judson?' said Keate from the bar.

'Don't know. Juddy's a damned good fellow, though. I wish to goodness he was on the *Mongoose* with us.'

The Lieutenant of the *Mongoose* dropped into a chair and read the mail-papers for an hour. Then he saw Bai-Jove-Judson in the street and shouted to him. Judson's eyes were very bright, and his figure was held very straight, and he moved joyously. Except for the Lieutenant of the *Mongoose*, the Club was empty.

'Juddy, there will be a beautiful row,' said that young man when he had heard the news delivered in an undertone. 'You'll probably have to fight, and yet I can't see what the old man's thinking of to—'

'My orders are not to row under any circumstances,' said Judson.
'Go-look-see? That all? When do you go?'

'To-night if I can. I must go down and see about things. I say, I
may want a few men for the day.'

'Anything on the *Mongoose* is at your service. There's my gig come
over now. I know that coast, dead, drunk, or asleep, and you'll need
all the knowledge you can get. If it had only been us two together!
Come along with me.'

For one whole hour Judson remained closeted in the stern cabin
of the *Mongoose*, listening, poring over chart upon chart and taking
notes, and for an hour the marine at the door heard nothing but
things like these: 'Now you'll have to lie in here if there's any sea
on. That current is ridiculously under-estimated, and it sets west at
this season of the year, remember. Their boats never come south of
this, see? So it's no good looking out for them.' And so on and so
forth, while Judson lay at length on the locker by the three-pounder,
and smoked and absorbed it all.

Next morning there was no flat-iron in Simon's Bay; only a little
smudge of smoke off Cape Hangklip to show that Mr. Davies, the
second-class engine-room artificer, was giving her all she could
carry. At the Admiral's house the ancient and retired bo'sun who
had seen many admirals come and go, brought out his paint and
brushes and gave a new coat of pure raw pea-green to the two big
cannon balls that stood one on each side of the Admiral's entrance-
gate. He felt dimly that great events were stirring.

And the flat-iron, constructed, as has been before said, solely for
the defence of rivers, met the great roll off Cape Agulhas and was
swept from end to end, and sat upon her twin screws, and leaped
as gracefully as a cow in a bog from one sea to another, till Mr.
Davies began to fear for the safety of his engines, and the Kroo boys
that made the majority of the crew were deathly sick. She ran along
a very badly-lighted coast, past bays that were no bays, where ugly
flat-topped rocks lay almost level with the water, and very many
extraordinary things happened that have nothing to do with the
story, but they were all duly logged by Bai-Jove-Judson.

At last the coast changed and grew green and low and
exceedingly muddy, and there were broad rivers whose bars were
little islands standing three or four miles out at sea, and Bai-Jove-
Judson hugged the shore more closely than ever, remembering
what the Lieutenant of the *Mongoose* had told him. Then he found

a river full of the smell of fever and mud, with green stuff growing
far into its waters, and a current that made the flat-iron gasp and
grunt.

'We will turn up here,' said Bai-Jove-Judson, and they turned up
accordingly; Mr. Davies wondering what in the world it all meant,
and the Kroo boys grinning merrily. Bai-Jove-Judson went forward
to the bows, and meditated, staring through the muddy waters.
After two hours of rooting through this desolation at an average
rate of five miles an hour, his eyes were cheered by the sight of one
white buoy in the coffee-hued midstream. The flat-iron crept up to
it cautiously, and a leadsman took soundings all round it from a
dinghy, while Bai-Jove-Judson smoked and thought, with his head
on one side.

'About seven feet, isn't there?' said he. 'That must be the tail-end
of the shoal. There's four fathom in the fairway. Knock that buoy
down with axes. I don't think it's picturesque, some how.' The
Kroo men hacked the wooden sides to pieces in three minutes, and
the mooring-chain sank with the last splinters of wood. Bai-Jove-
Judson laid the flat-iron carefully over the site, while Mr. Davies
watched, biting his nails nervously.

'Can you back her against this current?' said Bai-Jove-Judson.
Mr. Davies could, inch by inch, but only inch by inch, and Bai-Jove-
Judson stood in the bows and gazed at various things on the bank
as they came into line or opened out. The flat-iron dropped down
over the tail of the shoal, exactly where the buoy had been, and
backed once more before Bai-Jove-Judson was satisfied. Then they
went up-stream for half an hour, put into shoal-water by the bank
and waited, with a slip-rope on the anchor.

'Seems to me,' said Mr. Davies deferentially, 'like as if I heard
some one a-firing off at intervals, so to say.'

There was beyond doubt a dull mutter in the air.

'Seems to me,' said Bai-Jove-Judson, 'as if I heard a screw. Stand
by to slip her moorings.'

Another ten minutes passed and the beat of engines grew plainer.
Then round the bend of the river came a remarkably prettily-built
white-painted gunboat with a blue and white flag bearing a red
boss in the centre.

'Unshackle abaft the windlass! Stream both buoys! Easy astern.
Let go, all!' The slip-rope flew out, the two buoys bobbed in the
water to mark where anchor and cable had been left, and the flat-

iron waddled out into midstream with the white ensign at her one
mast-head.

'Give her all you can. That thing has the legs of us,' said Judson.
'And down we go.'

'It's war – bloody war! He's going to fire,' said Mr. Davies,
looking up through the engine-room hatch.

The white gunboat without a word of explanation fired three
guns at the flat-iron, cutting the trees on the banks into green chips.
Bai-Jove-Judson was at the wheel, and Mr. Davies and the current
helped the boat to an almost respectable degree of speed.

It was an exciting chase, but it did not last for more than five
minutes. The white gunboat fired again, and Mr. Davies in his
engine-room gave a wild shout.

'What's the matter? Hit?' said Bai-Jove-Judson.

'No, I've just seized of your roos-de-gare. Beg y' pardon, sir.'

'Right O! Just the half a fraction of a point more.' The wheel turned
under the steady hand, as Bai-Jove-Judson watched his marks on
the bank falling in line swiftly as troops anxious to aid. The flat-iron
smelt the shoal-water under her, checked for an instant, and went
on. 'Now we're over. Come along, you thieves, there!' said Judson.

The white gunboat, too hurried even to fire, was storming in the
wake of the flat-iron, steering as she steered. This was unfortunate,
because the lighter craft was dead over the missing buoy.

'What you do here?' shouted a voice from the bows.

'I'm going on. Sit tight. Now you're arranged for.'

There was a crash and a clatter as the white gunboat's nose took
the shoal, and the brown mud boiled up in oozy circles under her
forefoot. Then the current caught her stern on the starboard side and
drove her broadside on to the shoal, slowly and gracefully. There
she heeled at an undignified angle, and her crew yelled aloud.

'Neat! Oh, damn neat!' quoth Mr. Davies, dancing on the engine-
room plates, while the Kroo stokers beamed.

The flat-iron turned up-stream again, and passed under the
hove-up starboard side of the white gunboat, to be received with
howls and imprecations in a strange tongue. The stranded boat,
exposed even to her lower strakes, was as defenceless as a turtle on
its back, without the advantage of the turtle's plating. And the one
big bluff gun in the bows of the flat-iron was unpleasantly near.

But the captain was valiant and swore mightily. Bai-Jove-Judson
took no sort of notice. His business was to go up the river.

'We will come in a flotilla of boats and ecrazer your vile tricks,' said the captain, with language that need not be published.

Then said Bai-Jove-Judson, who was a linguist: 'You stayo where you areo, or I'll leave a holo in your bottomo that will make you muchos perforatados.'

There was a great deal of mixed language in reply, but Bai-Jove-Judson was out of hearing in a few minutes, and Mr. Davies, himself a man of few words, confided to one of his subordinates that Lieutenant Judson was 'a most remarkable prompt officer in a way of putting it.'

For two hours the flat-iron pawed madly through the muddy water, and that which had been at first a mutter became a distinct rumble.

'Was war declared?' said Mr. Davies, and Bai-Jove-Judson laughed. 'Then, damn his eyes, he might have spoilt my pretty little engines. There's war up there, though.'

The next bend brought them full in sight of a small but lively village, built round a white-washed mud house of some pretensions. There were scores and scores of saddle-coloured soldiery in dirty white uniforms running to and fro and shouting round a man in a litter, and on a gentle slope that ran inland for four or five miles something like a brisk battle was raging round a rude stockade. A smell of unburied carcases floated through the air and vexed the sensitive nose of Mr. Davies, who spat over the side.

'I want to get this gun on that house,' said Bai-Jove-Judson, indicating the superior dwelling over whose flat roof floated the blue and white flag. The little twin-screws kicked up the water exactly as a hen's legs kick in the dust before she settles down to a bath. The little boat moved uneasily from left to right, backed, yawed again, went ahead, and at last the gray, blunt gun's nose was held as straight as a rifle-barrel on the mark indicated. Then Mr. Davies allowed the whistle to speak as it is not allowed to speak in Her Majesty's service on account of waste of steam. The soldiery of the village gathered into knots and groups and bunches, and the firing up the hill ceased, and every one except the crew of the flat-iron yelled aloud. Something like an English cheer came down wind.

'Our chaps in mischief for sure, probably,' said Mr. Davies. 'They must have declared war weeks ago, in a kind of way, seems to me.'

'Hold her steady, you son of a soldier,' shouted Bai-Jove-Judson, as the muzzle fell off the white house.

Something rang as loudly as a ship's bell on the forward plates of the flat-iron, something spluttered in the water, and another thing cut a groove in the deck planking an inch in front of Bai-Jove-Judson's left foot. The saddle-coloured soldiery were firing as the mood took them, and the man in the litter waved a shining sword. The muzzle of the big gun kicked down a fraction as it was laid on the mud wall at the bottom of the house garden. Ten pounds of gunpowder shut up in a hundred pounds of metal was its charge. Three or four yards of the mud wall jumped up a little, as a man jumps when he is caught in the small of the back with a knee-cap, and then fell forward, spreading fan-wise in the fall. The soldiery fired no more that day, and Judson saw an old black woman climb to the flat roof of the house. She fumbled for a time with the flag halliards, then, finding that they were jammed, took off her one garment, which happened to be an Isabella-coloured petticoat, and waved it impatiently. The man in the litter flourished a white handkerchief, and Bai-Jove-Judson grinned. 'Now we'll give 'em one up the hill. Round with her, Mr. Davies. Curse the man who invented these floating gun-platforms! When can I pitch in a notice without slaying one of those little devils?'

The side of the slope was speckled with men returning in a disorderly fashion to the river-front. Behind them marched a small but very compact body of men who had filed out of the stockade. These last dragged quick-firing guns with them.

'Bai Jove, it's a regular army. I wonder whose,' said Bai-Jove-Judson, and he waited developments. The descending troops met and mixed with the troops in the village, and, with the litter in the centre, crowded down to the river, till the men with the quick-firing guns came up behind them. Then they divided left and right and the detachment marched through.

'Heave these damned things over!' said the leader of the party, and one after another ten little gatlings splashed into the muddy water. The flatiron lay close to the bank.

'When you're *quite* done,' said Bai-Jove-Judson politely, 'would you mind telling me what's the matter? I'm in charge here.'

'We're the Pioneers of the General Development Company,' said the leader. 'These little bounders have been hammering us in lager for twelve hours, and we're getting rid of their gatlings. Had to climb out and take them; but they've snaffled the lock-actions. Glad to see you.'

'Any one hurt?'

'No one killed exactly; but we're very dry.'

'Can you hold your men?'

The man turned round and looked at his command with a grin. There were seventy of them, all dusty and unkempt.

'We shan't sack this ash-bin, if that's what you mean. We're mostly gentlemen here, though we don't look it.'

'All right. Send the head of this post, or fort, or village, or whatever it is, aboard, and make what arrangements you can for your men.'

'We'll find some barrack accommodation somewhere. Hullo! You in the litter there, go aboard the gunboat.' The command wheeled round, pushed through the dislocated soldiery, and began to search through the village for spare huts.

The little man in the litter came aboard smiling nervously. He was in the fullest of full uniform, with many yards of gold lace and dangling chains. Also he wore very large spurs; the nearest horse being not more than four hundred miles away. 'My children,' said he, facing the silent soldiery, 'lay aside your arms.'

Most of the men had dropped them already and were sitting down to smoke. 'Let nothing,' he added in his own tongue, 'tempt you to kill these who have sought your protection.'

'Now,' said Bai-Jove-Judson, on whom the last remark was lost, 'will you have the goodness to explain what the deuce you mean by all this nonsense?'

'It was of a necessitate,' said the little man. 'The operations of war are unconformible. I am the Governor and I operate Captain. Be'old my little sword!'

'Confound your little sword, sir. I don't want it. You've fired on our flag. You've been firing at our people here for a week, and I've been fired at coming up the river.'

'Ah! The *Guadala*. She have misconstrued you for a slaver possibly. How are the *Guadala*?'

'Mistook a ship of Her Majesty's navy for a slaver! *You* mistake *any* craft for a slaver. Bai Jove, sir, I've a good mind to hang you at the yard-arm!'

There was nothing nearer that terrible spar than the walking-stick in the rack of Judson's cabin. The Governor looked at the one mast and smiled a deprecating smile.

'The position is embarrassment,' he said. 'Captain, do you think those illustrious traders burn my capital? My people will give them beer.'

'Never mind the traders, I want an explanation.'

'Hum! There are popular uprising in Europe, Captain – in my country.' His eye wandered aimlessly round the horizon.

'What has that to do with—'

'Captain, you are very young. There is still uproariment. But I,' – here he slapped his chest till his epaulets jingled – 'I am loyalist to pits of *all* my stomachs.'

'Go on,' said Judson, and his mouth quivered.

'An order arrive to me to establish a custom-houses here, and to collect of the taximent from the traders when she are come here necessarily. That was on account of political understandings with your country and mine. But to that arrangement there was no money also. Not one damn little cowrie! I desire damnably to extend all commercial things, and why? I am loyalist and there is rebellion – yes, I tell you – Republics in my country for to just begin. You do not believe? See some time how it exist. I cannot make this custom-houses and pay so the high-paid officials. The people too in my country they say the King she has no regardance into Honour of her nation. He throw away everything – Gladstone her all, you say, hey?'

'Yes, that's what we say,' said Judson with a grin.

'Therefore they say, let us be Republics on hot cakes. But I – I am loyalist to all my hands' ends. Captain, once I was attaché at Mexico. I say the Republics are no good. The peoples have her stomach high. They desire – they desire – Oh, course for the bills.'

'What on earth is that?'

'The cock-fight for pay at the gate. You give something, pay for see bloody-row. Do I make my comprehension?'

'A run for their money – is that what you mean? Gad, you're a sporting Governor!'

'So I say. I am loyalist too.' He smiled more easily. 'Now how can anything do herself for the customs-houses; but when the Company's mens she arrives, *then* a cock-fight for pay-at-gate that is, quite correct. My army he says it will Republic and shoot me off upon walls if I have not give her blood. An army, Captain, are terrible in her angries – especialment when she are not paid. I know too,' here he laid his hand on Judson's shoulder, 'I know too we are old friends. Yes! Badajos, Almeida, Fuentes d'Onor – time ever since; and a little, little cock-fight for pay-at-gate that is good for my King. More sit her tight on throne behind, you see? Now,' he waved his free hand round the decayed village, 'I say to my armies, Fight! Fight the Company's men when she come, but fight not so very strong that you are any dead. It is all in the raporta that I send. But you understand, Captain, we are good friends all the time. Ah! Ciudad Rodrigo, you remember? No? Perhaps your father then? So you see no one are dead, and we fight a fight, and it is all in the raporta, to please the people in our country; and my armies they do not put me against the walls, you see?'

'Yes; but the *Guadala*. She fired on us. Was that part of your game, my joker?'

'The *Guadala*. Ah! No, I think not. Her captain he is too big fool. But I thought she have gone down the coast. Those your gunboats poke her nose and shove her oar in every place. How is *Guadala*?'

'On a shoal. Stuck till I take her off.'

'There are any deads?'

'No.'

The Governor drew a breath of deep relief. 'There are no deads here. So you see none are deads anywhere, and nothing is done. Captain, you talk to the Company's mens. I think they are not pleased.'

'Naturally.'

'They have no senses. I thought to go backwards again they would. I leave her stockade alone all night to let them out, but they stay and come facewards to me, not backwards. They did not know we must conquer much in all these battles, or the King, he is kicked off her throne. Now we have won this battle – this great battle,' he waved his arms abroad, 'and I think you will say so that we have won, Captain. You are loyalist also? You would not disturb to the peaceful Europe? Captain, I tell you this. Your Queen she know too. She would not fight her cousin. It is a – a hand-up thing.'

'What?'

'Hand-up thing. Jobe you put. How you say?'

'Put-up job?'

'Yes. Put-up job. Who is hurt? We win. You lose. All righta!'

Bai-Jove-Judson had been exploding at intervals for the last five minutes. Here he broke down completely and roared aloud.

'But look here, Governor,' he said at last, 'I've got to think of other things than your riots in Europe. You've fired on our flag.'

'Captain, if you are me, you would have done how? And also, and also,' he drew himself up to his full height, 'we are both brave men of bravest countries. Our honour is the honour of our King,' here he uncovered, 'and of our Queen,' here he bowed low. 'Now, Captain, you shall shell my palace and I will be your prisoner.'

'Skittles!' said Bai-Jove-Judson. 'I can't shell that old hencoop.'

'Then come to dinner. Madeira, she are still to us, and I have of the best she manufac.'

He skipped over the side beaming, and Bai-Jove-Judson went into the cabin to laugh his laugh out. When he had recovered a little he sent Mr. Davies to the head of the Pioneers, the dusty man with the gatlings, and the troops who had abandoned the pursuit of arms watched the disgraceful spectacle of two men reeling with laughter on the quarter-deck of a gunboat.

'I'll put my men to build him a custom-house,' said the head of the Pioneers gasping. 'We'll make him one decent road at least. That Governor ought to be knighted. I'm glad now that we didn't fight 'em in the open, or we'd have killed some of them. So he's won great battles, has he? Give him the compliments of the victims, and tell him I'm coming to dinner. You haven't such a thing as a dress-suit, have you? I haven't seen one for six months.'

That evening there was a dinner in the village – a general and enthusiastic dinner, whose head was in the Governor's house, and whose tail threshed at large throughout all the streets. The Madeira was everything that the Governor had said, and more, and it was tested against two or three bottles of Bai-Jove-Judson's best Vanderhum, which is Cape brandy ten years in the bottle, flavoured with orange-peel and spices. Before the coffee was removed (by the lady who had made the flag of truce) the Governor had given the whole of his governorship and its appurtenances, once to Bai-Jove-Judson for services rendered by Judson's grandfather in the Peninsular War; and once to the head of the Pioneers, in consideration of that gentleman's good friendship. After the negotiation he retreated for a while into an inner apartment, and there evolved a true and complete account of the defeat of the English arms, which he read with his cocked hat over one eye to Judson and his companion. It was Judson who suggested the sinking of the flat-iron with all hands, and the head of the Pioneers who supplied the list of killed and wounded (not more than two hundred) in his command.

'Gentlemen,' said the Governor from under his cocked hat, 'the peace of Europe are saved by this raporta. You shall all be Knights of the Golden Hide. She shall go by the *Guadala*.'

'Great Heavens!' said Bai-Jove-Judson, flushed but composed, 'That reminds me that I've left that boat stuck on her broadside down the river. I must go down and soothe the commandante. He'll be blue with rage. Governor, let us go a sail on the river to cool our heads. A picnic, you understand.'

'Ya-as: everything I understand. Ho! A picnica! You are all my prisoner, but I am a good gaoler. We shall picnic on the river, and we shall take *all* the girls. Come on, my prisoners.'

'I do hope,' said the head of the Pioneers, staring from the verandah into the roaring village, 'that my chaps won't set the town alight by accident. Hullo! Hullo! A guard of honour for His Excellency, the most illustrious Governor!'

Some thirty men answered the call, made a swaying line upon a more swaying course, and bore the Governor most swayingly of all high in their arms as they staggered down to the river. And the song that they sang bade them, 'Swing, swing together, their body between their knees'; and they obeyed the words of the song faithfully, except that they were anything but 'steady from stroke to bow.' His Excellency the Governor slept on his uneasy litter, and did not wake when the chorus dropped him on the deck of the flat-iron.

'Good-night and good-bye,' said the head of the Pioneers to Judson. 'I'd give you my card if I had it, but I'm so damned drunk I hardly know my own Club. Oh yes! It's the Travellers. If ever we meet in town, remember me. I must stay here and look after my fellows. We're all right in the open, now. I s'pose you'll return the Governor some time. This is a political crisis. Good-night.'

The flat-iron went down-stream through the dark. The Governor slept on deck, and Judson took the wheel, but how he steered, and why he did not run into each bank many times, that officer does not remember. Mr. Davies did not note anything unusual, for there are two ways of taking too much, and Judson was only ward-room, not fo'c's'le drunk. As the night grew colder the Governor woke up, and expressed a desire for whisky and soda. When that came they were nearly abreast of the stranded *Guadala*, and His Excellency saluted the flag that he could not see with loyal and patriotic strains.

'They do not see. They do not hear,' he cried. 'Ten thousand saints! They sleep, and *I* have won battles! Ha!'

He started forward to the gun, which, very naturally, was loaded, pulled the lanyard, and woke the dead night with the roar of the full charge behind a common shell. That shell, mercifully, just missed the stern of the *Guadala*, and burst on the bank. 'Now you shall salute your Governor,' said he, as he heard feet running in all directions within the iron skin. 'Why you demand so base a quarter? I am here with all my prisoners.'

In the hurly-burly and the general shriek for mercy his reassurances were not heard.

'Captain,' said a grave voice from the ship, 'we have surrendered. Is it the custom of the English to fire on a helpless ship?'

'Surrendered! Holy Virgin! I go to cut off all their heads. You shall be ate by wild ants – flog and drowned! Throw me a balcony. It is I, the Governor! You shall never surrender. Judson of my soul, ascend her inside, and send me a bed, for I am sleepy; but, oh, I will multiple time kill that captain!'

'Oh!' said the voice in the darkness, 'I begin to comprehend.' And a rope-ladder was thrown, up which the Governor scrambled, with Judson at his heels.

'Now we will enjoy executions,' said the Governor on the deck. 'All these Republicans shall be shot. Little Judson, if I am not drunk, why are so sloping the boards which do not support?'

The deck, as I have said, was at a very stiff cant. His Excellency sat down, slid to leeward, and fell asleep again.

The captain of the *Guadala* bit his moustache furiously, and muttered in his own tongue: '"This land is the father of great villains and the step-father of honest men." You see our material, Captain. It is so everywhere with us. You have killed some of the rats, I hope?'

'Not a rat,' said Judson genially.

'That is a pity. If they were dead, our country might send us men, but our country is dead too, and I am dishonoured on a mud-bank through your English treachery.'

'Well, it seems to me that firing on a little tub of our size without a word of warning when you knew that the countries were at peace is treachery enough in a small way.'

'If one of my guns had touched you, you would have gone to the bottom, all of you. I would have taken the risk with my Government. By that time it would have been—'

'A Republic. So you really *did* mean fighting on your own hook! You're rather a dangerous officer to cut loose in a navy like yours. Well, what are you going to do now?'

'Stay here. Go away in boats. What does it matter? That drunken cat' – he pointed to the shadow in which the Governor slept – 'is here. I must take him back to his hole.'

'Very good. I'll tow you off at daylight if you get steam up.'

'Captain, I warn you that as soon as she floats again I will fight you.'

'Humbug! You'll have lunch with me, and then you'll take the Governor up the river.'

The captain was silent for some time. Then he said: 'Let us drink. What must be, must be, and after all we have not forgotten the Peninsular. You will admit, Captain, that it is bad to be run upon a shoal like a mud-dredger?'

'Oh, we'll pull you off before you can say knife. Take care of His Excellency. I shall try to get a little sleep now.'

They slept on both ships till the morning, and then the work of towing off the *Guadala* began. With the help of her own engines, and the tugging and puffing of the flat-iron, she slid off the mud bank sideways into deep water, the flat-iron immediately under her stern, and the big eye of the four-inch gun almost peering through the window of the captain's cabin.

Remorse in the shape of a violent headache had overtaken the Governor. He was uneasily conscious that he might perhaps have exceeded his powers, and the captain of the *Guadala*, in spite of all his patriotic sentiments, remembered distinctly that no war had been declared between the two countries. He did not need the Governor's repeated reminders that war, serious war, meant a Republic at home, possible supersession in his command, and much shooting of living men against dead walls.

'We have satisfied our honour,' said the Governor in confidence. 'Our army is appeased, and the raporta that you take home will show that we were loyal and brave. That other captain? Bah! He is a boy. He will call this a – a – Judson of my soul, how you say this is – all this affairs which have transpired between us?'

Judson was watching the last hawser slipping through the fairlead. 'Call it? Oh, I should call it rather a lark. Now your boat's all right, Captain. When will you come to lunch?'

'I told you,' said the Governor, 'it would be a larque to him.'

'Mother of the Saints! Then what is his seriousness?' said the Captain. 'We shall be happy to come when you will. Indeed, we have no other choice,' he added bitterly.

'Not at all,' said Judson, and as he looked at the three or four shot blisters on the bows of his boat a brilliant idea took him. 'It is we who are at your mercy. See how His Excellency's guns knocked us about.'

'Senor Capitan,' said the Governor pityingly, 'that is very sad. You are most injured, and your deck too, it is all shot over. We shall not be too severe on a beat man, shall we, Captain?'

'You couldn't spare us a little paint, could you? I'd like to patch up a little after the – action,' said Judson meditatively, fingering his upper lip to hide a smile.

'Our storeroom is at your disposition,' said the captain of the *Guadala*, and his eye brightened; for a few lead splashes on gray paint make a big show.

'Mr. Davies, go aboard and see what they have to spare – to spare, remember. Their spar-colour with a little working up should be just our freeboard tint.'

'Oh yes. I'll spare them,' said Mr. Davies savagely. 'I don't understand this how-d'you-do and damn-your-eyes business coming one atop of the other, in a manner o' speaking! By all rights, they're our lawful prize, after a manner o' sayin'.'

The Governor and the Captain came to lunch in the absence of Mr. Davies. Bai-Jove-Judson had not much to offer them, but what he had was given as by a beaten foeman to a generous conqueror. When they were a little warmed – the Governor genial and the Captain almost effusive – he explained quite casually over the opening of a bottle that it would not be to his interest to report the affair seriously, and it was in the highest degree improbable that the Admiral would treat it in any grave fashion.

'When my decks are cut up' (there was one groove across four planks), 'and my plates buckled' (there were five lead patches on three plates), 'and I meet such a boat as the *Guadala*, and a mere accident saves me from being blown out of the water—'

'Yes. Yes. A mere accident, Captain. The shoal buoy has been lost,' said the Captain of the *Guadala*.

'Ah? I do not know this river. That was very sad. But as I was saying, when an accident saves me from being sunk, what can I do but go away – if that is possible? But I fear that I have no coal for the sea-voyage. It is very sad.' Judson had compromised on what he knew of the French tongue as a medium of communication.

'It is enough,' said the Governor, waving a generous hand. 'Judson of my soul, the coal is yours and you shall be repaired – yes, repaired all over, of your battle's wounds. You shall go with all the honours of all the wars. Your flag shall fly. Your drum shall beat. Your, ah! – jolly-boys shall spoke their bayonets! Is it not so, Captain?'

'As you say, Excellency. But those traders in the town. What of them?'

The Governor looked puzzled for an instant. He could not quite remember what had happened to those jovial men who had cheered him overnight. Judson interrupted swiftly: 'His Excellency has set them to forced works on barracks and magazines, and, I think, a custom-house. When that is done they will be released, I hope, Excellency.'

'Yes, they shall be released for your sake, little Judson of my heart.' Then they drank the health of their respective sovereigns, while Mr. Davies superintended the removal of the scarred plank and the shot-marks on the deck and the bowplates.

'Oh, this is too bad,' said Judson when they went on deck. 'That idiot has exceeded his instructions, but – but you must let me pay for this!'

Mr. Davies, his legs in the water as he sat on a staging slung over the bows, was acutely conscious that he was being blamed in a foreign tongue. He twisted uneasily, and went on with his work.

'What is it?' said the Governor.

'That thick-head has thought that we needed some gold-leaf, and he has borrowed that from your storeroom, but I must make it good.' Then in English, 'Stand up, Mr. Davies! What the Furnace in Tophet do you mean by taking their gold-leaf? My—, are we a set of hairy pirates to scoff the storeroom out of a painted Levantine bumboat. Look contrite, you butt-ended, broad-breeched, bottle-bellied, swivel-eyed son of a tinker, you! My Soul alive, can't I maintain discipline in my own ship without a hired blacksmith of a boiler-riveter putting me to shame before a yellow-nosed picaroon! Get off the staging, Mr. Davies, and go to the engine-room! Put down that leaf first, though, and leave the books where they are. I'll send for you in a minute. Go aft!'

Now, only the upper half of Mr. Davies's round face was above the bulwarks when this torrent of abuse descended upon him; and it rose inch by inch as the shower continued, blank amazement, bewilderment, rage, and injured pride chasing each other across it till he saw his superior officer's left eyelid flutter on the cheek twice. Then he fled to the engine-room, and wiping his brow with a handful of cotton-waste, sat down to overtake circumstances.

'I am desolated,' said Judson to his companions, 'but you see the material that they give us. This leaves me more in your debt than before. The stuff I can replace' [gold-leaf is never carried on floating gun-platforms] 'but for the insolence of that man how shall I apologise?'

Mr. Davies's mind moved slowly, but after a while he transferred the cotton-waste from his forehead to his mouth and bit on it to prevent laughter. He began a second dance on the engine-room plates. 'Neat! Oh, damned neat!' he chuckled. 'I've served with a good few, but there never was one so neat as him. And I thought he was the new kind that don't know how to throw a few words, as it were.'

'Mr. Davies, you can continue your work,' said Judson down the engine-room hatch. 'These officers have been good enough to speak in your favour. Make a thorough job of it while you are about it. Slap on every man you have. Where did you get hold of it?'

'Their storeroom is a regular theatre, sir. You couldn't miss it. There's enough for two first-rates, and I've scoffed the best half of it.'

'Look sharp then. We shall be coaling from her this afternoon. You'll have to cover it all up.'

'Neat! Oh, damned neat!' said Mr. Davies under his breath, as he gathered his subordinates together, and set about accomplishing the long-deferred wish of Judson's heart.

· · · · ·

It was the *Martin Frobisher*, the flagship, a great war-boat when she was new, in the days when men built for sail as well as for steam. She could turn twelve knots under full sail, and it was under that that she stood up the mouth of the river, a pyramid of silver beneath the moon. The Admiral, fearing that he had given Judson a task beyond his strength, was coming to look for him, and incidentally to do a little diplomatic work along the coast. There was hardly wind enough to move the *Frobisher* a couple of knots an hour, and the silence of the land closed about her as she entered the fairway. Her yards sighed a little from time to time, and the ripple under her bows answered the sigh. The full moon rose over the steaming swamps, and the Admiral gazing upon it thought less of Judson and more of the softer emotions. In answer to the very mood of his mind there floated across the silver levels of the water, mellowed by distance to a most poignant sweetness, the throb of a mandolin, and the voice of one who called upon a genteel Julia – upon Julia, and upon Love. The song ceased, and the sighing of the yards was all that broke the silence of the big ship.

Again the mandolin began, and the commander on the lee side of the quarter-deck grinned a grin that was reflected in the face of the signal-midshipman. Not a word of the song was lost, and the voice of the singer was the voice of Judson.

> 'Last week down our alley came a toff,
> Nice old geyser with a nasty cough,
> Sees my missus, takes his topper off,
> Quite in a gentlemanly way'–

and so on to the end of the verse. The chorus was borne by several voices, and the signal-midshipman's foot began to tap the deck furtively.

> '"What cheer!" all the neighbours cried.
> "'Oo are you goin' to meet, Bill?
> 'ave you bought the street, Bill?"
> Laugh? – I thought I should ha' died
> When I knocked 'em in the Old Kent Road.'

It was the Admiral's gig, rowing softly, that came into the midst of that merry little smoking-concert. It was Judson, with the beribboned mandolin round his neck, who received the Admiral as he came up the side of the *Guadala*, and it may or may not have been the Admiral who stayed till three in the morning and delighted the hearts of the Captain and the Governor. He had come as an unbidden guest, and he departed as an honoured one, but strictly unofficial throughout. Judson told his tale next day in the Admiral's cabin as well as he could in the face of the Admiral's gales of laughter; but the most amazing tale was that told by Mr. Davies to his friends in the dockyard at Simon's Town from the point of view of a second-class engine-room artificer, all unversed in diplomacy.

And if there be no truth either in my tale, which is Judson's tale, or the tales of Mr. Davies, you will *not* find in harbour at Simon's Town today a flat-bottomed, twin-screw gunboat, designed solely for the defence of rivers, about two hundred and seventy tons displacement and five feet draught, wearing in open defiance of the rules of the Service a gold line on her gray paint. It follows also that you will be compelled to credit that version of the fray which, signed by His Excellency the Governor and despatched in the *Guadala*, satisfied the self-love of a great and glorious people, and saved a monarchy from the ill-considered despotism which is called a Republic.

[First published in *Many Inventions* (London: Macmillan; New York: D. Appleton, 1893).]

⚑ ⚑ ⚑

In 1892 Kipling married Caroline Balastier and went to live in her hometown of Brattleboro', Vermont, in the United States. So began a time of reflection about the sea, during which he mixed an interest in the fishing fleets which worked out of nearby Gloucester, Massachusetts, and other east coast ports, with a great romantic yearning for Britain and its seafaring traditions. During this productive period he wrote many poems, a series of stories, including 'The White Seal', which formed part of *The Jungle Book*, and 'The Ship That Found Herself', as well as a brilliant short novel, *Captains Courageous* (1897).

SOMETHING OF MYSELF

WE WENT ONCE OR twice to Gloucester, Mass., on a summer visit, when I attended the annual Memorial Service to the men drowned or lost in the cod-fishing schooners fleet. Gloucester was then the metropolis of that industry.

Now our Dr. Conland had served in that fleet when he was young. One thing leading to another, as happens in this world, I embarked on a little book which was called *Captains Courageous*. My part was the writing; his the details. This book took us (he rejoicing to escape from the dread respectability of our little town) to the shore-front, and the old T-wharf of Boston Harbour, and to queer meals in sailors' eating-houses, where he renewed his youth among ex-shipmates or their kin. We assisted hospitable tug-masters to help haul three- and four-stick schooners of Pocahontas coal all round the harbour; we boarded every craft that looked as if she might be useful, and we delighted ourselves to the limit of delight. Charts we got – old and new – and the crude implements of navigation such as they used off the Banks, and a battered boat-compass, still a treasure with me. (Also, by pure luck, I had sight of the first sickening uprush and vomit of iridescent coal-dusted water into the hold of a ship, a crippled iron hulk, sinking at her moorings.) And Conland took large cod and the appropriate knives with which they are prepared for the hold, and demonstrated anatomically and surgically so that I could make no mistake about treating them in print. Old tales, too, he dug up, and the lists of dead and gone schooners whom he had loved, and I revelled in profligate abundance of detail – not necessarily for publication but for the joy of it. And he sent me – may he be forgiven! – out on a pollock-fisher, which is ten times fouler than any cod-schooner, and I was immortally sick, even though they tried to revive me with a fragment of unfresh pollock.

[First published as *Something of Myself* (1937).]

✖ ✖ ✖

THE SEA-WIFE

THERE DWELLS A WIFE by the Northern Gate,
　　And a wealthy wife is she;
She breeds a breed o' rovin' men
　　And casts them over sea.

And some are drowned in deep water,
　　And some in sight o' shore,
And word goes back to the weary wife
　　And ever she sends more.

For since that wife had gate or gear,
　　Or hearth or garth or bield,

She willed her sons to the white harvest,
　And that is a bitter yield.

She wills her sons to the wet ploughing,
　To ride the horse of tree,
And syne her sons come back again
　Far-spent from out the sea.

The good wife's sons come home again
　With little into their hands,
But the lore of men that ha' dealt with men
　In the new and naked lands;

But the faith of men that ha' brothered men
　By more than easy breath,
And the eyes o' men that ha' read wi' men
　In the open books of death.

Rich are they, rich in wonders seen,
　But poor in the goods o' men;
So what they ha' got by the skin o' their teeth
　They sell for their teeth again.

For whether they lose to the naked life
　Or win to their hearts' desire,
They tell it all to the weary wife
　That nods beside the fire.

Her hearth is wide to every wind
　That makes the white ash spin;
And tide and tide and 'tween the tides
　Her sons go out and in;

(Out with great mirth that do desire
　Hazard of trackless ways,
In with content to wait their watch
　And warm before the blaze);

And some return by failing light,
　And some in waking dream,

For she hears the heels of the dripping ghosts
   That ride the rough roof-beam.

Home, they come home from all the ports,
   The living and the dead;
The good wife's sons come home again
   For her blessing on their head!

[This first appeared as the untitled introduction to John Arthur Barry's *Steve Brown's Bunyip* (London and Sydney: Remington and Co., 1893). This seems to have been a labour of love on Kipling's part. The book was a collection of short stories, and its author a favourite of the three old ladies of Warwick Gardens (Mary and Georgina Craik and Hannah Winward) whom Kipling had got to know in his schooldays. The poem was first collected in *The Seven Seas* (1896).]

✠ ✠ ✠

THE DEEP-SEA CABLES

THE WRECKS DISSOLVE ABOVE US; their dust drops down from
   afar –
Down to the dark, to the utter dark, where the blind white sea-
   snakes are.
There is no sound, no echo of sound, in the deserts of the deep,
Or the great grey level plains of ooze where the shell-burred cables
   creep.

Here in the womb of the world – here on the tie-ribs of earth
Words, and the words of men, flicker and flutter and beat –
Warning, sorrow and gain, salutation and mirth –
For a Power troubles the Still that has neither voice nor feet.

They have wakened the timeless Things; they have killed their
   father Time;
Joining hands in the gloom, a league from the last of the sun.
Hush! Men talk to-day o'er the waste of the ultimate slime,
And a new Word runs between: whispering, 'Let us be one!'

[First published in the *English Illustrated Magazine*, May 1893, as one of the six sub-sectional poems to 'A Song of the English', and then collected in *The Seven Seas* (1896).]

✠   ✠   ✠

THE MERCHANTMEN

KING SOLOMON DREW MERCHANTMEN,
    Because of his desire
For peacocks, apes, and ivory,
    From Tarshish unto Tyre,
With cedars out of Lebanon
    Which Hiram rafted down;
But we be only sailormen
    That use in London town.

Coastwise – cross-seas – round the world and back again –
    Where the flaw shall head us or the full Trade suits –
Plain-sail – storm-sail – lay your board and tack again –
    And that's the way we'll pay Paddy Doyle for his boots!

We bring no store of ingots,
    Of spice or precious stones,
But what we have we gathered
    With sweat and aching bones:
In flame beneath the Tropics,
    In frost upon the floe,
And jeopardy of every wind
    That does between them go.

And some we got by purchase,
    And some we had by trade,
And some we found by courtesy
    Of pike and carronade –
At midnight, 'mid-sea meetings,
    For charity to keep,
And light the rolling homeward-bound
    That rowed a foot too deep!

By sport of bitter weather
   We're walty, strained, and scarred
From the kentledge on the kelson
   To the slings upon the yard.
Six oceans had their will of us
   To carry all away –
Our galley's in the Baltic,
   And our boom's in Mossel Bay.

We've floundered off the Texel,
   Awash with sodden deals,
We've slipped from Valparaiso
   With the Norther at our heels:
We've ratched beyond the Crossets
   That tusk the Southern Pole,
And dipped our gunnels under
   To the dread Agulhas roll.
Beyond all outer charting
   We sailed where none have sailed,
And saw the land-lights burning
   On islands none have hailed;
Our hair stood up for wonder,
   But, when the night was done,
There danced the deep to windward
   Blue-empty 'neath the sun!

Strange consorts rode beside us
   And brought us evil luck;
The witch-fire climbed our channels,
   And flared on vane and truck,
Till, through the red tornado,
   That lashed us nigh to blind,
We saw The Dutchman plunging,
   Full canvas, head to wind!

We've heard the Midnight Leadsman
   That calls the black deep down –
Ay, thrice we've heard The Swimmer,
   The Thing that may not drown.
On frozen bunt and gasket

The sleet-cloud drave her hosts,
When, manned by more than signed with us,
We passed the Isle of Ghosts!

And north, amid the hummocks,
A biscuit-toss below,
We met the silent shallop
That frighted whalers know;
For, down a cruel ice-lane,
That opened as he sped,
We saw dead Hendrick Hudson
Steer, North by West, his dead.

So dealt God's waters with us
Beneath the roaring skies,
So walked His signs and marvels
All naked to our eyes:
But we were heading homeward
With trade to lose or make –
Good Lord, they slipped behind us
In the tailing of our wake!

Let go, let go the anchors;
Now shamed at heart are we
To bring so poor a cargo home
That had for gift the sea!
Let go the great bow-anchor –
Ah, fools were we and blind –
The worst we stored with utter toil,
The best we left behind!

Coastwise – cross-seas – round the world and back again,
Whither flaw shall fail us or the Trades drive down:
Plain-sail – storm-sail – lay your board and tack again –
And all to bring a cargo up to London Town!

[First published in *McClure's Magazine*, July 1893, and then collected in *The Seven Seas* (1896).]

✠ ✠ ✠

THE WHITE SEAL

Oh! hush thee, my baby, the night is behind us,
And black are the waters that sparkled so green.
The moon, o'er the combers, looks downward to find us
At rest in the hollows that rustle between.
Where billow meets billow, then soft be thy pillow,
Ah, weary wee flipperling, curl at thy ease!
The storm shall not wake thee, nor shark overtake thee,
Asleep in the arms of the slow-swinging seas!

[Seal Lullaby]

ALL THESE THINGS HAPPENED several years ago at a place called Novastoshnah, or North East Point, on the Island of St. Paul, away and away in the Bering Sea. Limmershin, the Winter Wren, told me the tale when he was blown on to the rigging of a steamer going to Japan, and I took him down into my cabin and warmed and fed him for a couple of days till he was fit to fly back to St. Paul's again. Limmershin is a very quaint little bird, but he knows how to tell the truth.

Nobody comes to Novastoshnah except on business, and the only people who have regular business there are the seals. They come in the summer months by hundreds and hundreds of thousands out of the cold gray sea. For Novastoshnah Beach has the finest accommodation for seals of any place in all the world.

Sea Catch knew that, and every spring would swim from whatever place he happened to be in – would swim like a torpedo-boat straight for Novastoshnah and spend a month fighting with his companions for a good place on the rocks, as close to the sea as possible. Sea Catch was fifteen years old, a huge gray fur seal with almost a mane on his shoulders, and long, wicked dog teeth. When he heaved himself up on his front flippers he stood more than four feet clear of the ground, and his weight, if anyone had been bold enough to weigh him, was nearly seven hundred pounds. He was scarred all over with the marks of savage fights, but he was always ready for just one fight more. He would put his head on one side, as though he were afraid to look his enemy in the face; then he would shoot it out like lightning, and when the big teeth were firmly fixed on the other seal's neck, the other seal might get away if he could, but Sea Catch would not help him.

Yet Sea Catch never chased a beaten seal, for that was against the Rules of the Beach. He only wanted room by the sea for his nursery. But as there were forty or fifty thousand other seals hunting for the same thing each spring, the whistling, bellowing, roaring, and blowing on the beach was something frightful.

From a little hill called Hutchinson's Hill, you could look over three and a half miles of ground covered with fighting seals; and the surf was dotted all over with the heads of seals hurrying to land and begin their share of the fighting. They fought in the breakers, they fought in the sand, and they fought on the smooth-worn basalt rocks of the nurseries, for they were just as stupid and unaccommodating as men. Their wives never came to the island until late in May or early in June, for they did not care to be torn to pieces; and the young two-, three-, and four-year-old seals who had not begun housekeeping went inland about half a mile through the ranks of the fighters and played about on the sand dunes in droves and legions, and rubbed off every single green thing that grew. They were called the holluschickie – the bachelors – and there were perhaps two or three hundred thousand of them at Novastoshnah alone.

Sea Catch had just finished his forty-fifth fight one spring when Matkah, his soft, sleek, gentle-eyed wife, came up out of the sea, and he caught her by the scruff of the neck and dumped her down on his reservation, saying gruffly: 'Late as usual. Where have you been?'

It was not the fashion for Sea Catch to eat anything during the four months he stayed on the beaches, and so his temper was generally bad. Matkah knew better than to answer back. She looked round and cooed: 'How thoughtful of you. You've taken the old place again.'

'I should think I had,' said Sea Catch. 'Look at me!'

He was scratched and bleeding in twenty places; one eye was almost out, and his sides were torn to ribbons.

'Oh, you men, you men!' Matkah said, fanning herself with her hind flipper. 'Why can't you be sensible and settle your places quietly? You look as though you had been fighting with the Killer Whale.'

'I haven't been doing anything but fight since the middle of May. The beach is disgracefully crowded this season. I've met at least a hundred seals from Lukannon Beach, house hunting. Why can't people stay where they belong?'

'I've often thought we should be much happier if we hauled out at Otter Island instead of this crowded place,' said Matkah.

'Bah! Only the holluschickie go to Otter Island. If we went there they would say we were afraid. We must preserve appearances, my dear.'

Sea Catch sunk his head proudly between his fat shoulders and pretended to go to sleep for a few minutes, but all the time he was keeping a sharp lookout for a fight. Now that all the seals and their wives were on the land, you could hear their clamor miles out to sea above the loudest gales. At the lowest counting there were over a million seals on the beach – old seals, mother seals, tiny babies, and holluschickie, fighting, scuffling, bleating, crawling, and playing together – going down to the sea and coming up from it in gangs and regiments, lying over every foot of ground as far as the eye could reach, and skirmishing about in brigades through the fog. It is nearly always foggy at Novastoshnah, except when the sun comes out and makes everything look all pearly and rainbow-colored for a little while.

Kotick, Matkah's baby, was born in the middle of that confusion, and he was all head and shoulders, with pale, watery blue eyes, as tiny seals must be, but there was something about his coat that made his mother look at him very closely.

'Sea Catch,' she said, at last, 'our baby's going to be white!'

'Empty clam-shells and dry seaweed!' snorted Sea Catch. 'There never has been such a thing in the world as a white seal.'

'I can't help that,' said Matkah; 'there's going to be now.' And she sang the low, crooning seal song that all the mother seals sing to their babies:

> You mustn't swim till you're six weeks old,
> Or your head will be sunk by your heels;
> And summer gales and Killer Whales
> Are bad for baby seals.
>
> Are bad for baby seals, dear rat,
> As bad as bad can be;
> But splash and grow strong,
> And you can't be wrong.
> Child of the Open Sea!

Of course the little fellow did not understand the words at first. He paddled and scrambled about by his mother's side, and learned to scuffle out of the way when his father was fighting with another seal, and the two rolled and roared up and down the slippery rocks. Matkah used to go to sea to get things to eat, and the baby was fed only once in two days, but then he ate all he could and throve upon it.

The first thing he did was to crawl inland, and there he met tens of thousands of babies of his own age, and they played together like puppies, went to sleep on the clean sand, and played again. The old people in the nurseries took no notice of them, and the holluschickie kept to their own grounds, and the babies had a beautiful playtime.

When Matkah came back from her deep-sea fishing she would go straight to their playground and call as a sheep calls for a lamb, and wait until she heard Kotick bleat. Then she would take the straightest of straight lines in his direction, striking out with her fore flippers and knocking the youngsters head over heels right and left. There were always a few hundred mothers hunting for their children through the playgrounds, and the babies were kept lively. But, as Matkah told Kotick, 'So long as you don't lie in muddy water and get mange, or rub the hard sand into a cut or scratch, and so long as you never go swimming when there is a heavy sea, nothing will hurt you here.'

Little seals can no more swim than little children, but they are unhappy till they learn. The first time that Kotick went down to the sea a wave carried him out beyond his depth, and his big head sank and his little hind flippers flew up exactly as his mother had told him in the song, and if the next wave had not thrown him back again he would have drowned.

After that, he learned to lie in a beach pool and let the wash of the waves just cover him and lift him up while he paddled, but he always kept his eye open for big waves that might hurt. He was two weeks learning to use his flippers; and all that while he floundered in and out of the water, and coughed and grunted and crawled up the beach and took catnaps on the sand, and went back again, until at last he found that he truly belonged to the water.

Then you can imagine the times that he had with his companions, ducking under the rollers; or coming in on top of a comber and landing with a swash and a splutter as the big wave went whirling far up the beach; or standing up on his tail and scratching his head as the old people did; or playing 'I'm the King of the Castle' on slippery, weedy rocks that just stuck out of the wash. Now and then he would see a thin fin, like a big shark's fin, drifting along close to shore, and he knew that that was the Killer Whale, the Grampus, who eats young seals when he can get them; and Kotick would head for the beach like an arrow, and the fin would jig off slowly, as if it were looking for nothing at all.

Late in October the seals began to leave St. Paul's for the deep sea, by families and tribes, and there was no more fighting over the nurseries, and the holluschickie played anywhere they liked. 'Next year,' said Matkah to Kotick, 'you will be a holluschickie; but this year you must learn how to catch fish.'

They set out together across the Pacific, and Matkah showed Kotick how to sleep on his back with his flippers tucked down by his side and his little nose just out of the water. No cradle is so comfortable as the long, rocking swell of the Pacific. When Kotick felt his skin tingle all over, Matkah told him he was learning the 'feel of the water,' and that tingly, prickly feelings meant bad weather coming, and he must swim hard and get away.

'In a little time,' she said, 'you'll know where to swim to, but just now we'll follow Sea Pig, the Porpoise, for he is very wise.' A school of porpoises were ducking and tearing through the water, and little Kotick followed them as fast as he could. 'How do you know where to go to?' he panted. The leader of the school rolled his white eye and ducked under. 'My tail tingles, youngster,' he said. 'That means there's a gale behind me. Come along! When you're south of the Sticky Water [he meant the Equator] and your tail tingles, that means there's a gale in front of you and you must head north. Come along! The water feels bad here.'

This was one of very many things that Kotick learned, and he was always learning. Matkah taught him to follow the cod and the halibut along the under-sea banks and wrench the rockling out of his hole among the weeds; how to skirt the wrecks lying a hundred fathoms below water and dart like a rifle bullet in at one porthole and out at another as the fishes ran; how to dance on the top of the waves when the lightning was racing all over the sky, and wave his flipper politely to the stumpy-tailed Albatross and the Man-of-war Hawk as they went down the wind; how to jump three or four feet clear of the water like a dolphin, flippers close to the side and tail curved; to leave the flying fish alone because they are all bony; to take the shoulder-piece out of a cod at full speed ten fathoms deep, and never to stop and look at a boat or a ship, but particularly a row-boat. At the end of six months what Kotick did not know about deep-sea fishing was not worth the knowing. And all that time he never set flipper on dry ground.

One day, however, as he was lying half asleep in the warm water somewhere off the Island of Juan Fernandez, he felt faint and lazy all over, just as human people do when the spring is in their legs, and he remembered the good firm beaches of Novastoshnah seven thousand miles away, the games his companions played, the smell of the seaweed, the seal roar, and the fighting. That very minute he turned north, swimming steadily, and as he went on he met scores of his mates, all bound for the same place, and they said: 'Greeting, Kotick! This year we are all holluschickie, and we can dance the Fire-dance in the breakers off Lukannon and play on the new grass. But where did you get that coat?'

Kotick's fur was almost pure white now, and though he felt very proud of it, he only said, 'Swim quickly! My bones are aching for the land.' And so they all came to the beaches where they had been born, and heard the old seals, their fathers, fighting in the rolling mist.

That night Kotick danced the Fire-dance with the yearling seals. The sea is full of fire on summer nights all the way down from Novastoshnah to Lukannon, and each seal leaves a wake like burning oil behind him and a flaming flash when he jumps, and the waves break in great phosphorescent streaks and swirls. Then they went inland to the holluschickie grounds and rolled up and down in the new wild wheat and told stories of what they had done while they had been at sea. They talked about the Pacific as boys would talk about a wood that they had been nutting in, and if anyone had understood them he could have gone away and made such a chart of that ocean as never was. The three- and four-year-old holluschickie romped down from Hutchinson's Hill crying: 'Out of the way, youngsters! The sea is deep and you don't know all that's in it yet. Wait till you've rounded the Horn. Hi, you yearling, where did you get that white coat?'

'I didn't get it,' said Kotick. 'It grew.' And just as he was going to roll the speaker over, a couple of black-haired men with flat red faces came from behind a sand dune, and Kotick, who had never seen a man before, coughed and lowered his head. The holluschickie just bundled off a few yards and sat staring stupidly. The men were no less than Kerick Booterin, the chief of the seal-hunters on the island, and Patalamon, his son. They came from the little village not half a mile from the sea nurseries, and they were deciding what seals they would drive up to the killing pens – for the seals were driven just like sheep – to be turned into seal-skin jackets later on.

'Ho!' said Patalamon. 'Look! There's a white seal!'

Kerick Booterin turned nearly white under his oil and smoke, for he was an Aleut, and Aleuts are not clean people. Then he began to mutter a prayer. 'Don't touch him, Patalamon. There has never been a white seal since – since I was born. Perhaps it is old Zaharrof's ghost. He was lost last year in the big gale.'

'I'm not going near him,' said Patalamon. 'He's unlucky. Do you really think he is old Zaharrof come back? I owe him for some gulls' eggs.'

'Don't look at him,' said Kerick. 'Head off that drove of four-year-olds. The men ought to skin two hundred to-day, but it's the beginning of the season and they are new to the work. A hundred will do. Quick!'

Patalamon rattled a pair of seal's shoulder bones in front of a herd of holluschickie and they stopped dead, puffing and blowing. Then he stepped near and the seals began to move, and Kerick headed them inland, and they never tried to get back to their companions. Hundreds and hundreds of thousands of seals watched them being driven, but they went on playing just the same. Kotick was the only one who asked questions, and none of his companions could tell him anything, except that the men always drove seals in that way for six weeks or two months of every year.

'I am going to follow,' he said, and his eyes nearly popped out of his head as he shuffled along in the wake of the herd.

'The white seal is coming after us,' cried Patalamon. 'That's the first time a seal has ever come to the killing-grounds alone.'

'Hsh! Don't look behind you,' said Kerick. 'It is Zaharrof's ghost! I must speak to the priest about this.'

The distance to the killing-grounds was only half a mile, but it took an hour to cover, because if the seals went too fast Kerick knew that they would get heated and then their fur would come off in patches when they were skinned. So they went on very slowly, past Sea Lion's Neck, past Webster House, till they came to the Salt House just beyond the sight of the seals on the beach.

Kotick followed, panting and wondering. He thought that he was at the world's end, but the roar of the seal nurseries behind him sounded as loud as the roar of a train in a tunnel. Then Kerick sat down on the moss and pulled out a heavy pewter watch and let the drove cool off for thirty minutes, and Kotick could hear the fog-dew dripping off the brim of his cap. Then ten or twelve men, each with an iron-bound club three or four feet long, came up, and Kerick pointed out one or two of the drove that were bitten by their companions or too hot, and the men kicked those aside with their heavy boots made of the skin of a walrus's throat, and then Kerick said, 'Let go!' and then the men clubbed the seals on the head as fast as they could.

Ten minutes later little Kotick did not recognize his friends any more, for their skins were ripped off from the nose to the hind flippers, whipped off and thrown down on the ground in a pile. That was enough for Kotick. He turned and galloped (a seal can gallop very swiftly for a short time) back to the sea; his little new mustache bristling with horror. At Sea Lion's Neck, where the great sea lions sit on the edge of the surf, he flung himself flipper-overhead into the cool water and rocked there, gasping miserably. 'What's here?' said a sea lion gruffly, for as a rule the sea lions keep themselves to themselves.

'Scoochnie! Ochen scoochnie!' ('I'm lonesome, very lonesome!') said Kotick. 'They're killing all the holluschickie on all the beaches!'

The Sea Lion turned his head inshore. 'Nonsense!' he said. 'Your friends are making as much noise as ever. You must have seen old Kerick polishing off a drove. He's done that for thirty years.'

'It's horrible,' said Kotick, backing water as a wave went over him, and steadying himself with a screw stroke of his flippers that brought him all standing within three inches of a jagged edge of rock.

'Well done for a yearling!' said the Sea Lion, who could appreciate good swimming. 'I suppose it is rather awful from your way of looking at it, but if you seals will come here year after year, of course the men get to know of it, and unless you can find an island where no men ever come you will always be driven.'

'Isn't there any such island?' began Kotick.

'I've followed the poltoos [the halibut] for twenty years, and I can't say I've found it yet. But look here – you seem to have a fondness for talking to your betters – suppose you go to Walrus

Islet and talk to Sea Vitch. He may know something. Don't flounce off like that. It's a six-mile swim, and if I were you I should haul out and take a nap first, little one.'

Kotick thought that that was good advice, so he swam round to his own beach, hauled out, and slept for half an hour, twitching all over, as seals will. Then he headed straight for Walrus Islet, a little low sheet of rocky island almost due northeast from Novastoshnah, all ledges and rock and gulls' nests, where the walrus herded by themselves.

He landed close to old Sea Vitch – the big, ugly, bloated, pimpled, fat-necked, long-tusked walrus of the North Pacific, who has no manners except when he is asleep – as he was then, with his hind flippers half in and half out of the surf.

'Wake up!' barked Kotick, for the gulls were making a great noise.

'Hah! Ho! Hmph! What's that?' said Sea Vitch, and he struck the next walrus a blow with his tusks and waked him up, and the next struck the next, and so on till they were all awake and staring in every direction but the right one.

'Hi! It's me,' said Kotick, bobbing in the surf and looking like a little white slug.

'Well! May I be — skinned!' said Sea Vitch, and they all looked at Kotick as you can fancy a club full of drowsy old gentlemen would look at a little boy. Kotick did not care to hear any more about skinning just then; he had seen enough of it. So he called out: 'Isn't there any place for seals to go where men don't ever come?'

'Go and find out,' said Sea Vitch, shutting his eyes. 'Run away. We're busy here.'

Kotick made his dolphin-jump in the air and shouted as loud as he could: 'Clam-eater! Clam-eater!' He knew that Sea Vitch never caught a fish in his life but always rooted for clams and seaweed; though he pretended to be a very terrible person. Naturally the Chickies and the Gooverooskies and the Epatkas – the Burgomaster Gulls and the Kittiwakes and the Puffins, who are always looking for a chance to be rude, took up the cry, and – so Limmershin told me – for nearly five minutes you could not have heard a gun fired on Walrus Islet. All the population was yelling and screaming 'Clam-eater! Stareek [old man]!' while Sea Vitch rolled from side to side grunting and coughing.

'Now will you tell?' said Kotick, all out of breath.

'Go and ask Sea Cow,' said Sea Vitch. 'If he is living still, he'll be able to tell you.'

'How shall I know Sea Cow when I meet him?' said Kotick, sheering off.

'He's the only thing in the sea uglier than Sea Vitch,' screamed a Burgomaster Gull, wheeling under Sea Vitch's nose. 'Uglier, and with worse manners! Stareek!'

Kotick swam back to Novastoshnah, leaving the gulls to scream. There he found that no one sympathized with him in his little attempt to discover a quiet place for the seals. They told him that men had always driven the holluschickie – it was part of the day's work – and that if he did not like to see ugly things he should not have gone to the killing-grounds. But none of the other seals had seen the killing, and that made the difference between him and his friends. Besides, Kotick was a white seal.

'What you must do,' said old Sea Catch, after he had heard his son's adventures, 'is to grow up and be a big seal like your father, and have a nursery on the beach, and then they will leave you alone. In another five years you ought to be able to fight for yourself.' Even gentle Matkah, his mother, said: 'You will never be able to stop the killing. Go and play in the sea, Kotick.' And Kotick went off and danced the Fire-dance with a very heavy little heart.

That autumn he left the beach as soon as he could, and set off alone because of a notion in his bullet-head. He was going to find Sea Cow, if there was such a person in the sea, and he was going to find a quiet island with good firm beaches for seals to live on, where men could not get at them. So he explored and explored by himself from the North to the South Pacific, swimming as much as three hundred miles in a day and a night. He met with more adventures than can be told, and narrowly escaped being caught by the Basking Shark, and the Spotted Shark, and the Hammerhead, and he met all the untrustworthy ruffians that loaf up and down the seas, and the heavy polite fish, and the scarlet spotted scallops that are moored in one place for hundreds of years, and grow very proud of it; but he never met Sea Cow, and he never found an island that he could fancy.

If the beach was good and hard, with a slope behind it for seals to play on, there was always the smoke of a whaler on the horizon, boiling down blubber, and Kotick knew what that meant. Or else he could see that seals had once visited the island and been killed off, and Kotick knew that where men had come once they would come again.

He picked up with an old stumpy-tailed albatross, who told him that Kerguelen Island was the very place for peace and quiet, and when Kotick went down there he was all but smashed to pieces against some wicked black cliffs in a heavy sleet-storm with lightning and thunder. Yet as he pulled out against the gale he could see that even there had once been a seal nursery. And it was so in all the other islands that he visited.

Limmershin gave a long list of them, for he said that Kotick spent five seasons exploring, with a four months' rest each year at Novastoshnah, when the holluschickie used to make fun of him and his imaginary islands. He went to the Gallapagos, a horrid dry place on the Equator, where he was nearly baked to death; he went to the Georgia Islands, the Orkneys, Emerald Island, Little Nightingale Island, Gough's Island, Bouvet's Island, the Crossets, and even to a little speck of an island south of the Cape of Good Hope. But everywhere the People of the Sea told him the same things. Seals had come to those islands once upon a time, but men had killed them all off. Even when he swam thousands of miles out of the Pacific and got to a place called Cape Corrientes (that was when he was coming back from Gough's Island), he found a few hundred mangy seals on a rock and they told him that men came there too.

That nearly broke his heart, and he headed round the Horn back to his own beaches; and on his way north he hauled out on an island full of green trees, where he found an old, old seal who was dying, and Kotick caught fish for him and told him all his sorrows. 'Now,' said Kotick, 'I am going back to Novastoshnah, and if I am driven to the killing-pens with the holluschickie I shall not care.'

The old seal said, 'Try once more. I am the last of the Lost Rookery of Masafuera, and in the days when men killed us by the hundred thousand there was a story on the beaches that some day a white seal would come out of the North and lead the seal people to a quiet place. I am old, and I shall never live to see that day, but others will. Try once more.'

And Kotick curled up his mustache (it was a beauty) and said, 'I am the only white seal that has ever been born on the beaches, and I am the only seal, black or white, who ever thought of looking for new islands.'

This cheered him immensely; and when he came back to Novastoshnah that summer, Matkah, his mother, begged him to marry and settle down, for he was no longer a holluschick but a full-grown sea-catch, with a curly white mane on his shoulders, as heavy, as big, and as fierce as his father. 'Give me another season,' he said. 'Remember, Mother, it is always the seventh wave that goes farthest up the beach.'

Curiously enough, there was another seal who thought that she would put off marrying till the next year, and Kotick danced the Fire-dance with her all down Lukannon Beach the night before he set off on his last exploration. This time he went westward, because he had fallen on the trail of a great shoal of halibut, and he needed at least one hundred pounds of fish a day to keep him in good condition. He chased them till he was tired, and then he curled himself up and went to sleep on the hollows of the ground swell that sets in to Copper Island. He knew the coast perfectly well, so about midnight, when he felt himself gently bumped on a weed-bed, he said, 'Hm, tide's running strong tonight,' and turning over under water opened his eyes slowly and stretched. Then he jumped like a cat, for he saw huge things nosing about in the shoal water and browsing on the heavy fringes of the weeds.

'By the Great Combers of Magellan!' he said, beneath his mustache. 'Who in the Deep Sea are these people?'

They were like no walrus, sea lion, seal, bear, whale, shark, fish, squid, or scallop that Kotick had ever seen before. They were between twenty and thirty feet long, and they had no hind flippers, but a shovel-like tail that looked as if it had been whittled out of wet leather. Their heads were the most foolish-looking things you ever saw, and they balanced on the ends of their tails in deep water when they weren't grazing, bowing solemnly to each other and waving their front flippers as a fat man waves his arm.

'Ahem!' said Kotick. 'Good sport, gentlemen?' The big things answered by bowing and waving their flippers like the Frog Footman. When they began feeding again Kotick saw that their upper lip was split into two pieces that they could twitch apart about a foot and bring together again with a whole bushel of seaweed between the splits. They tucked the stuff into their mouths and chumped solemnly.

'Messy style of feeding, that,' said Kotick. They bowed again, and Kotick began to lose his temper. 'Very good,' he said. 'If you do happen to have an extra joint in your front flipper you needn't show off so. I see you bow gracefully, but I should like to know your names.' The split lips moved and twitched; and the glassy green eyes stared, but they did not speak.

'Well!' said Kotick. 'You're the only people I've ever met uglier than Sea Vitch – and with worse manners.'

Then he remembered in a flash what the Burgomaster Gull had screamed to him when he was a little yearling at Walrus Islet, and he tumbled backward in the water, for he knew that he had found Sea Cow at last.

The sea cows went on schlooping and grazing and chumping in the weed, and Kotick asked them questions in every language that he had picked up in his travels; and the Sea People talk nearly as many languages as human beings. But the sea cows did not answer because Sea Cow cannot talk. He has only six bones in his neck where he ought to have seven, and they say under the sea that that prevents him from speaking even to his companions. But, as you know, he has an extra joint in his foreflipper, and by waving it up and down and about he makes what answers to a sort of clumsy telegraphic code.

By daylight Kotick's mane was standing on end and his temper was gone where the dead crabs go. Then the Sea Cow began to travel northward very slowly, stopping to hold absurd bowing councils from time to time, and Kotick followed them, saying to himself, 'People who are such idiots as these are would have been killed long ago if they hadn't found out some safe island. And what is good enough for the Sea Cow is good enough for the Sea Catch. All the same, I wish they'd hurry.'

It was weary work for Kotick. The herd never went more than forty or fifty miles a day, and stopped to feed at night, and kept close to the shore all the time; while Kotick swam round them, and over them, and under them, but he could not hurry them up one half-mile. As they went farther north they held a bowing council every few hours, and Kotick nearly bit off his mustache with impatience till he saw that they were following up a warm current of water, and then he respected them more.

One night they sank through the shiny water – sank like stones – and for the first time since he had known them began to swim quickly. Kotick followed, and the pace astonished him, for he never dreamed that Sea Cow was anything of a swimmer. They headed for a cliff by the shore – a cliff that ran down into deep water, and plunged into a dark hole at the foot of it, twenty fathoms under the sea. It was a long, long swim, and Kotick badly wanted fresh air before he was out of the dark tunnel they led him through.

'My wig!' he said, when he rose, gasping and puffing, into open water at the farther end. 'It was a long dive, but it was worth it.'

The sea cows had separated and were browsing lazily along the edges of the finest beaches that Kotick had ever seen. There were long stretches of smooth-worn rock running for miles, exactly fitted to make seal-nurseries, and there were playgrounds of hard sand sloping inland behind them, and there were rollers for seals to dance in, and long grass to roll in, and sand dunes to climb up and down, and, best of all, Kotick knew by the feel of the water, which never deceives a true sea catch, that no men had ever come there.

The first thing he did was to assure himself that the fishing was good, and then he swam along the beaches and counted up the delightful low sandy islands half hidden in the beautiful rolling fog. Away to the northward, out to sea, ran a line of bars and shoals and rocks that would never let a ship come within six miles of the beach, and between the islands and the mainland was a stretch of deep water that ran up to the perpendicular cliffs, and somewhere below the cliffs was the mouth of the tunnel.

'It's Novastoshnah over again, but ten times better,' said Kotick. 'Sea Cow must be wiser than I thought. Men can't come down the cliffs, even if there were any men; and the shoals to seaward would knock a ship to splinters. If any place in the sea is safe, this is it.'

He began to think of the seal he had left behind him, but though he was in a hurry to go back to Novastoshnah, he thoroughly explored the new country, so that he would be able to answer all questions.

Then he dived and made sure of the mouth of the tunnel, and raced through to the southward. No one but a sea cow or a seal would have dreamed of there being such a place, and when he looked back at the cliffs even Kotick could hardly believe that he had been under them.

He was six days going home, though he was not swimming slowly; and when he hauled out just above Sea Lion's Neck the first person he met was the seal who had been waiting for him, and she saw by the look in his eyes that he had found his island at last.

But the holluschickie and Sea Catch, his father, and all the other seals laughed at him when he told them what he had discovered, and a young seal about his own age said, 'This is all very well, Kotick, but you can't come from no one knows where and order us off like this. Remember we've been fighting for our nurseries, and that's a thing you never did. You preferred prowling about in the sea.'

The other seals laughed at this, and the young seal began twisting his head from side to side. He had just married that year, and was making a great fuss about it.

'I've no nursery to fight for,' said Kotick. 'I only want to show you all a place where you will be safe. What's the use of fighting?'

'Oh, if you're trying to back out, of course I've no more to say,' said the young seal with an ugly chuckle.

'Will you come with me if I win?' said Kotick. And a green light came into his eye, for he was very angry at having to fight at all.

'Very good,' said the young seal carelessly. 'If you win, I'll come.'

He had no time to change his mind, for Kotick's head was out and his teeth sunk in the blubber of the young seal's neck. Then he threw himself back on his haunches and hauled his enemy down the beach, shook him, and knocked him over. Then Kotick roared to the seals: 'I've done my best for you these five seasons past. I've found you the island where you'll be safe, but unless your heads are dragged off your silly necks you won't believe. I'm going to teach you now. Look out for yourselves!'

Limmershin told me that never in his life – and Limmershin sees ten thousand big seals fighting every year – never in all his little life did he see anything like Kotick's charge into the nurseries. He flung himself at the biggest sea catch he could find, caught him by the throat, choked him and bumped him and banged him till he grunted for mercy, and then threw him aside and attacked the next. You see, Kotick had never fasted for four months as the big seals did every year, and his deep-sea swimming trips kept him in perfect condition, and, best of all, he had never fought before. His curly white mane stood up with rage, and his eyes flamed, and his big dog teeth glistened, and he was splendid to look at. Old Sea Catch, his father, saw him tearing past, hauling the grizzled old seals about as though they had been halibut, and upsetting the young bachelors in all directions; and Sea Catch gave a roar and shouted: 'He may be a fool, but he is the best fighter on the beaches! Don't tackle your father, my son! He's with you!'

Kotick roared in answer, and old Sea Catch waddled in with his mustache on end, blowing like a locomotive, while Matkah and the seal that was going to marry Kotick cowered down and admired their men-folk. It was a gorgeous fight, for the two fought as long as there was a seal that dared lift up his head, and when there were none they paraded grandly up and down the beach side by side, bellowing.

At night, just as the Northern Lights were winking and flashing through the fog, Kotick climbed a bare rock and looked down on the scattered nurseries and the torn and bleeding seals. 'Now,' he said, 'I've taught you your lesson.'

'My wig!' said old Sea Catch, boosting himself up stiffly, for he was fearfully mauled. 'The Killer Whale himself could not have cut them up worse. Son, I'm proud of you, and what's more, I'll come with you to your island – if there is such a place.'

'Hear you, fat pigs of the sea. Who comes with me to the Sea Cow's tunnel? Answer, or I shall teach you again,' roared Kotick.

There was a murmur like the ripple of the tide all up and down the beaches. 'We will come,' said thousands of tired voices. 'We will follow Kotick, the White Seal.'

Then Kotick dropped his head between his shoulders and shut his eyes proudly. He was not a white seal any more, but red from head to tail. All the same he would have scorned to look at or touch one of his wounds.

A week later he and his army (nearly ten thousand holluschickie and old seals) went away north to the Sea Cow's tunnel, Kotick leading them, and the seals that stayed at Novastoshnah called them idiots. But next spring, when they all met off the fishing banks of the Pacific, Kotick's seals told such tales of the new beaches beyond Sea Cow's tunnel that more and more seals left Novastoshnah. Of course it was not all done at once, for the seals are not very clever, and they need a long time to turn things over in their minds, but year after year more seals went away from Novastoshnah, and Lukannon, and the other nurseries, to the quiet, sheltered beaches where Kotick sits all the summer through, getting bigger and fatter and stronger each year, while the holluschickie play around him, in that sea where no man comes.

[First published in the *National Review*, 1893, and then collected in *The Jungle Book* (London: Macmillan; New York, Century, 1894).]

✠ ✠ ✠

THE SHIP THAT FOUND HERSELF

IT WAS HER FIRST voyage, and though she was but a cargo-steamer of twenty-five hundred tons, she was the very best of her kind, the outcome of forty years of experiments and improvements in framework and machinery; and her designers and owner thought as much of her as though she had been the *Lucania*. Any one can make a floating hotel that will pay expenses, if he puts enough money into the saloon, and charges for private baths, suites of rooms, and such like; but in these days of competition and low freights every square inch of a cargo-boat must be built for cheapness, great hold-capacity, and a certain steady speed. This boat was, perhaps, two hundred and forty feet long and thirty-two feet wide, with arrangements that enabled her to carry cattle on her main and sheep on her upper deck if she wanted to; but her great glory was the amount of cargo that she could store away in her holds. Her owners – they were a very well known Scotch firm – came round with her from the north, where she had been launched and christened and fitted, to Liverpool, where she was to take cargo for New York; and the owner's daughter, Miss Frazier, went to and fro on the clean decks, admiring the new paint and the brass work, and the patent winches, and particularly the strong, straight bow, over which she had cracked a bottle of champagne when she named the steamer the *Dimbula*. It was a beautiful September afternoon, and the boat in all her newness – she was painted lead-colour with a red funnel – looked very fine indeed. Her house-flag was flying, and her whistle from time to time acknowledged the salutes of friendly boats, who saw that she was new to the High and Narrow Seas and wished to make her welcome.

'And now,' said Miss Frazier, delightedly, to the captain, 'she's a real ship, isn't she? It seems only the other day father gave the order for her, and now – and now – isn't she a beauty!' The girl was proud of the firm, and talked as though she were the controlling partner.

'Oh, she's no so bad,' the skipper replied cautiously. 'But I'm sayin' that it takes more than christenin' to mak' a ship. In the nature o' things, Miss Frazier, if ye follow me, she's just irons and rivets and plates put into the form of a ship. She has to find herself yet.'

'I thought father said she was exceptionally well found.'

'So she is,' said the skipper, with a laugh. 'But it's this way wi' ships, Miss Frazier. She's all here, but the parrts of her have not learned to work together yet. They've had no chance.'

'The engines are working beautifully. I can hear them.'

'Yes, indeed. But there's more than engines to a ship. Every inch of her, ye'll understand, has to be livened up and made to work wi' its neighbour – sweetenin' her, we call it, technically.'

'And how will you do it?' the girl asked.

'We can no more than drive and steer her and so forth; but if we have rough weather this trip – it's likely – she'll learn the rest by heart! For a ship, ye'll obsairve, Miss Frazier, is in no sense a reegid body closed at both ends. She's a highly complex structure o' various an' conflictin' strains, wi' tissues that must give an' tak' accordin' to her personal modulus of elasteecity.' Mr. Buchanan, the chief engineer, was coming towards them. 'I'm sayin' to Miss Frazier, here, that our little *Dimbula* has to be sweetened yet, and nothin' but a gale will do it. How's all wi' your engines, Buck?'

'Well enough – true by plumb an' rule, o' course; but there's no spontaneeity yet.' He turned to the girl. 'Take my word, Miss Frazier, and maybe ye'll comprehend later; even after a pretty girl's christened a ship it does not follow that there's such a thing as a ship under the men that work her.'

'I was sayin' the very same, Mr. Buchanan,' the skipper interrupted.

'That's more metaphysical than I can follow,' said Miss Frazier, laughing.

'Why so? Ye're good Scotch, an' – I knew your mother's father, he was fra' Dumfries – ye've a vested right in metapheesics, Miss Frazier, just as ye have in the *Dimbula*,' the engineer said.

'Eh, well, we must go down to the deep watters, an' earn Miss Frazier her deevidends. Will you not come to my cabin for tea?' said the skipper. 'We'll be in dock the night, and when you're goin' back to Glasgie ye can think of us loadin' her down an' drivin' her forth – all for your sake.'

In the next few days they stowed some four thousand tons dead-weight into the *Dimbula*, and took her out from Liverpool. As soon as she met the lift of the open water, she naturally began to talk. If you lay your ear to the side of the cabin, the next time you are in a steamer, you will hear hundreds of little voices in every direction, thrilling and buzzing, and whispering and popping, and gurgling and sobbing and squeaking exactly like a telephone in a thunderstorm. Wooden ships shriek and growl and grunt, but iron vessels throb and quiver through all their hundreds of ribs and thousands of rivets. The *Dimbula* was very strongly built, and every piece of her had a letter or a number, or both, to describe it; and every piece had been hammered, or forged, or rolled, or punched by man, and had lived in the roar and rattle of the shipyard for months. Therefore, every piece had its own separate voice, in exact proportion to the amount of trouble spent upon it. Cast-iron, as a rule, says very little; but mild steel plates and wrought-iron, and ribs and beams that have been much bent and welded and riveted, talk continuously. Their conversation, of course, is not half as wise as our human talk, because they are all, though they do not know it, bound down one to the other in a black darkness, where they cannot tell what is happening near them, nor what will overtake them next.

As soon as she had cleared the Irish coast, a sullen, grey-headed old wave of the Atlantic climbed leisurely over her straight bows, and sat down on the steam-capstan used for hauling up the anchor. Now the capstan and the engine that drove it had been newly painted red and green; besides which, nobody likes being ducked.

'Don't you do that again,' the capstan sputtered through the teeth of his cogs. 'Hi! Where's the fellow gone?'

The wave had slouched overside with a plop and a chuckle; but 'Plenty more where he came from,' said a brother-wave, and went through and over the capstan, who was bolted firmly to an iron plate on the iron deck-beams below.

'Can't you keep still up there?' said the deck-beams. 'What's the matter with you? One minute you weigh twice as much as you ought to, and the next you don't!'

'It isn't my fault,' said the capstan. 'There's a green brute outside that comes and hits me on the head.'

'Tell that to the shipwrights. You've been in position for months and you've never wriggled like this before. If you aren't careful you'll strain us.'

'Talking of strain,' said a low, rasping, unpleasant voice, are any of you fellows – you deck-beams, we mean – aware that those exceedingly ugly knees of yours happen to be riveted into our structure – ours?'

'Who might you be?' the deck-beams inquired.

'Oh, nobody in particular,' was the answer. 'We're only the port and starboard upper-deck stringers; and if you persist in heaving and hiking like this, we shall be reluctantly compelled to take steps.'

Now the stringers of the ship are long iron girders, so to speak, that run lengthways from stern to bow. They keep the iron frames (what are called ribs in a wooden ship) in place, and also help to hold the ends of the deck-beams, which go from side to side of the ship. Stringers always consider themselves most important, because they are so long.

'You will take steps – will you?' This was a long echoing rumble. It came from the frames – scores and scores of them, each one about eighteen inches distant from the next, and each riveted to the stringers in four places. 'We think you will have a certain amount of trouble in that'; and thousands and thousands of the little rivets that held everything together whispered: 'You will! You will! Stop quivering and be quiet. Hold on, brethren! Hold on! Hot Punches! What's that?'

Rivets have no teeth, so they cannot chatter with fright; but they did their best as a fluttering jar swept along the ship from stern to bow, and she shook like a rat in a terrier's mouth.

An unusually severe pitch, for the sea was rising, had lifted the big throbbing screw nearly to the surface, and it was spinning round in a kind of soda-water – half sea and half air – going much faster than was proper, because there was no deep water for it to work in. As it sank again, the engines – and they were triple expansion, three cylinders in a row – snorted through all their three pistons. 'Was that a joke, you fellow outside? It's an uncommonly poor one. How are we to do our work if you fly off the handle that way?'

'I didn't fly off the handle,' said the screw, twirling huskily at the end of the screw-shaft. 'If I had, you'd have been scrap-iron by this time. The sea dropped away from under me, and I had nothing to catch on to. That's all.'

'That's all, d'you call it?' said the thrust-block, whose business it is to take the push of the screw; for if a screw had nothing to hold it back it would crawl right into the engine-room. (It is the holding back of the screwing action that gives the drive to a ship.) 'I know I do my work deep down and out of sight, but I warn you I expect justice. All I ask for is bare justice. Why can't you push steadily and evenly, instead of whizzing like a whirligig, and making me hot under all my collars?' The thrust-block had six collars, each faced with brass, and he did not wish to get them heated.

All the bearings that supported the fifty feet of screw-shaft as it ran to the stern whispered: 'Justice – give us justice.'

'I can only give you what I can get,' the screw answered. 'Look out! It's coming again!'

He rose with a roar as the *Dimbula* plunged, and 'whack – flack – whack – whack' went the engines, furiously, for they had little to check them.

'I'm the noblest outcome of human ingenuity – Mr. Buchanan says so,' squealed the high-pressure cylinder. 'This is simply ridiculous!' The piston went up savagely, and choked, for half the steam behind it was mixed with dirty water. 'Help! Oiler! Fitter! Stoker! Help I'm choking,' it gasped. 'Never in the history of maritime invention has such a calamity over-taken one so young and strong. And if I go, who's to drive the ship?'

'Hush! Oh, hush!' whispered the Steam, who, of course, had been to sea many times before. He used to spend his leisure ashore in a cloud, or a gutter, or a flower-pot, or a thunder-storm, or anywhere else where water was needed. 'That's only a little priming, a little carrying-over, as they call it. It'll happen all night, on and off. I don't say it's nice, but it's the best we can do under the circumstances.'

'What difference can circumstances make? I'm here to do my work – on clean, dry steam. Blow circumstances!' the cylinder roared.

'The circumstances will attend to the blowing. I've worked on the North Atlantic run a good many times – it's going to be rough before morning.'

'It isn't distressingly calm now,' said the extra strong frames – they were called web-frames – in the engine-room. 'There's an upward thrust that we don't understand, and there's a twist that is very bad for our brackets and diamond-plates, and there's a sort of west-northwesterly pull, that follows the twist, which seriously annoys us. We mention this because we happened to cost a good deal of money, and we feel sure that the owner would not approve of our being treated in this frivolous way.'

'I'm afraid the matter is out of owner's hands for the present,' said the Steam, slipping into the condenser. 'You're left to your own devices till the weather betters.'

'I wouldn't mind the weather,' said a flat bass voice below; 'it's this confounded cargo that's breaking my heart. I'm the garboard-strake, and I'm twice as thick as most of the others, and I ought to know something.'

The garboard-strake is the lowest plate in the bottom of a ship, and the *Dimbula*'s garboard-strake was nearly three-quarters of an inch mild steel.

'The sea pushes me up in a way I should never have expected,' the strake grunted, 'and the cargo pushes me down, and, between the two, I don't know what I'm supposed to do.'

'When in doubt, hold on,' rumbled the Steam, making head in the boilers.

'Yes; but there's only dark, and cold, and hurry, down here; and how do I know whether the other plates are doing their duty? Those bulwark-plates up above, I've heard, ain't more than five-sixteenths of an inch thick – scandalous, I call it.'

'I agree with you,' said a huge web-frame, by the main cargo-hatch. He was deeper and thicker than all the others, and curved half-way across the ship in the shape of half an arch, to support the deck where deck-beams would have been in the way of cargo coming up and down. 'I work entirely unsupported, and I observe that I am the sole strength of this vessel, so far as my vision extends. The responsibility, I assure you, is enormous. I believe the money-value of the cargo is over one hundred and fifty thousand pounds. Think of that!'

'And every pound of it is dependent on my personal exertions.' Here spoke a sea-valve that communicated directly with the water outside, and was seated not very far from the garboard-strake. 'I rejoice to think that I am a Prince-Hyde Valve, with best Para rubber facings. Five patents cover me – I mention this without pride – five separate and several patents, each one finer than the other. At present I am screwed fast. Should I open, you would immediately be swamped. This is incontrovertible!'

Patent things always use the longest words they can. It is a trick that they pick up from their inventors.

'That's news,' said a big centrifugal bilge-pump. 'I had an idea that you were employed to clean decks and things with. At least,

I've used you for that more than once. I forget the precise number, in thousands, of gallons which I am guaranteed to throw per hour; but I assure you, my complaining friends, that there is not the least danger. I alone am capable of clearing any water that may find its way here. By my Biggest Deliveries, we pitched then!'

The sea was getting up in workmanlike style. It was a dead westerly gale, blown from under a ragged opening of green sky, narrowed on all sides by fat, grey clouds; and the wind bit like pincers as it fretted the spray into lacework on the flanks of the waves.

'I tell you what it is,' the foremast telephoned down its wire-stays. 'I'm up here, and I can take a dispassionate view of things. There's an organised conspiracy against us. I'm sure of it, because every single one of these waves is heading directly for our bows. The whole sea is concerned in it – and so's the wind. It's awful!'

'What's awful?' said a wave, drowning the capstan for the hundredth time.

'This organised conspiracy on your part,' the capstan gurgled, taking his cue from the mast.

'Organised bubbles and spindrift! There has been a depression in the Gulf of Mexico. Excuse me!' He leaped overside; but his friends took up the tale one after another.

'Which has advanced—' That wave hove green water over the funnel.

'As far as Cape Hatteras—' He drenched the bridge.

'And is now going out to sea – to sea – to sea!' The third went out in three surges, making a clean sweep of a boat, which turned bottom up and sank in the darkening troughs alongside, while the broken falls whipped the davits.

'That's all there is to it,' seethed the white water roaring through the scuppers. 'There's no animus in our proceedings. We're only meteorological corollaries.'

'Is it going to get any worse?' said the bow-anchor chained down to the deck, where he could only breathe once in five minutes.

'Not knowing, can't say. Wind may blow a bit by midnight. Thanks awfully. Good-bye.'

The wave that spoke so politely had travelled some distance aft, and found itself all mixed up on the deck amidships, which was a well-deck sunk between high bulwarks. One of the bulwark-plates, which was hung on hinges to open outward, had swung out, and passed the bulk of the water back to the sea again with a clean smack.

'Evidently that's what I'm made for,' said the plate, closing again with a sputter of pride. 'Oh, no, you don't, my friend!' The top of a wave was trying to get in from the outside, but as the plate did not open in that direction, the defeated water spurted back.

'Not bad for five-sixteenths of an inch,' said the bulwark-plate. 'My work, I see, is laid down for the night'; and it began opening and shutting, as it was designed to do, with the motion of the ship.

'We are not what you might call idle,' groaned all the frames together, as the *Dimbula* climbed a big wave, lay on her side at the top, and shot into the next hollow, twisting in the descent. A huge swell pushed up exactly under her middle, and her bow and stern hung free with nothing to support them. Then one joking wave caught her up at the bow, and another at the stern, while the rest of the water slunk away from under her just to see how she would like it; so she was held up at her two ends only, and the weight of the cargo and the machinery fell on the groaning iron keels and bilge-stringers.

'Ease off! Ease off; there!' roared the garboard-strake. 'I want one-eighth of an inch fair play. D'you hear me, you rivets!'

'Ease off! Ease off!' cried the bilge-stringers. 'Don't hold us so tight to the frames!'

'Ease off!' grunted the deck-beams, as the *Dimbula* rolled fearfully. 'You've cramped our knees into the stringers, and we can't move. Ease off; you flat-headed little nuisances.'

Then two converging seas hit the bows, one on each side, and fell away in torrents of streaming thunder.

'Ease off!' shouted the forward collision-bulkhead. 'I want to crumple up, but I'm stiffened in every direction. Ease off; you dirty little forge-filings. Let me breathe!'

All the hundreds of plates that are riveted to the frames, and make the outside skin of every steamer, echoed the call, for each plate wanted to shift and creep a little, and each plate, according to its position, complained against the rivets.

'We can't help it! We can't help it!' they murmured in reply. 'We're put here to hold you, and we're going to do it; you never pull us twice in the same direction. If you'd say what you were going to do next, we'd try to meet your views.'

'As far as I could feel,' said the upper-deck planking, and that was four inches thick, 'every single iron near me was pushing or pulling in opposite directions. Now, what's the sense of that? My friends, let us all pull together.'

'Pull any way you please,' roared the funnel, 'so long as you don't try your experiments on me. I need fourteen wire-ropes, all pulling in different directions, to hold me steady. Isn't that so?'

'We believe you, my boy!' whistled the funnel-stays through their clinched teeth, as they twanged in the wind from the top of the funnel to the deck.

'Nonsense! We must all pull together,' the decks repeated. 'Pull lengthways.'

'Very good,' said the stringers; 'then stop pushing sideways when you get wet. Be content to run gracefully fore and aft, and curve in at the ends as we do.'

'No – no curves at the end. A very slight workmanlike curve from side to side, with a good grip at each knee, and little pieces welded on,' said the deck-beams.

'Fiddle!' cried the iron pillars of the deep, dark hold. 'Who ever heard of curves? Stand up straight; be a perfectly round column, and carry tons of good solid weight – like that! There!' A big sea smashed on the deck above, and the pillars stiffened themselves to the load.

'Straight up and down is not bad,' said the frames, who ran that way in the sides of the ship, 'but you must also expand yourselves sideways. Expansion is the law of life, children. Open out! open out!'

'Come back!' said the deck-beams, savagely, as the upward heave of the sea made the frames try to open. 'Come back to your bearings, you slack-jawed irons!'

'Rigidity! Rigidity! Rigidity!' thumped the engines. 'Absolute, unvarying rigidity – rigidity!'

'You see!' whined the rivets, in chorus. 'No two of you will ever pull alike, and – and you blame it all on us. We only know how to go through a plate and bite down on both sides so that it can't, and mustn't, and sha'n't move.'

'I've got one fraction of an inch play, at any rate,' said the garboard-strake, triumphantly. So he had, and all the bottom of the ship felt the easier for it.

'Then we're no good,' sobbed the bottom rivets. 'We were ordered – we were ordered – never to give; and we've given, and the sea will come in, and we'll all go to the bottom together! First we're blamed for everything unpleasant, and now we haven't the consolation of having done our work.'

'Don't say I told you,' whispered the Steam, consolingly; 'but, between you and me and the last cloud I came from, it was bound to happen sooner or later. You had to give a fraction, and you've given without knowing it. Now, hold on, as before.'

'What's the use?' a few hundred rivets chattered. 'We've given – we've given; and the sooner we confess that we can't keep the ship together, and go off our little heads, the easier it will be. No rivet forged can stand this strain.'

'No one rivet was ever meant to. Share it among you,' the Steam answered.

'The others can have my share. I'm going to pull out,' said a rivet in one of the forward plates.

'If you go, others will follow,' hissed the Steam. 'There's nothing so contagious in a boat as rivets going. Why, I knew a little chap like you – he was an eighth of an inch fatter, though – on a steamer – to be sure, she was only twelve hundred tons, now I come to think of it in exactly the same place as you are. He pulled out in a bit of a bobble of a sea, not half as bad as this, and he started all his friends on the same butt-strap, and the plates opened like a furnace door, and I had to climb into the nearest fog-bank, while the boat went down.'

'Now that's peculiarly disgraceful,' said the rivet. 'Fatter than me, was he, and in a steamer not half our tonnage? Reedy little peg! I blush for the family, sir.' He settled himself more firmly than ever in his place, and the Steam chuckled.

'You see,' he went on, quite gravely, 'a rivet, and especially a rivet in your position, is really the one indispensable part of the ship.'

The Steam did not say that he had whispered the very same thing to every single piece of iron aboard. There is no sense in telling too much.

And all that while the little *Dimbula* pitched and chopped, and swung and slewed, and lay down as though she were going to die, and got up as though she had been stung, and threw her nose round and round in circles half a dozen times as she dipped, for the gale was at its worst. It was inky black, in spite of the tearing white froth on the waves, and, to top everything, the rain began to fall in sheets, so that you could not see your hand before your face.

This did not make much difference to the ironwork below, but it troubled the foremast a good deal.

'Now it's all finished,' he said dismally. 'The conspiracy is too strong for us. There is nothing left but to—'

'Hurraar! Brrrraaah! Brrrrrrp!' roared the Steam through the fog-horn, till the decks quivered. 'Don't be frightened, below. It's only me, just throwing out a few words, in case any one happens to be rolling round to-night.'

'You don't mean to say there's any one except us on the sea in such weather?' said the funnel, in a husky snuffle.

'Scores of 'em,' said the Steam, clearing its throat. 'Rrrrrraaa! Brraaaaa! Prrrrp! It's a trifle windy up here; and, Great Boilers! how it rains!'

'We're drowning,' said the scuppers. They had been doing nothing else all night, but this steady thrash of rain above them seemed to be the end of the world.

'That's all right. We'll be easier in an hour or two. First the wind and then the rain. Soon you may make sail again! Grrraaaaaah! Drrrraaaa! Drrrp! I have a notion that the sea is going down already. If it does you'll learn something about rolling. We've only pitched till now. By the way, aren't you chaps in the hold a little easier than you were?'

There was just as much groaning and straining as ever, but it was not so loud or squeaky in tone; and when the ship quivered she did not jar stiffly, like a poker hit on the floor, but gave with a supple little waggle, like a perfectly balanced golf-club.

'We have made a most amazing discovery,' said the stringers, one after another. 'A discovery that entirely changes the situation. We have found, for the first time in the history of ship-building, that the inward pull of the deck-beams and the outward thrust of the frames locks us, as it were, more closely in our places, and enables us to endure a strain which is entirely without parallel in the records of marine architecture.'

The Steam turned a laugh quickly into a roar up the fog-horn. 'What massive intellects you great stringers have,' he said softly, when he had finished.

'We also,' began the deck-beams, 'are discoverers and geniuses. We are of opinion that the support of the hold-pillars materially helps us. We find that we lock up on them when we are subjected to a heavy and singular weight of sea above.'

Here the *Dimbula* shot down a hollow, lying almost on her side; righting at the bottom with a wrench and a spasm.

'In these cases – are you aware of this, Steam? – the plating at the bows, and particularly at the stern – we would also mention the floors beneath us – help us to resist any tendency to spring.' The frames spoke, in the solemn awed voice which people use when they have just come across something entirely new for the very first time.

'I'm only a poor puffy little flutterer,' said the Steam, 'but I have to stand a good deal of pressure in my business. It's all tremendously interesting. Tell us some more. You fellows are so strong.'

'Watch us and you'll see,' said the bow-plates, proudly. 'Ready, behind there! Here's the father and mother of waves coming! Sit tight, rivets all!' A great sluicing comber thundered by, but through the scuffle and confusion the Steam could hear the low, quick cries of the ironwork as the various strains took them – cries like these: 'Easy, now – easy! Now push for all your strength! Hold out! Give a fraction! Hold up! Pull in! Shove crossways! Mind the strain at the ends! Grip, now! Bite tight! Let the water get away from under – and there she goes!'

The wave raced off into the darkness, shouting, 'Not bad, that, if it's your first run!' and the drenched and ducked ship throbbed to the beat of the engines inside her. All three cylinders were white with the salt spray that had come down through the engine-room hatch; there was white fur on the canvas-bound steam-pipes, and even the bright-work deep below was speckled and soiled; but the cylinders had learned to make the most of steam that was half water, and were pounding along cheerfully.

'How's the noblest outcome of human ingenuity hitting it?' said the Steam, as he whirled through the engine-room.

'Nothing for nothing in this world of woe,' the cylinders answered, as though they had been working for centuries, 'and precious little for seventy-five pounds head. We've made two knots this last hour and a quarter! Rather humiliating for eight hundred horse-power, isn't it?'

'Well, it's better than drifting astern, at any rate. You seem rather less – how shall I put it – stiff in the back than you were.'

'If you'd been hammered as we've been this night, you wouldn't be stiff-iff-iff, either. Theoreti-retti-retti-cally, of course, rigidity is the thing. Purrr-purr-practically, there has to be a little give and take. We found that out by working on our sides for five minutes at a stretch-chch-chh. How's the weather?'

'Sea's going down fast,' said the Steam.

'Good business,' said the high-pressure cylinder. 'Whack her up, boys. They've given us five pounds more steam'; and he began humming the first bars of 'Said the young Obadiah to the old Obadiah,' which, as you may have noticed, is a pet tune among engines not built for high speed. Racing-liners with twin-screws sing 'The Turkish Patrol' and the overture to the 'Bronze Horse,' and 'Madame Angot,' till something goes wrong, and then they render Gounod's 'Funeral March of a Marionette,' with variations.

'You'll learn a song of your own some fine day,' said the Steam, as he flew up the fog-horn for one last bellow.

Next day the sky cleared and the sea dropped a little, and the *Dimbula* began to roll from side to side till every inch of iron in her was sick and giddy. But luckily they did not all feel ill at the same time: otherwise she would have opened out like a wet paper box.

The Steam whistled warnings as he went about his business: it is in this short, quick roll and tumble that follows a heavy sea that most of the accidents happen, for then everything thinks that the worst is over and goes off guard. So he orated and chattered till the beams and frames and floors and stringers and things had learned how to lock down and lock up on one another, and endure this new kind of strain.

They found ample time to practise, for they were sixteen days at sea, and it was foul weather till within a hundred miles of New York. The *Dimbula* picked up her pilot, and came in covered with salt and red rust. Her funnel was dirty-grey from top to bottom; two boats had been carried away; three copper ventilators looked like hats after a fight with the police; the bridge had a dimple in the middle of it; the house that covered the steam steering-gear was split as with hatchets; there was a bill for small repairs in the engine-room almost as long as the screw-shaft; the forward cargo-hatch fell into bucket-staves when they raised the iron cross-bars; and the steam-capstan had been badly wrenched on its bed. Altogether, as the skipper said, it was 'a pretty general average.'

'But she's soupled,' he said to Mr. Buchanan. 'For all her dead-weight she rode like a yacht. Ye mind that last blow off the Banks – I am proud of her, Buck.'

'It's vera good,' said the chief engineer, looking along the dishevelled decks. 'Now, a man judgin' superfeecially would say we were a wreck, but we know otherwise – by experience.'

Naturally everything in the *Dimbula* fairly stiffened with pride, and the foremast and the forward collision-bulkhead, who are pushing creatures, begged the Steam to warn the Port of New York of their arrival. 'Tell those big boats all about us,' they said. 'They seem to take us quite as a matter of course.'

It was a glorious, clear, dead calm morning, and in single file, with less than half a mile between each, their bands playing and their tugboats shouting and waving handkerchiefs, were the *Majestic*, the *Paris*, the *Touraine*, the *Servia*, the *Kaiser Wilhelm II*, and the *Werkendam*, all statelily going out to sea. As the *Dimbula* shifted her helm to give the great boats clear way, the Steam (who knows far too much to mind making an exhibition of himself now and then) shouted:

'Oyez! Oyez! Oyez! Princes, Dukes, and Barons of the High Seas! Know ye by these presents, we are the *Dimbula*, fifteen days nine hours from Liverpool, having crossed the Atlantic with four thousand ton of cargo for the first time in our career! We have not foundered. We are here. 'Eer! 'Eer! We are not disabled. But we have had a time wholly unparalleled in the annals of ship-building! Our decks were swept! We pitched; we rolled! We thought we were going to die! Hi! Hi! But we didn't. We wish to give notice that we have come to New York all the way across the Atlantic, through the worst weather in the world; and we are the *Dimbula*! We are – arr – ha – ha – ha-r-r-r!'

The beautiful line of boats swept by as steadily as the procession of the Seasons. The *Dimbula* heard the *Majestic* say, 'Hmph!' and the *Paris* grunted, 'How!' and the *Touraine* said, 'Oui!' with a little coquettish flicker of steam; and the *Servia* said, 'Haw!' and the *Kaiser* and the *Werkendam* said, 'Hoch!' Dutch fashion – and that was absolutely all.

'I did my best,' said the Steam, gravely, 'but I don't think they were much impressed with us, somehow. Do you?'

'It's simply disgusting,' said the bow-plates. 'They might have seen what we've been through. There isn't a ship on the sea that has suffered as we have – is there, now?'

'Well, I wouldn't go so far as that,' said the Steam, 'because I've worked on some of those boats, and sent them through weather quite as bad as the fortnight that we've had, in six days; and some of them are a little over ten thousand tons, I believe. Now I've seen the *Majestic*, for instance, ducked from her bows to her funnel; and I've helped the *Arizona*, I think she was, to back off an iceberg she met with one dark night; and I had to run out of the *Paris*'s engine-room, one day, because there was thirty foot of water in it. Of course, I don't deny—' The Steam shut off suddenly, as a tugboat, loaded with a political club and a brass band, that had been to see a New York Senator off to Europe, crossed their bows, going to Hoboken. There was a long silence that reached, without a break, from the cut-water to the propeller-blades of the *Dimbula*.

Then a new, big voice said slowly and thickly, as though the owner had just waked up: 'It's my conviction that I have made a fool of myself.'

The Steam knew what had happened at once; for when a ship finds herself all the talking of the separate pieces ceases and melts into one voice, which is the soul of the ship.

'Who are you?' he said, with a laugh.

'I am the *Dimbula*, of course. I've never been anything else except that – and a fool!'

The tugboat, which was doing its very best to be run down, got away just in time; its band playing clashily and brassily a popular but impolite air:

> In the days of old Rameses – are you on?
> In the days of old Rameses – are you on?
> In the days of old Rameses,
> That story had paresis,
> Are you on – are you on – are you on?

'Well, I'm glad you've found yourself,' said the Steam. 'To tell the truth, I was a little tired of talking to all those ribs and stringers. Here's Quarantine. After that we'll go to our wharf and clean up a little, and – next month we'll do it all over again.'

[First published in the *Idler Magazine*, December 1895 and then collected in *The Day's Work* (London: Macmillan; New York, Doubleday, 1898).]

✠　✠　✠

CAPTAINS COURAGEOUS

Chapter VIII

To THE END OF his days, Harvey will never forget that sight. The sun was just clear of the horizon they had not seen for nearly a week, and his low red light struck into the riding-sails of three fleets of anchored schooners – one to the north, one to the westward, and one to the south. There must have been nearly a hundred of them, of every possible make and build, with, far away, a square-rigged Frenchman, all bowing and courtesying one to the other. From every boat dories were dropping away like bees from a crowded hive, and the clamour of voices, the rattling of ropes and blocks, and the splash of the oars carried for miles across the heaving water. The sails turned all colours, black, pearly-gray, and white, as the sun mounted; and more boats swung up through the mists to the southward.

The dories gathered in clusters, separated, reformed, and broke again, all heading one way; while men hailed and whistled and cat-called and sang, and the water was speckled with rubbish thrown overboard.

'It's a town,' said Harvey. 'Disko was right. It IS a town!'

'I've seen smaller,' said Disko. 'There's about a thousand men here; an' yonder's the Virgin.' He pointed to a vacant space of greenish sea, where there were no dories.

The *We're Here* skirted round the northern squadron, Disko waving his hand to friend after friend, and anchored as nearly as a racing yacht at the end of the season. The Bank fleet pass good seamanship in silence; but a bungler is jeered all along the line.

'Jest in time fer the caplin,' cried the *Mary Chilton*.

'Salt 'most wet?' asked the *King Philip*.

'Hey, Tom Platt! Come t' supper to-night?' said the *Henry Clay*; and so questions and answers flew back and forth. Men had met one another before, dory-fishing in the fog, and there is no place for gossip like the Bank fleet. They all seemed to know about Harvey's rescue, and asked if he were worth his salt yet. The young bloods jested with Dan, who had a lively tongue of his own, and inquired after their health by the town-nicknames they least liked. Manuel's countrymen jabbered at him in their own language; and even the silent cook was seen riding the jib-boom and shouting Gaelic to a friend as black as himself. After they had buoyed the cable – all around the Virgin is rocky bottom, and carelessness means chafed ground-tackle and danger from drifting – after they had buoyed the cable, their dories went forth to join the mob of boats anchored about a mile away. The schooners rocked and dipped at a safe distance, like mother ducks watching their brood, while the dories behaved like mannerless ducklings.

As they drove into the confusion, boat banging boat, Harvey's ears tingled at the comments on his rowing. Every dialect from Labrador to Long Island, with Portuguese, Neapolitan, Lingua Franca, French, and Gaelic, with songs and shoutings and new oaths, rattled round him, and he seemed to be the butt of it all. For the first time in his life he felt shy – perhaps that came from living so long with only the *We're Heres* – among the scores of wild faces that rose and fell with the reeling small craft. A gentle, breathing swell, three furlongs from trough to barrel, would quietly shoulder up a string of variously painted dories. They hung for an instant, a wonderful frieze against the sky-line, and their men pointed and hailed. Next moment the open mouths, waving arms, and bare chests disappeared, while on another swell came up an entirely new line of characters like paper figures in a toy theatre. So Harvey stared. 'Watch out!' said Dan, flourishing a dip-net. 'When I tell you dip, you dip. The caplin'll school any time from naow on. Where'll we lay, Tom Platt?'

Pushing, shoving, and hauling, greeting old friends here and warning old enemies there, Commodore Tom Platt led his little fleet well to leeward of the general crowd, and immediately three or four men began to haul on their anchors with intent to lee-bow the *We're Heres*. But a yell of laughter went up as a dory shot from her station with exceeding speed, its occupant pulling madly on the roding.

'Give her slack!' roared twenty voices. 'Let him shake it out.'

'What's the matter?' said Harvey, as the boat flashed away to the southward. 'He's anchored, isn't he?'

'Anchored, sure enough, but his graound-tackle's kinder shifty,' said Dan, laughing. 'Whale's fouled it. . . . Dip Harve! Here they come!'

The sea round them clouded and darkened, and then frizzed up in showers of tiny silver fish, and over a space of five or six acres the cod began to leap like trout in May; while behind the cod three or four broad gray-backs broke the water into boils.

Then everybody shouted and tried to haul up his anchor to get among the school, and fouled his neighbour's line and said what was in his heart, and dipped furiously with his dip-net, and shrieked cautions and advice to his companions, while the deep fizzed like freshly opened soda-water, and cod, men, and whales together flung in upon the luckless bait. Harvey was nearly knocked overboard by the handle of Dan's net. But in all the wild tumult he noticed, and never forgot, the wicked, set little eye – something like a circus elephant's eye – of a whale that drove along almost level with the water, and, so he said, winked at him. Three boats found their rodings fouled by these reckless mid-sea hunters, and were towed half a mile ere their horses shook the line free.

Then the caplin moved off, and five minutes later there was no sound except the splash of the sinkers overside, the flapping of the cod, and the whack of the muckles as the men stunned them. It was wonderful fishing. Harvey could see the glimmering cod below, swimming slowly in droves, biting as steadily as they swam. Bank law strictly forbids more than one hook on one line when the dories are on the Virgin or the Eastern Shoals; but so close lay the boats that even single hooks snarled, and Harvey found himself in hot argument with a gentle, hairy Newfoundlander on one side and a howling Portuguese on the other.

Worse than any tangle of fishing-lines was the confusion of the dory-rodings below water. Each man had anchored where it seemed good to him, drifting and rowing round his fixed point. As the fish struck on less quickly, each man wanted to haul up and get to better ground; but every third man found himself intimately connected with some four or five neighbours. To cut another's roding is crime unspeakable on the Banks; yet it was done, and done without detection, three or four times that day. Tom Platt caught a Maine man in the black act and knocked him over the gunwale with an oar, and Manuel served a fellow-countryman in the same way. But Harvey's anchor-line was cut, and so was Penn's, and they were turned into relief-boats to carry fish to the *We're Here* as the dories filled. The caplin schooled once more at twilight, when the mad clamour was repeated; and at dusk they rowed back to dress down by the light of kerosene-lamps on the edge of the pen.

It was a huge pile, and they went to sleep while they were dressing. Next day several boats fished right above the cap of the

Virgin; and Harvey, with them, looked down on the very weed of that lonely rock, which rises to within twenty feet of the surface. The cod were there in legions, marching solemnly over the leathery kelp. When they bit, they bit all together; and so when they stopped. There was a slack time at noon, and the dories began to search for amusement. It was Dan who sighted the *Hope of Prague* just coming up, and as her boats joined the company they were greeted with the question: 'Who's the meanest man in the Fleet?'

Three hundred voices answered cheerily: 'Nick Bra-ady.' It sounded like an organ chant.

'Who stole the lampwicks?' That was Dan's contribution.

'Nick Bra-ady,' sang the boats.

'Who biled the salt bait fer soup?' This was an unknown back-biter a quarter of a mile away.

Again the joyful chorus. Now, Brady was not especially mean, but he had that reputation, and the Fleet made the most of it. Then they discovered a man from a Truro boat who, six years before, had been convicted of using a tackle with five or six hooks – a 'scrowger,' they call it – in the Shoals. Naturally, he had been christened 'Scrowger Jim'; and though he had hidden himself on the Georges ever since, he found his honours waiting for him full blown. They took it up in a sort of firecracker chorus: 'Jim! O Jim! Jim! O Jim! Sssscrowger Jim!' That pleased everybody. And when a poetical Beverly man – he had been making it up all day, and talked about it for weeks – sang, 'The *Carrie Pitman*'s anchor doesn't hold her for a cent' the dories felt that they were indeed fortunate. Then they had to ask that Beverly man how he was off for beans, because even poets must not have things all their own way. Every schooner and nearly every man got it in turn. Was there a careless or dirty cook anywhere? The dories sang about him and his food. Was a schooner badly found? The Fleet was told at full length. Had a man hooked tobacco from a mess-mate? He was named in meeting; the name tossed from roller to roller. Disko's infallible judgments, Long Jack's market-boat that he had sold years ago, Dan's sweetheart (oh, but Dan was an angry boy!), Penn's bad luck with dory-anchors, Salter's views on manure, Manuel's little slips from virtue ashore, and Harvey's ladylike handling of the oar – all were laid before the public; and as the fog fell around them in silvery sheets beneath the sun, the voices sounded like a bench of invisible judges pronouncing sentence.

The dories roved and fished and squabbled till a swell underran the sea. Then they drew more apart to save their sides, and some one called that if the swell continued the Virgin would break. A reckless Galway man with his nephew denied this, hauled up anchor, and rowed over the very rock itself. Many voices called them to come away, while others dared them to hold on. As the smooth-backed rollers passed to the southward, they hove the dory high and high into the mist, and dropped her in ugly, sucking, dimpled water, where she spun round her anchor, within a foot or two of the hidden rock. It was playing with death for mere bravado; and the boats looked on in uneasy silence till Long Jack rowed up behind his countrymen and quietly cut their roding.

'Can't ye hear ut knockin'?' he cried. 'Pull for you miserable lives! Pull!'

The men swore and tried to argue as the boat drifted; but the next swell checked a little, like a man tripping on a carpet. There was a deep sob and a gathering roar, and the Virgin flung up a couple of acres of foaming water, white, furious, and ghastly over the shoal sea. Then all the boats greatly applauded Long Jack, and the Galway men held their tongue.

'Ain't it elegant?' said Dan, bobbing like a young seal at home. 'She'll break about once every ha'af hour now, 'les the swell piles up good. What's her reg'lar time when she's at work, Tom Platt?'

'Once ivry fifteen minutes, to the tick. Harve, you've seen the greatest thing on the Banks; an' but for Long Jack you'd seen some dead men too.'

There came a sound of merriment where the fog lay thicker and the schooners were ringing their bells. A big bark nosed cautiously out of the mist, and was received with shouts and cries of, 'Come along, darlin',' from the Irishry.

'Another Frenchman?' said Harvey.

'Hain't you eyes? She's a Baltimore boat; goin' in fear an' tremblin',' said Dan. 'We'll guy the very sticks out of her. Guess it's the fust time her skipper ever met up with the Fleet this way.'

She was a black, buxom, eight-hundred-ton craft. Her mainsail was looped up, and her topsail flapped undecidedly in what little wind was moving. Now a bark is feminine beyond all other daughters of the sea, and this tall, hesitating creature, with her white and gilt figurehead, looked just like a bewildered woman half lifting her skirts to cross a muddy street under the jeers of bad little boys. That was very much her situation. She knew she was somewhere in the neighbourhood of the Virgin, had caught the roar of it, and was, therefore, asking her way. This is a small part of what she heard from the dancing dories:

'The Virgin? Fwhat are you talkin' of? "This is Le Have on a Sunday mornin'". Go home an' sober up.'

'Go home, ye tarrapin! Go home an' tell 'em we're comin'.'

Half a dozen voices together, in a most tuneful chorus, as her stern went down with a roll and a bubble into the troughs: 'Thay-aah – she – strikes!'

'Hard up! Hard up fer your life! You're on top of her now.'

'Daown! Hard daown! Let go everything!'

'All hands to the pumps!'

'Daown jib an' pole her!'

Here the skipper lost his temper and said things. Instantly fishing was suspended to answer him, and he heard many curious facts about his boat and her next port of call. They asked him if he were insured; and whence he had stolen his anchor, because, they said, it belonged to the *Carrie Pitman*; they called his boat a mud-scow, and accused him of dumping garbage to frighten the fish; they offered to tow him and charge it to his wife; and one audacious youth slipped up almost under the counter, smacked it with his open palm, and yelled: 'Gid up, Buck!'

The cook emptied a pan of ashes on him, and he replied with cod-heads. The bark's crew fired small coal from the galley, and the dories threatened to come aboard and 'razee' her. They would have warned her at once had she been in real peril; but, seeing her well clear of the Virgin, they made the most of their chances. The fun was spoilt when the rock spoke again, a half-mile to windward, and the tormented bark set everything that would draw and went her ways; but the dories felt that the honours lay with them.

All that night the Virgin roared hoarsely; and next morning, over an angry, white-headed sea, Harvey saw the Fleet with flickering masts waiting for a lead. Not a dory was hove out till ten o'clock, when the two Jeraulds of the *Day's Eye*, imagining a lull which did not exist, set the example. In a minute half the boats were out and bobbing in the cockly swells, but Troop kept the *We're Here*s at work dressing down. He saw no sense in 'dares'; and as the storm grew that evening they had the pleasure of receiving wet strangers only too glad to make any refuge in the gale. The boys stood by the dory-tackles with lanterns, the men ready to haul, one eye cocked for the sweeping wave that would make them drop everything and hold on for dear life. Out of the dark would come a yell of 'Dory, dory!' They would hook up and haul in a drenched man and a half-sunk boat, till their decks were littered down with nests of dories and the bunks were full. Five times in their watch did Harvey, with Dan, jump at the foregaff where it lay lashed on the boom, and cling with arms, legs, and teeth to rope and spar and sodden canvas as a big wave filled the decks. One dory was smashed to pieces, and the sea pitched the man head first on to the decks, cutting his forehead open; and about dawn, when the racing seas glimmered white all along their cold edges, another man, blue and ghastly, crawled in with a broken hand, asking news of his brother. Seven extra mouths sat down to breakfast: A Swede; a Chatham skipper; a boy from Hancock, Maine; one Duxbury, and three Provincetown men.

There was a general sorting out among the Fleet next day; and though no one said anything, all ate with better appetites when boat after boat reported full crews aboard. Only a couple of Portuguese and an old man from Gloucester were drowned, but many were cut or bruised; and two schooners had parted their tackle and been blown to the southward, three days' sail. A man died on a Frenchman – it was the same bark that had traded tobacco with the *We're Here*s. She slipped away quite quietly one wet, white morning, moved to a patch of deep water, her sails all hanging anyhow, and Harvey saw the funeral through Disko's spy-glass. It was only an oblong bundle slid overside. They did not seem to have any form of service, but in the night, at anchor, Harvey heard them across the star-powdered black water, singing something that sounded like a hymn. It went to a very slow tune.

> 'La brigantine
> Qui va tourner,
> Roule et s'incline
> Pour m'entrainer.
> Oh, Vierge Marie,
> Pour moi priez Dieu!
> Adieu, patrie;
> Quebec, adieu!'

Tom Platt visited her, because, he said, the dead man was his brother as a Freemason. It came out that a wave had doubled the poor fellow over the heel of the bowsprit and broken his back. The news spread like a flash, for, contrary to general custom, the Frenchman held an auction of the dead man's kit, – he had no friends at St Malo or Miquelon, – and everything was spread out on the top of the house, from his red knitted cap to the leather belt with the sheath-knife at the back. Dan and Harvey were out on twenty-fathom water in the *Hattie S.*, and naturally rowed over to join the crowd. It was a long pull, and they stayed some little time while Dan bought the knife, which had a curious brass handle. When they dropped overside and pushed off into a drizzle of rain and a lop of sea, it occurred to them that they might get into trouble for neglecting the lines.

'Guess 'twon't hurt us any to be warmed up,' said Dan, shivering under his oilskins, and they rowed on into the heart of a white fog, which, as usual, dropped on them without warning.

'There's too much blame tide hereabouts to trust to your instinks,' he said. 'Heave over the anchor, Harve, and we'll fish a piece till the thing lifts. Bend on your biggest lead. Three pound ain't any too much in this water. See how she's tightened on her rodin' already.'

There was quite a little bubble at the bows, where some irresponsible Bank current held the dory full stretch on her rope; but they could not see a boat's length in any direction. Harvey turned up his collar and bunched himself over his reel with the air of a wearied navigator. Fog had no special terrors for him now. They fished a while in silence, and found the cod struck on well. Then Dan drew the sheath-knife and tested the edge of it on the gunwale.

'That's a daisy,' said Harvey. 'How did you get it so cheap?'

'On account o' their blame Cath'lic superstitions,' said Dan, jabbing with the bright blade. 'They don't fancy takin' iron from off a dead man, so to speak. 'See them Arichat Frenchmen step back when I bid?'

'But an auction ain't taking anythink off a dead man. It's business.'

'We know it ain't, but there's no goin' in the teeth o' superstition. That's one o' the advantages o' livin' in a progressive country.' And Dan began whistling:

'Oh, Double Thatcher, how are you?
Now Eastern Point comes inter view.
The girls an' boys we soon shall see,
At anchor off Cape Ann!'

'Why didn't that Eastport man bid, then? He bought his boots. Ain't Maine progressive?'

'Maine? Pshaw! They don't know enough, or they hain't got money enough, to paint their haouses in Maine. I've seen 'em. The Eastport man he told me that the knife had been used – so the French captain told him – used up on the French coast last year.'

'Cut a man? Heave's the muckle.' Harvey hauled in his fish, rebaited, and threw over.

'Killed him! Course, when I heard that I was keener'n ever to get it.'

'Christmas! I didn't know it,' said Harvey, turning round. 'I'll give you a dollar for it when I — get my wages. Say, I'll give you two dollars.'

'Honest? D'you like it as much as all that?' said Dan, flushing. 'Well, to tell the truth, I kinder got it for you – to give; but I didn't let on till I saw how you'd take it. It's yours and welcome, Harve, because we're dory-mates, and so on and so forth, an' so followin'. Catch a-holt!'

He held it out, belt and all.

'But look at here. Dan, I don't see—'

'Take it. 'Tain't no use to me. I wish you to hev it.' The temptation was irresistible. 'Dan, you're a white man,' said Harvey. 'I'll keep it as long as I live.'

'That's good hearin',' said Dan, with a pleasant laugh; and then, anxious to change the subject: 'Look's if your line was fast to somethin'.'

'Fouled, I guess,' said Harve, tugging. Before he pulled up he fastened the belt round him, and with deep delight heard the tip of the sheath click on the thwart. 'Concern the thing!' he cried. 'She acts as though she were on strawberry-bottom. It's all sand here, ain't it?'

Dan reached over and gave a judgmatic tweak. 'Hollbut'll act that way 'f he's sulky. Thet's no strawberry-bottom. Yank her once or twice. She gives, sure. Guess we'd better haul up an' make certain.'

They pulled together, making fast at each turn on the cleats, and the hidden weight rose sluggishly.

'Prize, oh! Haul!' shouted Dan, but the shout ended in a shrill, double shriek of horror, for out of the sea came the body of the dead Frenchman buried two days before! The hook had caught him under the right armpit, and he swayed, erect and horrible, head and shoulders above water. His arms were tied to his side, and – he had no face. The boys fell over each other in a heap at the bottom of the dory, and there they lay while the thing bobbed alongside, held on the shortened line.

'The tide – the tide brought him!' said Harvey with quivering lips, as he fumbled at the clasp of the belt.

'Oh, Lord! Oh, Harve!' groaned Dan, 'be quick. He's come for it. Let him have it. Take it off.'

'I don't want it! I don't want it!' cried Harvey. 'I can't find the bu-buckle.'

'Quick, Harve! He's on your line!'

Harvey sat up to unfasten the belt, facing the head that had no face under its streaming hair. 'He's fast still,' he whispered to Dan, who slipped out his knife and cut the line, as Harvey flung the belt far overside. The body shot down with a plop, and Dan cautiously rose to his knees, whiter than the fog.

'He come for it. He come for it. I've seen a stale one hauled up on a trawl and I didn't much care, but he come to us special.'

'I wish – I wish I hadn't taken the knife. Then he'd have come on your line.'

'Dunno as thet would ha' made any differ. We're both scared out o' ten years' growth. Oh, Harve, did ye see his head?'

'Did I? I'll never forget it. But look at here, Dan; it couldn't have been meant. It was only the tide.'

'Tide! He come for it, Harve. Why, they sunk him six miles to south'ard o' the Fleet, an' we're two miles from where she's lyin' now. They told me he was weighted with a fathom an' a half o' chain-cable.'

'Wonder what he did with the knife – up on the French coast?'

'Something bad. 'Guess he's bound to take it with him to the Judgment, an' so— What are you doin' with the fish?'

'Heaving 'em overboard,' said Harvey.

'What for? We sha'n't eat 'em.'

'I don't care. I had to look at his face while I was takin' the belt off. You can keep your catch if you like. I've no use for mine.'

Dan said nothing, but threw his fish over again.

'Guess it's best to be on the safe side,' he murmured at last. 'I'd give a month's pay if this fog 'u'd lift. Things go abaout in a fog that ye don't see in clear weather – yo-hoes an' hollerers and such like. I'm sorter relieved he come the way he did instid o' walkin'. He might ha' walked.'

'Don't, Dan! We're right on top of him now. 'Wish I was safe aboard, hem' pounded by Uncle Salters.'

'They'll be lookin' fer us in a little. Gimme the tooter.' Dan took the tin dinner-horn, but paused before he blew.

'Go on,' said Harvey. 'I don't want to stay here all night'

'Question is, haow he'd take it. There was a man frum down the coast told me once he was in a schooner where they darsen't ever blow a horn to the dories, becaze the skipper – not the man he was with, but a captain that had run her five years before – he'd drowned a boy alongside in a drunk fit; an' ever after, that boy he'd row alongside too and shout, "Dory! dory!" with the rest.'

'Dory! dory!' a muffled voice cried through the fog. They cowered again, and the horn dropped from Dan's hand.

'Hold on!' cried Harvey; 'it's the cook.'

'Dunno what made me think o' thet fool tale, either,' said Dan. 'It's the doctor, sure enough.'

'Dan! Danny! Oooh, Dan! Harve! Harvey! Oooh, Haarveee!'

'We're here,' sung both boys together. They heard oars, but could see nothing till the cook, shining and dripping, rowed into them.

'What iss happened?' said he. 'You will be beaten at home.'

'Thet's what we want. Thet's what we're sufferin' for,' said Dan. 'Anything homey's good enough fer us. We've had kinder depressin' company.' As the cook passed them a line, Dan told him the tale.

'Yess! He come for hiss knife,' was all he said at the end.

Never had the little rocking *We're Here* looked so deliciously home-like as when the cook, born and bred in fogs, rowed them back to her. There was a warm glow of light from the cabin and a satisfying smell of food forward, and it was heavenly to hear Disko and the others, all quite alive and solid, leaning over the rail and promising them a first-class pounding. But the cook was a black; master of strategy. He did not get the dories aboard till he had given the more striking points of the tale, explaining as he backed and bumped round the counter how Harvey was the mascot to destroy any possible bad luck. So the boys came over-side as rather uncanny heroes, and every one asked them questions instead of pounding them for making trouble. Little Penn delivered quite a speech on the folly of superstitions; but public opinion was against him and in favour of Long Jack, who told the most excruciating ghost-stories, till nearly midnight. Under that influence no one except Salters and Penn said anything about 'idolatry,' when the cook put a lighted candle, a cake of flour and water, and a pinch of salt on a shingle, and floated them out astern to keep the Frenchman quiet in case he was still restless. Dan lit the candle because he had bought the belt, and the cook grunted and muttered charms as long as he could see the ducking point of flame.

Said Harvey to Dan, as they turned in after watch: 'How about progress and Catholic superstitions?'

'Huh! I guess I'm as enlightened and progressive as the next man, but when it comes to a dead St. Malo deck-hand scarin' a couple o' pore boys stiff fer the sake of a thirty-cent knife, why, then, the cook can take hold fer all o' me. I mistrust furriners, livin' or dead.'

Next morning all, except the cook, were rather ashamed of the ceremonies, and went to work double tides, speaking gruffly to one another.

The *We're Here* was racing neck and neck for her last few loads against the *Parry Norman*; and so close was the struggle that the Fleet took side and betted tobacco. All hands worked at the lines or dressing-down till they fell asleep where they stood – beginning before dawn and ending when it was too dark to see. They even used the cook as pitcher, and turned Harvey into the hold to pass salt, while Dan helped to dress down. Luckily a *Parry Norman* man sprained his ankle falling down the foc'sle, and the *We're Heres* gained. Harvey could not see how one more fish could be crammed into her, but Disko and Tom Platt stowed and stowed, and planked the mass down with big stones from the ballast, and there was always 'jest another day's work.' Disko did not tell them when all the salt was wetted. He rolled to the lazarette aft the cabin and began hauling out the big mainsail. This was at ten in the morning. The riding-sail was down and the main- and topsail were up by noon, and dories came alongside with letters for home, envying their good fortune. At last she cleared decks, hoisted her flag, – as is the right of the first boat off the Banks, – up-anchored, and began to move. Disko pretended that he wished to accomodate folk who had not sent in their mail, and so worked her gracefully in and out among the schooners. In reality, that was his little triumphant procession, and for the fifth year running it showed what kind of mariner he was. Dan's accordion and Tom Platt's fiddle supplied the music of the magic verse you must not sing till all the salt is wet:

> 'Hih! Yih! Yoho! Send your letters raound!
> All our salt is wetted, an' the anchor's off the graound!
> Bend, oh, bend your mains'l, we're back to Yankeeland –
>   With fifteen hunder' quintal,
>   An' fifteen hunder' quintal,
>   'Teen hunder' toppin' quintal,
> 'Twix' old 'Queereau an' Grand.'

The last letters pitched on deck wrapped round pieces of coal, and the Gloucester men shouted messages to their wives and womenfolks and owners, while the *We're Here* finished the musical ride through the Fleet, her headsails quivering like a man's hand when he raises it to say good-bye.

Harvey very soon discovered that the *We're Here*, with her riding-sail, strolling from berth to berth, and the *We're Here* headed west by south under home canvas, were two very different boats. There was a bite and kick to the wheel even in 'boy's' weather; he could feel the dead weight in the hold flung forward mightily across the surges, and the streaming line of bubbles overside made his eyes dizzy.

Disko kept them busy fiddling with the sails; and when those were flattened like a racing yacht's, Dan had to wait on the big topsail, which was put over by hand every time she went about. In spare moments they pumped, for the packed fish dripped brine, which does not improve a cargo. But since there was no fishing, Harvey had time to look at the sea from another point of view. The low-sided schooner was naturally on most intimate terms with her surroundings. They saw little of the horizon save when she topped a swell; and usually she was elbowing, fidgeting, and coasting her steadfast way through gray, gray-blue, or black hollows laced across and across with streaks of shivering foam; or rubbing herself caressingly along the flank of some bigger water-hill. It was as if she said: 'You wouldn't hurt me, surely? I'm only the little *We're Here*.' Then she would slide away chuckling softly to herself till she was brought up by some fresh obstacle. The dullest of folk cannot see this kind of thing hour after hour through long days without noticing it; and Harvey, being anything but dull, began to comprehend and enjoy the dry chorus of wave-tops turning over with a sound of incessant tearing; the hurry of the winds working across open spaces and herding the purple-blue cloud-shadows; the splendid upheaval of the red sunrise; the folding and packing away of the morning mists, wall after wall withdrawn across the white floors; the salty glare and blaze of noon; the kiss of rain falling over thousands of dead, flat square miles; the chilly blackening of everything at the day's end; and the million wrinkles of the sea under the moonlight, when the jib-boom solemnly poked at the low stars, and Harvey went down to get a doughnut from the cook.

But the best fun was when the boys were put on the wheel together, Tom Platt within hail, and she cuddled her lee-rail down to the crashing blue, and kept a little home-made rainbow arching unbroken over her windlass. Then the jaws of the booms whined against the masts, and the sheets creaked, and the sails filled with roaring; and when she slid into a hollow she trampled like a woman tripped in her own silk dress, and came out, her jib wet half-way up, yearning and peering for the tall twin-lights of Thatcher's Island.

They left the cold gray of the Bank sea, saw the lumber-ships making for Quebec by the Straits of St. Lawrence, with the Jersey salt-brigs from Spain and Sicily; found a friendly northeaster off Artimon Bank that drove them within view of the East light of Sable Island, – a sight Disko did not linger over, – and stayed with them past Western and Le Have, to the northern fringe of George's. From there they picked up the deeper water, and let her go merrily.

'Hattie's pulling on the string,' Dan confided to Harvey. 'Hattie an' Ma. Next Sunday you'll be hirin' a boy to throw water on the windows to make ye go to sleep. 'Guess you'll keep with us till your folks come. Do you know the best of gettin' ashore again?'

'Hot bath?' said Harvey. His eyebrows were all white with dried spray.

'That's good, but a night-shirt's better. I've been dreamin' o' night-shirts ever since we bent our mainsail. Ye can wiggle your toes then. Ma'll hev a new one fer me, all washed soft. It's home, Harve. It's home! Ye can sense it in the air. We're runnin' into the aidge of a hot wave naow, an' I can smell the bayberries. Wonder if we'll get in fer supper. Port a trifle.'

The hesitating sails flapped and lurched in the close air as the deep smoothed out, blue and oily, round them. When they whistled for a wind only the rain came in spiky rods, bubbling and drumming, and behind the rain the thunder and the lightning of mid-August. They lay on the deck with bare feet and arms, telling one another what they would order at their first meal ashore; for now the land was in plain sight. A Gloucester swordfish-boat drifted alongside, a man in the little pulpit on the bowsprit flourished his harpoon, his bare head plastered down with the wet. 'And all's well!' he sang cheerily, as though he were watch on a big liner. 'Wouverman's waiting fer you, Disko. What's the news o' the Fleet?'

Disko shouted it and passed on, while the wild summer storm pounded overhead and the lightning flickered along the capes from four different quarters at once. It gave the low circle of hills round Gloucester Harbor, Ten Pound Island, the fish-sheds, with the broken line of house-roofs, and each spar and buoy on the water, in blinding photographs that came and went a dozen times to the minute as the *We're Here* crawled in on half-flood, and the whistling-buoy moaned and mourned behind her. Then the storm died out in long, separated, vicious dags of blue-white flame, followed by a single roar like the roar of a mortar-battery, and the shaken air tingled under the stars as it got back to silence.

'The flag, the flag!' said Disko, suddenly, pointing upward.

'What is ut?' said Long Jack.

'Otto! Ha'af mast. They can see us frum shore now.'

'I'd clean forgot. He's no folk to Gloucester, has he?'

'Girl he was goin' to be married to this fall.'

'Mary pity her!' said Long Jack, and lowered the little flag half-mast for the sake of Otto, swept overboard in a gale off Le Have three months before.

Disko wiped the wet from his eyes and led the *We're Here* to Wouverman's wharf, giving his orders in whispers, while she swung round moored tugs and night-watchmen hailed her from the ends of inky-black piers. Over and above the darkness and the mystery of the procession, Harvey could feel the land close round him once more, with all its thousands of people asleep, and the smell of earth after rain, and the familiar noise of a switching-engine coughing to herself in a freight-yard; and all those things made his heart beat and his throat dry up as he stood by the foresheet. They heard the anchor-watch snoring on a lighthouse-tug, nosed into a pocket of darkness where a lantern glimmered on either side; somebody waked with a grunt, threw them a rope, and they made fast to a silent wharf flanked with great iron-roofed sheds fall of warm emptiness, and lay there without a sound.

Then Harvey sat down by the wheel, and sobbed and sobbed as though his heart would break, and a tall woman who had been sitting on a weigh-scale dropped down into the schooner and kissed Dan once on the cheek; for she was his mother, and she had seen the *We're Here* by the lightning flashes. She took no notice of Harvey till he had recovered himself a little and Disko had told her his story. Then they went to Disko's house together as the dawn was breaking; and until the telegraph office was open and he could wire his folk, Harvey Cheyne was perhaps the loneliest boy in all America. But the curious thing was that Disko and Dan seemed to think none the worse of him for crying.

Wouverman was not ready for Disko's prices till Disko, sure that the *We're Here* was at least a week ahead of any other Gloucester boat, had given him a few days to swallow them; so all hands played about the streets, and Long Jack stopped the Rocky Neck trolley, on principle, as he said, till the conductor let him ride free. But Dan went about with his freckled nose in the air, bung-full of mystery and most haughty to his family.

'Dan, I'll hev to lay inter you ef you act this way,' said Troop, pensively. 'Sence we've come ashore this time you've bin a heap too fresh.'

'I'd lay into him naow ef he was mine,' said Uncle Salters, sourly. He and Penn boarded with the Troops.

'Oho!' said Dan, shuffling with the accordion round the backyard, ready to leap the fence if the enemy advanced. 'Dad, you're welcome to your own judgment, but remember I've warned ye. Your own flesh an' blood ha' warned ye! 'Tain't any o' my fault ef you're mistook, but I'll be on deck to watch ye. An' ez fer yeou, Uncle Salters, Pharaoh's chief butler ain't in it 'longside o' you! You watch aout an' wait. You'll be plowed under like your own blamed clover; but me – Dan Troop – I'll flourish like a green bay-tree because I warn't stuck on my own opinion.'

Disko was smoking in all his shore dignity and a pair of beautiful carpet-slippers. 'You're gettin' ez crazy as poor Harve. You two go araound gigglin' an' squinchin' an' kickin' each other under the table till there's no peace in the haouse,' said he.

'There's goin' to be a heap less – fer some folks,' Dan replied. 'You wait an' see.'

He and Harvey went out on the trolley to East Gloucester, where they tramped through the bayberry bushes to the lighthouse, and lay down on the big red boulders and laughed themselves hungry. Harvey had shown Dan a telegram, and the two swore to keep silence till the shell burst.

'Harve's folk?' said Dan, with an unruffled face after supper. 'Well, I guess they don't amount to much of anything, or we'd ha' heard from 'em by naow. His pop keeps a kind o' store out West. Maybe he'll give you 's much as five dollars, Dad.'

'What did I tell ye?' said Salters. 'Don't sputter over your vittles, Dan.'

[First published in serial form in *McClure's Magazine*, November 1896. The first book edition was published by Macmillan in London and New York in 1897.]

✠ ✠ ✠

THE DEVIL AND THE DEEP SEA

All supplies very bad and dear, and there are no facilities for even the smallest repairs.

– sailing directions.

HER NATIONALITY WAS BRITISH, but you will not find her house-flag in the list of our mercantile marine. She was a nine-hundred-ton, iron, schooner-rigged, screw cargo-boat, differing externally in no way from any other tramp of the sea. But it is with steamers as it is with men. There are those who will for a consideration sail extremely close to the wind; and, in the present state of a fallen world, such people and such steamers have their use. From the hour that the *Aglaia* first entered the Clyde – new, shiny, and innocent, with a quart of cheap champagne trickling down her cut-water – Fate and her owner, who was also her captain, decreed that she should deal with embarrassed crowned heads, fleeing Presidents, financiers of over-extended ability, women to whom change of air was imperative, and the lesser law-breaking Powers. Her career led her sometimes into the Admiralty Courts, where the sworn statements of her skipper filled his brethren with envy. The mariner cannot tell or act a lie in the face of the sea, or mislead a tempest; but, as lawyers have discovered, he makes up for chances withheld when he returns to shore, an affidavit in either hand.

The *Aglaia* figured with distinction in the great Mackinaw salvage-case. It was her first slip from virtue, and she learned how to change her name, but not her heart, and to run across the sea. As the *Guiding Light* she was very badly wanted in a South American port for the little matter of entering harbour at full speed, colliding with a coal-hulk and the State's only man-of-war, just as that man-of-war was going to coal. She put to sea without explanations, though three forts fired at her for half an hour. As the *Julia M'Gregor* she had been concerned in picking up from a raft certain gentlemen who should have stayed in Noumea, but who preferred making themselves vastly unpleasant to authority in quite another quarter of the world; and as the *Shah-in-Shah* she had been overtaken on the high seas, indecently full of munitions of war, by the cruiser of an agitated Power at issue with its neighbour. That time she was very nearly sunk, and her riddled hull gave eminent lawyers of two countries great profit. After a season she reappeared as the *Martin Hunt* painted a dull slate-colour, with pure saffron funnel, and boats of robin's-egg blue, engaging in the Odessa trade till she was invited (and the invitation could not well be disregarded) to keep away from Black Sea ports altogether.

She had ridden through many waves of depression. Freights might drop out of sight, Seamen's Unions throw spanners and nuts at certificated masters, or stevedores combine till cargo perished on the dock-head; but the boat of many names came and went, busy, alert, and inconspicuous always. Her skipper made no complaint of hard times, and port officers observed that her crew signed and signed again with the regularity of Atlantic liner boatswains. Her name she changed as occasion called; her well-paid crew never; and a large percentage of the profits of her voyages was spent with an open hand on her engine-room. She never troubled the underwriters, and very seldom stopped to talk with a signal-station, for her business was urgent and private.

But an end came to her tradings, and she perished in this manner. Deep peace brooded over Europe, Asia, Africa, America, Australasia, and Polynesia. The Powers dealt together more or less honestly; banks paid their depositors to the hour; diamonds of price came safely to the hands of their owners; Republics rested content with their Dictators; diplomats found no one whose presence in the least incommoded them; monarchs lived openly with their lawfully wedded wives. It was as though the whole earth had put on its best Sunday bib and tucker; and business was very bad for the *Martin Hunt*. The great, virtuous calm engulfed her, slate sides, yellow funnel, and all, but cast up in another hemisphere the steam whaler *Haliotis*, black and rusty, with a manure-coloured funnel, a litter of dingy white boats, and an enormous stove, or furnace, for boiling blubber on her forward well-deck. There could be no doubt that her trip was successful, for she lay at several ports not too well known, and the smoke of her trying-out insulted the beaches.

Anon she departed, at the speed of the average London four-wheeler, and entered a semi-inland sea, warm, still, and blue, which is, perhaps, the most strictly preserved water in the world. There she stayed for a certain time, and the great stars of those mild skies beheld her playing puss-in-the-corner among islands where whales are never found. All that while she smelt abominably, and the smell, though fishy, was not whalesome. One evening calamity descended upon her from the island of Pygang-Watai, and she fled, while her crew jeered at a fat black-and-brown gunboat puffing far behind. They knew to the last revolution the capacity of every boat, on those seas, that they were anxious to avoid. A British ship with a good conscience does not, as a rule, flee from the man-of-war of a foreign Power, and it is also considered a breach of etiquette to stop and search British ships at sea. These things the skipper of the *Haliotis* did not pause to prove, but held on at an inspiriting eleven knots an hour till nightfall. One thing only he overlooked.

The Power that kept an expensive steam-patrol moving up and down those waters (they had dodged the two regular ships of the station with an ease that bred contempt) had newly brought up a third and a fourteen-knot boat with a clean bottom to help the work; and that was why the *Haliotis*, driving hard from the east to the west, found herself at daylight in such a position that she could not help seeing an arrangement of four flags, a mile and a half behind, which read: 'Heave to, or take the consequences!'

She had her choice, and she took it. The end came when, pre suming on her lighter draught, she tried to draw away northward over a friendly shoal. The shell that arrived by way of the Chief Engineer's cabin was some five inches in diameter, with a practice, not a bursting, charge. It had been intended to cross her bows, and that was why it knocked the framed portrait of the Chief Engineer's wife – and she was a very pretty girl – on to the floor, splintered his wash-hand stand, crossed the alleyway into the engine-room, and striking on a grating, dropped directly in front of the forward engine, where it burst, neatly fracturing both the bolts that held the connecting-rod to the forward crank.

What follows is worth consideration. The forward engine had no more work to do. Its released piston-rod, therefore, drove up fiercely, with nothing to check it, and started most of the nuts of the cylinder-cover. It came down again, the full weight of the steam behind it, and the foot of the disconnected connecting-rod, useless as the leg of a man with a sprained ankle, flung out to the right and struck the starboard, or right-hand, cast-iron supporting-column of the forward engine, cracking it clean through about six inches above the base, and wedging the upper portion outwards three inches towards the ship's side. There the connecting-rod jammed. Meantime, the after-engine, being as yet unembarrassed, went on with its work, and in so doing brought round at its next revolution the crank of the forward engine, which smote the already jammed connecting-rod, bending it and therewith the piston-rod cross-head – the big cross-piece that slides up and down so smoothly.

The cross-head jammed sideways in the guides, and, in addition to putting further pressure on the already broken starboard supporting-column, cracked the port, or left-hand, supporting-column in two or three places. There being nothing more that could be made to move, the engines brought up, all standing, with a hiccup that seemed to lift the *Haliotis* a foot out of the water; and the engine-room staff, opening every steam outlet that they could find in the confusion, arrived on deck somewhat scalded, but calm. There was a sound below of things happening – a rushing, clicking, purring, grunting, rattling noise that did not last for more than a minute. It was the machinery adjusting itself, on the spur of the moment, to a hundred altered conditions. Mr. Wardrop, one foot on the upper grating, inclined his ear sideways, and groaned. You cannot stop engines working at twelve knots an hour in three seconds without disorganising them. The *Haliotis* slid forward in a cloud of steam, shrieking like a wounded horse. There was nothing more to do. The five-inch shell with a reduced charge had settled the situation. And when you are full, all three holds, of strictly preserved pearls; when you have cleaned out the Tanna Bank, the Sea-Horse Bank, and four other banks from one end to the other of the Amanala Sea – when you have ripped out the very heart of a rich Government monopoly so that five years will not repair your wrong-doings – you must smile and take what is in store. But the skipper reflected, as a launch put out from the man-of-war, that he had been bombarded on the high seas, with the British flag – several of them – picturesquely disposed above him, and tried to find comfort from the thought.

'Where,' said the stolid naval lieutenant hoisting himself aboard, 'where are those dam' pearls?'

They were there beyond evasion. No affidavit could do away with the fearful smell of decayed oysters, the diving-dresses, and the shell-littered hatches. They were there to the value of seventy thousand pounds, more or less; and every pound poached.

The man-of-war was annoyed; for she had used up many tons of coal, she had strained her tubes, and, worse than all, her officers and crew had been hurried. Every one on the *Haliotis* was arrested and rearrested several times, as each officer came aboard; then they were told by what they esteemed to be the equivalent of a midshipman that they were to consider themselves prisoners, and finally were put under arrest.

'It's not the least good,' said the skipper, suavely. 'You'd much better send us a tow—'

'Be still – you are arrest!' was the reply.

'Where the devil do you expect we are going to escape to?'

'We're helpless. You've got to tow us into somewhere, and explain why you fired on us. Mr. Wardrop, we're helpless, aren't we?'

'Ruined from end to end,' said the man of machinery. 'If she rolls, the forward cylinder will come down and go through her bottom. Both columns are clean cut through. There's nothing to hold anything up.'

The council of war clanked off to see if Mr. Wardrop's words were true. He warned them that it was as much as a man's life was worth to enter the engine-room, and they contented themselves with a distant inspection through the thinning steam. The *Haliotis* lifted to the long, easy swell, and the starboard supporting-column ground a trifle, as a man grits his teeth under the knife. The forward cylinder was depending on that unknown force men call the pertinacity of materials, which now and then balances that other heartbreaking power, the perversity of inanimate things.

'You see!' said Mr. Wardrop, hurrying them away. 'The engines aren't worth their price as old iron.'

'We tow,' was the answer. 'Afterwards we shall confiscate.'

The man-of-war was short-handed, and did not see the necessity for putting a prize-crew aboard the *Haliotis*. So she sent one sublieutenant, whom the skipper kept very drunk, for he did not wish to make the tow too easy, and, moreover, he had an inconspicuous little rope hanging from the stem of his ship.

Then they began to tow at an average speed of four knots an hour. The *Haliotis* was very hard to move, and the gunnery-lieutenant, who had fired the five-inch shell, had leisure to think upon consequences. Mr. Wardrop was the busy man. He borrowed all the crew to shore up the cylinders with spars and blocks from the bottom and sides of the ship. It was a day's risky work; but anything was better than drowning at the end of a tow-rope; and if the forward cylinder had fallen, it would have made its way to the sea-bed, and taken the *Haliotis* after.

'Where are we going to, and how long will they tow us?' he asked of the skipper.

'God knows! and this prize-lieutenant's drunk. What do you think you can do?'

'There's just the bare chance,' Mr. Wardrop whispered, though no one was within hearing – 'there's just the bare chance o' repairin' her, if a man knew how. They've twisted the very guts out of her, bringing her up with that jerk; but I'm saying that, with time and patience, there's just the chance o' making steam yet. *We* could do it.'

The skipper's eye brightened. 'Do you mean,' he began, 'that she is any good?'

'Oh, no,' said Mr. Wardrop. 'She'll need three thousand pounds in repairs, at the lowest, if she's to take the sea again, an' that apart from any injury to her structure. She's like a man fallen down five pair o' stairs. We can't tell for months what has happened; but we know she'll never be good again without a new inside. Ye should see the condenser-tubes an' the steam connections to the donkey, for two things only. I'm not afraid of them repairin' her. I'm afraid of them stealin' things.'

'They've fired on us. They'll have to explain that.'

'Our reputation's not good enough to ask for explanations. Let's take what we have and be thankful. Ye would not have consuls remembern' the *Guidin' Light,* an' the *Shah-in-Shah,* an' the *Aglaia,* at this most alarmin' crisis. We've been no better than pirates these ten years. Under Providence we're no worse than thieves now. We've much to be thankful for – if we e'er get back to her.'

'Make it your own way, then,' said the skipper. 'If there's the least chance—'

'I'll leave none,' said Mr. Wardrop – 'none that they'll dare to take. Keep her heavy on the tow, for we need time.'

The skipper never interfered with the affairs of the engine-room, and Mr. Wardrop – an artist in his profession – turned to and composed a work terrible and forbidding. His background was the dark-grained sides of the engine-room; his material the metals of power and strength, helped out with spars, baulks, and ropes. The man-of-war towed sullenly and viciously. The *Haliotis* behind her hummed like a hive before swarming. With extra and totally unneeded spars her crew blocked up the space round the forward engine till it resembled a statue in its scaffolding, and the butts of the shores interfered with every view that a dispassionate eye might wish to take. And that the dispassionate mind might be swiftly shaken out of its calm, the well-sunk bolts of the shores were wrapped round untidily with loose ends of ropes, giving a studied effect of most dangerous insecurity. Next, Mr. Wardrop took up a collection from the after-engine, which, as you will remember, had not been affected in the general wreck. The cylinder escape-valve he abolished with a flogging-hammer. It is difficult in far-off ports to come by such valves, unless, like Mr. Wardrop, you keep duplicates in store. At the same time men took off the nuts of two of the great holding-down bolts that serve to keep the engines in place on their solid bed. An engine violently arrested in mid-career may easily jerk off the nut of a holding-down bolt, and this accident looked very natural.

Passing along the tunnel, he removed several shaft coupling-bolts and -nuts, scattering other and ancient pieces of iron underfoot. Cylinder-bolts he cut off to the number of six from the after-engine cylinder, so that it might match its neighbour, and stuffed the bilge – and feed-pumps with cotton-waste. Then he made up a neat bundle of the various odds and ends that he had gathered from the engines – little things like nuts and valve-spindles, all carefully tallowed – and retired with them under the floor of the engine-room, where he sighed, being fat, as he passed from manhole to manhole of the double bottom, and in a fairly dry submarine compartment hid them. Any engineer, particularly in an unfriendly port, has a right to keep his spare stores where he chooses; and the foot of one of the cylinder shores blocked all entrance into the regular store-room, even if that had not been already closed with steel wedges. In conclusion, he disconnected the after-engine, laid piston and connecting-rod, carefully tallowed, where it would be most inconvenient to the casual visitor, took out three of the eight collars of the thrust-block, hid them where only he could find them again, filled the boilers by hand, wedged the sliding doors of the coal-bunkers, and rested from his labours. The engine-room was a cemetery, and it did not need the contents of the ash-lift through the skylight to make it any worse.

He invited the skipper to look at the completed work.

'Saw ye ever such a forsaken wreck as that?' said he, proudly. 'It almost frights *me* to go under those shores. Now, what d' you think they'll do to us?'

'Wait till we see,' said the skipper. 'It'll be bad enough when it comes.'

He was not wrong. The pleasant days of towing ended all too soon, though the *Haliotis* trailed behind her a heavily weighted jib stayed out into the shape of a pocket; and Mr. Wardrop was no longer an artist of imagination, but one of seven-and-twenty prisoners in a prison full of insects. The man-of-war had towed them to the nearest port, not to the headquarters of the colony, and when Mr. Wardrop saw the dismal little harbour, with its ragged line of Chinese junks, its one crazy tug, and the boat-building shed that, under the charge of a philosophical Malay, represented a dockyard, he sighed and shook his head.

'I did well,' he said. 'This is the habitation o' wreckers an' thieves. We're at the uttermost ends of the earth. Think you they'll ever know in England?'

'Doesn't look like it,' said the skipper.

They were marched ashore with what they stood up in, under a generous escort, and were judged according to the customs of the

country, which, though excellent, are a little out of date. There were
the pearls; there were the poachers; and there sat a small but hot
Governor. He consulted for a while, and then things began to move
with speed, for he did not wish to keep a hungry crew at large on
the beach, and the man-of-war had gone up the coast. With a wave
of his hand – a stroke of the pen was not necessary – he consigned
them to the *blackgang-tana*, the back-country, and the hand of the
Law removed them from his sight and the knowledge of men. They
were marched into the palms, and the back-country swallowed
them up – all the crew of the *Haliotis*.

Deep peace continued to brood over Europe, Asia, Africa,
America, Australasia, and Polynesia.

It was the firing that did it. They should have kept their counsel;
but when a few thousand foreigners are bursting with joy over the
fact that a ship under the British flag has been fired at on the high
seas, news travels quickly; and when it came out that the pearl-
stealing crew had not been allowed access to their consul (there
was no consul within a few hundred miles of that lonely port) even
the friendliest of Powers has a right to ask questions. The great
heart of the British public was beating furiously on account of the
performance of a notorious race-horse, and had not a throb to waste
on distant accidents; but somewhere deep in the hull of the ship of
State there is machinery which more or less accurately takes charge
of foreign affairs. That machinery began to revolve, and who so
shocked and surprised as the Power that had captured the *Haliotis*?
It explained that colonial governors and far-away men-of-war were
difficult to control, and promised that it would most certainly make
an example both of the Governor and the vessel. As for the crew
reported to be pressed into military service in tropical climes, it
would produce them as soon as possible, and it would apologise,
if necessary. Now, no apologies were needed. When one nation
apologises to another, millions of amateurs who have no earthly
concern with the difficulty hurl themselves into the strife and
embarrass the trained specialist. It was requested that the crew be
found, if they were still alive – they had been eight months beyond
knowledge – and it was promised that all would be forgotten.

The little Governor of the little port was pleased with himself.
Seven-and-twenty white men made a very compact force to throw
away on a war that had neither beginning nor end – a jungle and

stockade fight that flickered and smouldered through the wet hot years in the hills a hundred miles away, and was the heritage of every wearied official. He had, he thought, deserved well of his country; and if only some one would buy the unhappy *Haliotis*, moored in the harbour below his verandah, his cup would be full. He looked at the neatly silvered lamps that he had taken from her cabins, and thought of much that might be turned to account. But his countrymen in that moist climate had no spirit. They would peep into the silent engine-room, and shake their heads. Even the men-of-war would not tow her further up the coast, where the Governor believed that she could be repaired. She was a bad bargain; but her cabin carpets were undeniably beautiful, and his wife approved of her mirrors.

Three hours later cables were bursting round him like shells, for, though he knew it not, he was being offered as a sacrifice by the nether to the upper millstone, and his superiors had no regard for his feelings. He had, said the cables, grossly exceeded his power, and failed to report on events. He would, therefore – at this he cast himself back in his hammock – produce the crew of the *Haliotis*. He would send for them, and, if that failed, he would put his dignity on a pony and fetch them himself. He had no conceivable right to make pearl-poachers serve in any war. He would be held responsible.

Next morning the cables wished to know whether he had found the crew of the *Haliotis*. They were to be found, freed and fed – he was to feed them – till such time as they could be sent to the nearest English port in a man-of-war. If you abuse a man long enough in great words flashed over the sea-beds, things happen. The Governor sent inland swiftly for his prisoners, who were also soldiers; and never was a militia regiment more anxious to reduce its strength. No power short of death could make these mad men wear the uniform of their service. They would not fight, except with their fellows, and it was for that reason the regiment had not gone to war, but stayed in a stockade, reasoning with the new troops. The autumn campaign had been a fiasco, but here were the Englishmen. All the regiment marched back to guard them, and the hairy enemy, armed with blow-pipes, rejoiced in the forest. Five of the crew had died, but there lined up on the Governor's verandah two-and-twenty men marked about the legs with the scars of leech-bites. A few of them wore fringes that had once been trousers; the others used loin-cloths of gay patterns; and they existed beautifully but simply in the Governor's verandah, and when he came out they sang at him. When you have lost seventy thousand pounds' worth of pearls, your pay, your ship, and all your clothes, and have lived in bondage for five months beyond the faintest pretences of civilisation, you know what true independence means, for you become the happiest of created things – natural man.

The Governor told the crew that they were evil, and they asked for food. When he saw how they ate, and when he remembered that none of the pearl patrol-boats were expected for two months, he sighed. But the crew of the *Haliotis* lay down in the verandah, and said that they were pensioners of the Governor's bounty. A grey-bearded man, fat and bald-headed, his one garment a green-and-yellow loin-cloth, saw the *Haliotis* in the harbour, and bellowed for joy. The men crowded to the verandah-rail, kicking aside the long cane chairs. They pointed, gesticulated, and argued freely, without shame. The militia regiment sat down in the Governor's garden. The Governor retired to his hammock – it was as easy to be killed lying as standing – and his women squeaked from the shuttered rooms.

'She sold?' said the grey-bearded man, pointing to the *Haliotis*. He was Mr. Wardrop.

'No good,' said the Governor, shaking his head. 'No one come buy.'

'He's taken my lamps, though,' said the skipper. He wore one leg of a pair of trousers, and his eye wandered along the verandah. The Governor quailed. There were cuddy camp-stools and the skipper's writing-table in plain sight.

'They've cleaned her out, o' course,' said Mr. Wardrop. 'They would. We'll go aboard and take an inventory. See!' He waved his hands over the harbour. 'We – live – there – now. Sorry?'

The Governor smiled a smile of relief.

'He's glad of that,' said one of the crew, reflectively. 'I shouldn't wonder.'

They flocked down to the harbour-front, the militia regiment clattering behind, and embarked themselves in what they found – it happened to be the Governor's boat. Then they disappeared over the bulwarks of the *Haliotis*, and the Governor prayed that they might find occupation inside.

Mr. Wardrop's first bound took him to the engine-room; and when the others were patting the well-remembered decks, they heard him giving God thanks that things were as he had left them. The wrecked engines stood over his head untouched; no inexpert hand had meddled with his shores; the steel wedges of the store-room were rusted home; and, best of all, the hundred and sixty tons of good Australian coal in the bunkers had not diminished.

'I don't understand it,' said Mr. Wardrop. 'Any Malay knows the use o' copper. They ought to have cut away the pipes. And with Chinese junks coming here, too. It's a special interposition o' Providence.'

'You think so,' said the skipper, from above. 'There's only been one thief here, and he's cleaned her out of all *my* things, anyhow.'

Here the skipper spoke less than the truth, for under the planking of his cabin, only to be reached by a chisel, lay a little money which never drew any interest – his sheet-anchor to windward. It was all in clean sovereigns that pass current the world over, and might have amounted to more than a hundred pounds.

'He's left me alone. Let's thank God,' repeated Mr. Wardrop.

'He's taken everything else; look!'

The *Haliotis*, except as to her engine-room, had been system-atically and scientifically gutted from one end to the other, and there was strong evidence that an unclean guard had camped in the skipper's cabin to regulate that plunder. She lacked glass, plate, crockery, cutlery, mattresses, cuddy carpets and chairs, all boats, and her copper ventilators. These things had been removed, with her sails and as much of the wire rigging as would not imperil the safety of the masts.

'He must have sold those,' said the skipper. 'The other things are in his house, I suppose.'

Every fitting that could be pried or screwed out was gone. Port, starboard, and masthead lights; teak gratings; sliding sashes of the deckhouse; the captain's chest of drawers, with charts and chart-table; photographs, brackets, and looking-glasses; cabin doors; rubber cuddy mats; hatch-irons; half the funnel-stays; cork fenders; carpenter's grindstone and tool-chest; holystones, swabs, squeegees; all cabin and pantry lamps; galley-fittings *en bloc*; flags and flag-locker; clocks, chronometers; the forward compass and the ship's bell and belfry, were among the missing.

There were great scarred marks on the deck-planking over which the cargo-derricks had been hauled. One must have fallen by the way, for the bulwark-rails were smashed and bent and the side-plates bruised.

'It's the Governor,' said the skipper. 'He's been selling her on the instalment plan.'

'Let's go up with spanners and shovels, and kill 'em all,' shouted the crew. 'Let's drown him, and keep the woman!'

'Then we'll be shot by that black-and-tan regiment – *our* regiment. What's the trouble ashore – They've camped our regiment on the beach.'

'We're cut off; that's all. Go and see what they want,' said Mr. Wardrop. 'You've the trousers.'

In his simple way the Governor was a strategist. He did not desire that the crew of the *Haliotis* should come ashore again, either singly or in detachments, and he proposed to turn their steamer into a convict-hulk. They would wait – he explained this from the quay to the skipper in the barge – and they would continue to wait till the man-of-war came along, exactly where they were. If one of them set foot ashore, the entire regiment would open fire, and he would not scruple to use the two cannon of the town. Meantime food would be sent daily in a boat under an armed escort. The skipper, bare to the waist, and rowing, could only grind his teeth; and the Governor improved the occasion, and revenged himself for the bitter words in the cables, by saying what he thought of the morals and manners of the crew. The barge returned to the *Haliotis* in silence, and the skipper climbed aboard, white on the cheek-bones and blue about the nostrils.

'I knew it,' said Mr. Wardrop; 'and they won't give us good food, either. We shall have bananas morning, noon, and night, an' a man can't work on fruit. *We* know that.'

Then the skipper cursed Mr. Wardrop for importing frivolous side-issues into the conversation; and the crew cursed one another, and the *Haliotis*, the voyage, and all that they knew or could bring to mind. They sat down in silence on the empty decks, and their eyes burned in their heads. The green harbour water chuckled at them overside. They looked at the palm-fringed hills inland, at the white houses above the harbour road, at the single tier of native craft by the quay, at the stolid soldiery sitting round the two cannon, and, last of all, at the blue bar of the horizon. Mr. Wardrop was buried in thought, and scratched imaginary lines with his untrimmed finger-nails on the planking.

'I make no promise,' he said, at last, 'for I can't say what may or may not have happened to them. But here's the ship, and here's us.'

There was a little scornful laughter at this, and Mr. Wardrop knitted his brows. He recalled that in the days when he wore trousers he had been Chief Engineer of the *Haliotis*.

'Harland, Mackesy, Noble, Hay, Naughton, Fink, O'Hara, Trumbull.'

'Here, sir!' The instinct of obedience waked to answer the roll-call of the engine-room.

'Below!'

They rose and went.

'Captain, I'll trouble you for the rest of the men as I want them. We'll get my stores out, and clear away the shores we don't need, and then we'll patch her up. *My* men will remember that they're in the *Haliotis*, – under me.'

He went into the engine-room, and the others stared. They were used to the accidents of the sea, but this was beyond their experience. None who had seen the engine-room believed that anything short of new engines from end to end could stir the *Haliotis* from her moorings.

The engine-room stores were unearthed, and Mr. Wardrop's face, red with the filth of the bilges and the exertion of travelling on his stomach, lit with joy. The spare gear of the *Haliotis* had been unusually complete, and two-and-twenty men, armed with screw-jacks, differential blocks, tackle, vices, and a forge or so, can look Kismet between the eyes without winking. The crew were ordered to replace the holding-down and shaft-bearing bolts, and return the collars of the thrust-block. When they had finished, Mr. Wardrop delivered a lecture on repairing compound engines without the aid of the shops, and the men sat about on the cold machinery. The cross-head jammed in the guides leered at them drunkenly, but offered no help. They ran their fingers hopelessly into the cracks of the starboard supporting-column, and picked at the ends of the ropes round the shores, while Mr. Wardrop's voice rose and fell echoing, till the quick tropic night closed down over the engine-room skylight.

Next morning the work of reconstruction began. It has been explained that the foot of the connecting-rod was forced against the foot of the starboard supporting-column, which it had cracked through and driven outward towards the ship's skin. To all appearance the job was more than hopeless, for rod and column seemed to have been welded into one. But herein Providence smiled on them for one moment to hearten them through the weary weeks ahead. The second engineer – more reckless than resourceful – struck at random with a cold chisel into the cast-iron of the column, and a greasy, grey flake of metal flew from under the imprisoned foot of the connecting-rod, while the rod itself fell away slowly, and brought up with a thunderous clang somewhere in the dark of the crank-pit. The guides-plates above were still jammed fast in the guides, but the first blow had been struck. They spent the rest of the day grooming the donkey-engine, which stood immediately forward of the engine-room hatch. Its tarpaulin, of course, had been stolen, and eight warm months had not improved the working parts. Further, the last dying hiccup of the *Haliotis* seemed – or it might have been the Malay from the boat-house – to have lifted the thing bodily on its bolts, and set it down inaccurately as regarded its steam connections.

'If we only had one single cargo-derrick!' Mr. Wardrop sighed. 'We can take the cylinder-cover off by hand, if we sweat; but to get the rod out o' the piston's not possible unless we use steam. Well, there'll be steam the morn, if there's nothing else. She'll fizzle!'

Next morning men from the shore saw the *Haliotis* through a cloud, for it was as though the deck smoked. Her crew were chasing steam through the shaken and leaky pipes to its work in the forward donkey-engine; and where oakum failed to plug a crack, they stripped off their loin-cloths for lapping, and swore, half-boiled and mother-naked. The donkey-engine worked – at a price – the price of constant attention and furious stoking – worked long enough to allow a wire-rope (it was made up of a funnel and a foremast-stay) to be led into the engine-room and made fast on the cylinder-cover of the forward engine. That rose easily enough, and was hauled through the skylight and on to the deck, many hands assisting the doubtful steam. Then came the tug of war, for it was necessary to get to the piston and the jammed piston-rod. They removed two of the piston junk-ring studs, screwed in two strong iron eye-bolts by way of handles, doubled the wire-rope, and set half a dozen men to smite with an extemporised battering-ram at the end of the piston-rod, where it peered through the piston, while the donkey-engine hauled upwards on the piston itself. After four hours of this furious work, the piston-rod suddenly slipped, and the piston rose with a jerk, knocking one or two men over into the engine-room. But when Mr. Wardrop declared that the piston had not split, they cheered, and thought nothing of their wounds; and the donkey-engine was hastily stopped; its boiler was nothing to tamper with.

And day by day their supplies reached them by boat. The skipper humbled himself once more before the Governor, and as a concession had leave to get drinking-water from the Malay boat-builder on the quay. It was not good drinking-water, but the Malay was anxious to supply anything in his power, if he were paid for it.

Now when the jaws of the forward engine stood, as it were, stripped and empty, they began to wedge up the shores of the cylinder itself. That work alone filled the better part of three days – warm and sticky days, when the hands slipped and sweat ran into the eyes. When the last wedge was hammered home there was no longer an ounce of weight on the supporting-columns; and Mr. Wardrop rummaged the ship for boiler-plate three-quarters of an inch thick, where he could find it. There was not much available, but what there was was more than beaten gold to him. In one desperate forenoon the entire crew, naked and lean, haled back, more or less into place, the starboard supporting-column, which, as you remember, was cracked clean through. Mr. Wardrop found them asleep where they had finished the work, and gave them a day's rest, smiling upon them as a father while he drew chalk-marks about the cracks. They woke to new and more trying labour; for over each one of those cracks a plate of three-quarter-inch boiler-iron was to be worked hot, the rivet-holes being drilled by hand. All that time they were fed on fruits, chiefly bananas, with some sago.

Those were the days when men swooned over the ratchet-drill and the hand-forge, and where they fell they had leave to lie unless their bodies were in the way of their fellows' feet. And so, patch upon patch, and a patch over all, the starboard supporting-column was clouted; but when they thought all was secure, Mr. Wardrop decreed that the noble patchwork would never support working engines; at the best, it could only hold the guide-bars approximately true. The deadweight of the cylinders must be borne by vertical struts; and, therefore, a gang would repair to the bows, and take out, with files, the big bow-anchor davits, each of which was some three inches in diameter. They threw hot coals at Wardrop, and threatened to kill him, those who did not weep (they were ready to weep on the least provocation); but he hit them with iron bars heated at the end, and they limped forward, and the davits came with them when they returned. They slept sixteen hours on the strength of it, and in three days two struts were in place, bolted from the foot of the starboard supporting-column to the under side of the cylinder. There remained now the port, or condenser-column, which, though not so badly cracked as its fellow, had also been strengthened in four places with boiler-plate patches, but needed struts. They took away the main stanchions of the bridge for that work, and, crazy with toil, did not see till all was in place that the rounded bars of iron must be flattened from top to bottom to allow the air-pump levers to clear them. It was Wardrop's oversight, and he wept bitterly before the men as he gave the order to unbolt the struts and flatten them with hammer and the flame. Now the broken engine was underpinned firmly, and they took away the wooden shores from under the cylinders, and gave them to the robbed bridge, thanking God for even half a day's work on gentle, kindly wood instead of the iron that had entered into their souls. Eight months in the back-country among the leeches, at a temperature of 84 degrees moist, is very bad for the nerves.

They had kept the hardest work to the last, as boys save Latin prose, and, worn though they were, Mr. Wardrop did not dare to give them rest. The piston-rod and connecting-rod were to be straightened, and this was a job for a regular dockyard with every appliance. They fell to it, cheered by a little chalk showing of work done and time consumed which Mr. Wardrop wrote up on the engine-room bulkhead. Fifteen days had gone – fifteen days of killing labour – and there was hope before them.

It is curious that no man knows how the rods were straightened. The crew of the *Haliotis* remember that week very dimly, as a fever patient remembers the delirium of a long night. There were fires everywhere, they say; the whole ship was one consuming furnace, and the hammers were never still. Now, there could not have been more than one fire at the most, for Mr. Wardrop distinctly recalls that no straightening was done except under his own eye. They remember, too, that for many years voices gave orders which they obeyed with their bodies, but their minds were abroad on all the seas. It seems to them that they stood through days and nights slowly sliding a bar backwards and forwards through a white glow that was part of the ship. They remember an intolerable noise in their burning heads from the walls of the stoke-hole, and they remember being savagely beaten by men whose eyes seemed asleep. When their shift was over they would draw straight lines in the air, anxiously and repeatedly, and would question one another in their sleep, crying, 'Is she straight?'

At last – they do not remember whether this was by day or by night – Mr. Wardrop began to dance clumsily, and wept the while; and they too danced and wept, and went to sleep twitching all over; and when they woke, men said that the rods were straightened, and no one did any work for two days, but lay on the decks and ate fruit. Mr. Wardrop would go below from time to time, and pat the two rods where they lay, and they heard him singing hymns.

Then his trouble of mind went from him, and at the end of the third day's idleness he made a drawing in chalk upon the deck, with letters of the alphabet at the angles. He pointed out that, though the piston-rod was more or less straight, the piston-rod cross-head – the thing that had been jammed sideways in the guides – had been badly strained, and had cracked the lower end of the piston-rod. He was going to forge and shrink a wrought-iron collar on the neck of the piston-rod where it joined the cross-head, and from the collar he would bolt a Y-shaped piece of iron whose lower arms should be bolted into the cross-head. If anything more were needed, they could use up the last of the boiler-plate.

So the forges were lit again, and men burned their bodies, but hardly felt the pain. The finished connection was not beautiful, but it seemed strong enough – at least, as strong as the rest of the machinery; and with that job their labours came to an end. All that remained was to connect up the engines, and to get food and water. The skipper and four men dealt with the Malay boat-builder by night chiefly; it was no time to haggle over the price of sago and dried fish. The others stayed aboard and replaced piston, piston-rod, cylinder-cover, cross-head, and bolts, with the aid of the faithful donkey-engine. The cylinder-cover was hardly steam-proof, and the eye of science might have seen in the connecting-rod a flexure something like that of a Christmas-tree candle which has melted and been straightened by hand over a stove, but, as Mr. Wardrop said, 'She didn't hit anything.'

As soon as the last bolt was in place, men tumbled over one another in their anxiety to get to the hand starting-gear, the wheel and worm, by which some engines can be moved when there is no steam aboard. They nearly wrenched off the wheel, but it was evident to the blindest eye that the engines stirred. They did not revolve in their orbits with any enthusiasm, as good machines should; indeed, they groaned not a little; but they moved over and came to rest in a way which proved that they still recognised man's hand. Then Mr. Wardrop sent his slaves into the darker bowels of the engine-room and the stoke-hole, and followed them with a flare-lamp. The boilers were sound, but would take no harm from a little scaling and cleaning. Mr. Wardrop would not have any one over-zealous, for he feared what the next stroke of the tool might show. 'The less we know about her now,' said he, 'the better for us all, I'm thinkin'. Ye'll understand me when I say that this is in no sense regular engineerin'.'

As his raiment, when he spoke, was his grey beard and uncut hair, they believed him. They did not ask too much of what they met, but polished and tallowed and scraped it to a false brilliancy.

'A lick of paint would make me easier in my mind,' said Mr. Wardrop, plaintively. 'I know half the condenser-tubes are started; and the propeller-shaftin' 's God knows how far out of the true, and we'll need a new air-pump, an' the main-steam leaks like a sieve, and there's worse each way I look; but – paint's like clothes to a man, an' ours is near all gone.'

The skipper unearthed some stale ropy paint of the loathsome green that they used for the galleys of sailing-ships, and Mr. Wardrop spread it abroad lavishly to give the engines self-respect.

His own was returning day by day, for he wore his loin-cloth continuously; but the crew, having worked under orders, did not feel as he did. The completed work satisfied Mr. Wardrop. He would at the last have made shift to run to Singapore, and gone home without vengeance taken to show his engines to his brethren in the craft; but the others and the captain forbade him. They had not yet recovered their self-respect.

'It would be safer to make what ye might call a trial trip, but beggars mustn't be choosers; an if the engines will go over to the hand-gear, the probability – I'm only saying it's a probability – the chance is that they'll hold up when we put steam on her.'

'How long will you take to get steam?' said the skipper.

'God knows! Four hours – a day – half a week. If I can raise sixty pound I'll not complain.'

'Be sure of her first; we can't afford to go out half a mile, and break down.'

'My soul and body, man, we're one continuous breakdown, fore an' aft! We might fetch Singapore, though.'

'We'll break down at Pygang-Watai, where we can do good,' was the answer, in a voice that did not allow argument. 'She's *my* boat, and – I've had eight months to think in.'

No man saw the *Haliotis* depart, though many heard her. She left at two in the morning, having cut her moorings, and it was none of her crew's pleasure that the engines should strike up a thundering half-seas-over chanty that echoed among the hills. Mr. Wardrop wiped away a tear as he listened to the new song.

'She's gibberin' – she's just gibberin',' he whimpered. 'Yon's the voice of a maniac.'

And if engines have any soul, as their masters believe, he was quite right. There were outcries and clamours, sobs and bursts of chattering laughter, silences where the trained ear yearned for the clear note, and torturing reduplications where there should have been one deep voice. Down the screw-shaft ran murmurs and warnings, while a heart-diseased flutter without told that the propeller needed re-keying.

'How does she make it?' said the skipper.

'She moves, but – but she's breakin' my heart. The sooner we're at Pygang-Watai, the better. She's mad, and we're waking the town.'

'Is she at all near safe?'

'What do *I* care how safe she is? She's mad. Hear that, now! To be sure, nothing's hittin' anything, and the bearin's are fairly cool, but – can ye not hear?'

'If she goes,' said the skipper, 'I don't care a curse. And she's *my* boat, too.'

She went, trailing a fathom of weed behind her. From a slow two knots an hour she crawled up to a triumphant four. Anything beyond that made the struts quiver dangerously, and filled the engine-room with steam. Morning showed her out of sight of land, and there was a visible ripple under her bows; but she complained bitterly in her bowels, and, as though the noise had called it, there shot along across the purple sea a swift, dark proa, hawk-like and curious, which presently ranged alongside and wished to know if the *Haliotis* were helpless. Ships, even the steamers of the white men, had been known to break down in those waters, and the honest Malay and Javanese traders would sometimes aid them in their own peculiar way. But this ship was not full of lady passengers and well-dressed officers. Men, white, naked and savage, swarmed down her sides – some with red-hot iron bars, and others with large hammers – threw themselves upon those innocent inquiring strangers, and, before any man could say what had happened, were in full possession of the proa, while the lawful owners bobbed in the water overside. Half an hour later the proa's cargo of sago and trepang, as well as a doubtful-minded compass, was in the *Haliotis*. The two huge triangular mat sails, with their seventy-foot yards and booms, had followed the cargo, and were being fitted to the stripped masts of the steamer.

They rose, they swelled, they filled, and the empty steamer visibly laid over as the wind took them. They gave her nearly three knots an hour, and what better could men ask? But if she had been forlorn before, this new purchase made her horrible to see. Imagine a respectable charwoman in the tights of a ballet-dancer rolling drunk along the streets, and you will come to some faint notion of the appearance of that nine-hundred-ton, well-decked, once schooner-rigged cargo-boat as she staggered under her new help, shouting and raving across the deep. With steam and sail that marvellous voyage continued; and the bright-eyed crew looked over the rail, desolate, unkempt, unshorn, shamelessly clothed beyond the decencies.

At the end of the third week she sighted the island of Pygang-Watai, whose harbour is the turning-point of a pearl sea-patrol. Here the gunboats stay for a week ere they retrace their line. There is no village at Pygang-Watai; only a stream of water, some palms, and a harbour safe to rest in till the first violence of the southeast monsoon has blown itself out. They opened up the low coral beach, with its mound of whitewashed coal ready for supply, the deserted huts for the sailors, and the flagless flagstaff.

Next day there was no *Haliotis* – only a little proa rocking in the warm rain at the mouth of the harbour, whose crew watched with hungry eyes the smoke of a gunboat on the horizon.

Months afterwards there were a few lines in an English newspaper to the effect that some gunboat of some foreign Power had broken her back at the mouth of some far-away harbour by running at full speed into a sunken wreck.

[First published in *The Graphic*, Christmas 1895, and then collected in *The Day's Work* (1898).]

✖ ✖ ✖

After only four years in the United States, Kipling returned to England in 1896 and, for the first time in his life, lived by the sea in Teignmouth and Rottingdean (before moving to Bateman's in the Sussex Weald in 1902). During these six years he developed his contacts in the Royal Navy. He visited the training ship HMS *Britannia* and the sculptor Hamo Thornycroft invited him to watch the trials of a new destroyer built by Thornycroft's brother's company. In 1897 Kipling renewed his friendship with Captain E.H. Bayly from South Africa, who was in command of a new ship, the HMS *Pelorus*, a cruiser, which Kipling joined on exercises in the English Channel and as far as Bantry Bay. The result was a series of articles in the *Morning Post*, which were collected in *A Fleet in Being* (1898).

Kipling followed this up with further voyages on HMS *Nile* during the Navy's annual manoeuvres in 1901. These different experiences contributed to several new poems, as well as to a series of stories which tried to portray life in the navy in human terms. His Pyecroft stories, which appeared over several years, starting in 1902, are the naval equivalent of his Mulvaney tales about army life in India.

A FLEET IN BEING:
NOTES OF TWO TRIPS WITH
THE CHANNEL SQUADRON

'. . . the sailor men
That sail upon the seas,
To fight the Wars and keep the Laws,
And live on yellow peas.'
                    – 'A Gunroom Ditty-Box.' G.S. Bowles.

SOME THIRTY OF HER Majesty's men-of-war were involved in this matter; say a dozen battleships of the most recent, and seventeen or eighteen cruisers; but my concern was limited to one of a new type commanded by an old friend. I had some dim knowledge of the interior of a warship, but none of the new world into which I stepped from a Portsmouth wherry one wonderful summer evening in '97.

With the exception of the Captain, the Chief Engineer, and maybe a few petty officers, nobody was more than twenty-eight years old. They ranged in the ward-room from this resourceful age to twenty-six or seven clear-cut, clean-shaved young faces with all manner of varied experience behind them. When one comes to think, it's only just that a light 20-knot cruiser should be handled, under guidance of an older head, by affable young gentlemen prepared, even sinfully delighted, to take chances not set down in books. She was new, they were new, the Admiral was new, and we were all off to the Manœuvres together thirty keels next day – threading their way in and out between a hundred and twenty moored vessels not so fortunate. We opened the ball, for the benefit of some foreign warships, with a piece of rather pretty steering. A consort was coming up a waterlane, between two lines of shipping, just behind us; and we nipped in immediately ahead of her, precisely as a hansom turning out of Bond Street nips in in front of a City 'bus. Distance on water is deceptive, and when I vowed that at one crisis I could have spat on the wicked ram of our next astern, pointed straight at our naked turning side, the ward-room laughed.

'Oh, that's nothing,' said a gentleman of twenty-two. 'Wait till we have to keep station to-night. It's my middle watch.'

'Close water-tight doors, then,' said a Sub-Lieutenant. 'I say' (this to the passenger) 'if you find a second-class cruiser's ram in the small of your back at midnight don't be alarmed.'

Fascinating Game of General Post

We were then strung out in a six-mile line, thirty ships, all heading Westwards. As soon as we found room the Flagship began to signal, and there followed a most fascinating game of general post. When I came to know our signalmen on the human side I appreciated it even more. The Admiral wreathed himself with flags, strings of them; the signalman on our high little, narrow little bridge, telescope jammed to his eye, read out the letters of that order; the Quartermaster spun the infantine wheel; the Officer of the Bridge rumbled requests down the speaking-tube to the engine-room, and away we fled to take up station at such and such a distance from our neighbours, ahead and astern, at such and such an angle on the Admiral, his bow or beam. The end of it was a miracle to lay eyes. The long line became four parallel lines of strength and beauty, a mile and a quarter from flank to flank, and thus we abode till evening. Two hundred yards or so behind us the ram of our next astern planed through the still water; an equal distance in front of us lay the oily water from the screw of our next ahead. So it was ordered, and so we did, as though glued into position. But our Captain took up the parable and bade me observe how slack we were, by reason of recent festivities, compared to what we should be in a few days. 'Now we're all over the shop. The ships haven't worked together, and station-keeping isn't as easy as it looks.' Later on I found this was perfectly true.

A Varying Strain

One thing more than all the rest impresses the passenger on a Queen's ship. She is seldom for three whole hours at the same speed. The liner clear of her dock strikes her pace and holds it to her journey's end, but the man-of-war must always have two or three knots up her sleeve in case the Admiral demands a spurt; she must also be ready to drop three or four knots at the wave of a flag; and on occasion she must lie still and meditate. This means a varying strain on all the mechanism, and constant strain on the people who control it.

I counted seven speeds in one watch, ranging from eight knots to seventeen, which, with eleven, was our point of maximum vibration. At eight knots you heard the vicious little twin-screws jigitting like restive horses; at seventeen they pegged away into the sea like a pair of short-gaited trotting ponies on a hard road. But one felt, even in dreams, that she was being held back. Those who talk of a liner's freedom from breakdown should take a 7,000 horsepower boat and hit her and hold her for a fortnight all across the salt seas.

In Club and Coteries

After a while I went to the galley to get light on these and other matters. Once forward of the deck torpedo-tubes you enter another and a fascinating world of seamen-gunners, artificers, cooks, Marines (we had twenty and a sergeant), ship's boys, signalmen, and the general democracy. Here the men smoke at the permitted times, and in clubs and coteries gossip and say what they please of each other and their superiors. Their speech is soft (if everyone spoke aloud you could not hear yourself think on a cruiser), their gestures are few (if a man swung his arms about he would interfere with his neighbour), their steps are noiseless as they pop in and out of the forward flats; they are at all times immensely interesting, and, as a rule, delightfully amusing. Their slang borrows from the engine-room, the working parts of guns, the drill-book, and the last music-hall song. It is delivered in a tight-lipped undertone; the more excruciatingly funny parts without a shade of expression. The first thing that strikes a casual observer is their superb health; next, their quiet adequateness; and thirdly, a grave courtesy. But under the shell of the new Navy beats the heart of the old. All Marryat's immortals are there, better fed, better tended, better educated, but at heart unchanged. I heard Swinburne laying down the law to his juniors by the ash-shoot; Chucks was there, too, inquiring in the politest manner in the world what a friend meant by spreading his limbs about the landscape; and a lineal descendant of Dispart fussed over a 4in. gun that some one had been rude to. They were men of the world, at once curiously simple and curiously wily (this makes the charm of the Naval man of all ranks), coming and going about their businesses like shadows.

Not From the Admiralty Standpoint

They were all keenly interested in the Manœuvres – not from the Admiralty standpoint, but the personal. Many of them had served under one or other of the Admirals, and they enlightened their fellows, as you shall later hear.

Then night fell, and our Fleet blazed 'like a lot of chemists' shops adrift,' as one truthfully put it – six lights to each ship; bewildering the tramps. There was a cove of refuge, by one of the forward 4-in.

guns, within touch of the traffic to the bridge, the break of the foc'sle, the crowded populations below, and the light banter near the galley. My vigil here was cheered by the society of a Marine, who delivered a lecture on the thickness of the skulls of the inhabitants of South America, as tested by his own hands. It ended thus: 'An' so I got ten days in one o' their stinkin' prisons. Fed me on grapes they did, along with one o' their own murderers. Funny people them South Americans. Oh, we 'adn't killed any one. We only skirmished through their bloomin' Suburbs lookin' for fun like.'

'Fun! *We*'ve got all the fun we want!' growled a voice in the shadow. A stoker had risen silently as a seal for a breath of air, and stood, chest to the breeze, scanning the Fleet lights.

''Ullo! Wot's the matter with *your* condenser?' said the Marine. 'You'd better take your mucky 'ands off them hammick-cloths or you'll be spoke to.'

'Our bunkers,' said the figure, addressing his grievance to the sea-line, 'are stuck all about like a lot o' women's pockets. They're stuck about like a lot o' bunion-plasters. That's what our bunkers are.' He slipped back into the darkness. Presently a signalman pattered by to relieve his mate on the bridge.

'You'll be 'ung,' said the Marine, who was a wit, and by the same token something of a prophet.

'Not if you're anywhere in the crowd I won't,' was the retort, always in a cautious, 'don't-wake-him' undertone. 'Wot are you doin' 'ere?'

'Never you mind. You go on up to the 'igh an' lofty bridge an' persecute your vocation. My Gawd! I wouldn't be a signalman, not for ever so.'

When I met my friend next morning 'persecuting his vocation' as sentry over the lifebuoy aft neither he nor I recognised each other; but I owe him some very nice tales.

Wheeling, Circling, and Returning

Next day both Fleets were exercised at steam tactics, which is a noble game; but I was too interested in the life of my own cruiser, unfolding hour by hour, to be intelligently interested in evolutions. All I remember is that we were eternally taking up positions at fifteen knots an hour amid a crowd of other cruisers, all precisely alike, all still as death, each with a wedge of white foam under her nose; wheeling, circling, and returning. The battleships danced stately quadrilles by themselves in another part of the deep. We of the light horse did barn-dances about the windy floors; and precisely as couples in the ball-room fling a word over their shoulders, so we and our friends, whirling past to take up fresh stations, snapped out an unofficial sentence or two by means of our bridge-semaphores. Cruisers are wondrous human. In the afternoon the battleships overtook us, their white upperworks showing like icebergs as they topped the sea-line. Then we sobered our faces, and the engineers had rest, and at a wave of the Admiral's flag off Land's End our Fleet was split in twain. One half would go outside Ireland, toying with the weight of the Atlantic *en route*, to Blacksod Bay, while we turned up the Irish Channel to Lough Swilly. There we would coal, and wait for War. After that it would be blind man's buff within a three hundred and fifty mile ring of the Atlantic. We of Lough Swilly would try to catch the Blacksod Fleet, which was supposed to have a rendezvous of its own somewhere out at sea, before it could return to the shelter of the Bay.

The Experts of the Lower Deck

There was, however, one small flaw in the rules, and as soon as they were in possession of the plan of campaign the experts of the lower deck put their horny thumbs on it – thus:

'Look 'ere. Their Admiral 'as to go out from Blacksod to some rendezvous known only to 'isself. Ain't that so?'

'We've 'eard all that.' This from an impertinent, new to War.

'Leavin' a cruiser be'ind 'im – *Blake* most likely, or *Blenheim* – to bring 'im word of the outbreak of 'ostilities. Ain't that so?'

'Get *on*. What are you drivin' at?'

'You'll see. When that cruiser overtakes 'im 'e 'as to navigate back to Blacksod from 'is precious rendezvous to get 'ome again before we intercepts the beggar.'

'Well?'

'Now I put it to you. What's to prevent 'im rendezvousin' out *slow* in order to be overtook by that cruiser; an' rendezvousin' back quick to Blacksod, before we intercepts 'im? I don't see that 'is steamin' rate is anywhere laid down. You mark my word, 'e'll take precious good care to be overtook by that cruiser of 'is. We won't catch 'im. There's an 'ole in the rules an' 'e'll slip through. *I* know 'im if you don't!'

The voice went on to describe "im,' the Admiral of our enemy – as a wily person, who would make the Admiralty sit up.

And truly, it came out in the end that the other Admiral had done almost exactly what his foc'sle friends expected. He went to his rendezvous slowly, was overtaken by his cruiser about a hundred miles from the rendezvous, turned back again to Blacksod, and having won the game of 'Pussy vants a corner,' played about in front of the Bay till we descended on him. Then he was affable, as he could afford to be, explained the situation, and I presume smiled. There was a 'hole in the rules,' and he sailed all his Fleet through it.

We, of the Northern Squadron, found Lough Swilly in full possession of a Sou'-west gale, and an assortment of dingy colliers lying where they could most annoy the anchoring Fleet. A collier came alongside with donkey-engines that would not lift more than half their proper load; she had no bags, no shovels, and her crazy derrick-boom could not be topped up enough to let the load clear our bulwarks. So we supplied our own bags and shovels, rearranged the boom, put two of our own men on the rickety donkey-engines, and fell to work in that howling wind and wet.

Coaling: A Preparation for War

As a preparation for War next day, it seemed a little hard on the crew, who worked like sailors – there is no stronger term. From time to time a red-eyed black demon, with flashing teeth, shot into the ward-room for a bite and a drink, cried out the number of tons aboard, added a few pious words on the collier's appliances, and our bunkers ('Like a lot of bunion-plasters,' the stoker had said), and tore back to where the donkey-engines wheezed, the bags crashed, the shovels rasped and scraped, the boom whined and creaked, and the First Lieutenant, carved in pure jet, said precisely what occurred to him. Before the collier cast off a full-blooded battleship sent over a boat to take some measurements of her hatch. The boat was in charge of a Midshipman aged, perhaps, seventeen, though he looked younger. He came dripping into the ward-room bloodless, with livid lips, for he had been invalided from the Mediterranean full of Malta fever.

'And what are you in?' said our Captain, who chanced to pass by. 'The *Victorious*, sir, and a smart ship!' He drank his little glass of Marsala, swirled his dank boat-cloak about him, and went out serenely to take his boat home through the dark and the dismal welter.

Now the *Victorious*, she is some fourteen thousand nine hundred tons, and he who gave her her certificate was maybe ten stone two, with a touch of Malta fever on him!

The Ward-Room Disported Itself

We cleaned up at last; the First Lieutenant's face relaxed a little, and some one called for the instruments of music. Out came two violins, a mandoline, and bagpipes, and the ward-room disported itself among tunes of three Nations till War should be declared. In the middle of a scientific experiment as to how the ship's kitten might be affected by bagpipes that hour struck, and even more swiftly than pussy fled under the sofa the trim mess-jackets melted away, the chaff ceased, the hull shivered to the power of the steam-capstan, the slapping of the water on our sides grew, and we glided through the moored Fleet to the mouth of Lough Swilly. Our orders were to follow and support another cruiser who had been already despatched towards Blacksod Bay to observe the enemy – or rather that cruiser who was bearing news of the outbreak of War to the enemy's Fleet.

It was then midnight of the 7th of July – by the rules of the game the main body could not move till noon of the 8th – and the North Atlantic, cold and lumpy, was waiting for us as soon as we had put out our lights. Then I began to understand why a certain type of cruiser is irreverently styled 'a commodious coffee-grinder.' We had the length of a smallish liner, but by no means her dead weight, so where the Red Duster would have driven heavily through the seas the White Ensign danced; and the twin-screws gave us more kick than was pleasant. At half-past five of a peculiarly cheerless dawn we picked up the big cruiser (who had seen nothing), stayed in her company till nearly seven, and ran back to rejoin the Fleet, whom we met coming out of Lough

Swilly about 1 p.m. of Thursday, the 8th. And the weather was vile. Once again we headed W.N.W. in company at an average speed of between thirteen and fourteen knots on a straightaway run of three hundred and fifty miles towards the Rockal Bank and the lonely rock that rises out of the sea there. The idea was that our enemy might have made this his rendezvous, in which case we had hope of catching him *en masse*.

Through that penitential day the little cruiser was disgustingly lively, but all we took aboard was spray, whereas the low-bowed battleships slugged their bluff noses into the surge and rose dripping like half-tide rocks. The Flagship might have manœuvred like half a dozen Nelsons, but I lay immediately above the twin-screws and thought of the Quartermaster on the reeling bridge who was not allowed to lie down. Through the cabin-door I could see the decks, dim with spray; hear the bugles calling to quarters; and catch glimpses of the uninterrupted life of the ship – a shining face under a sou'wester; a pair of sea-legs cloaked in oil-skins; a hurrying signalman with a roiling and an anxious eye; a warrant officer concerned for the proper housing of his quick-firers, as they disappeared in squirts of foam; or a Lieutenant serenely reporting men and things 'present' or 'correct.' Behind all, as the cruiser flung herself carelessly abroad, great grey and slate-coloured scoops of tormented sea. About midnight the scouting cruiser – same we had left that morning on the look-out for the *Blake* or the *Blenheim* – rejoined the Fleet; but the Fleet might have gone down as one keel so far as one unhappy traveller was concerned.

By noon of July 9th we had covered 325½ miles in twenty-four hours, with never a sight of the enemy to cheer us, and had reached the limit of our ground. Here we turned, and, on a front of twenty-four miles from wing to wing, swept down 250 miles South-eastward to the offing of Blacksod Bay.

'Missed!'

Mercifully the weather began to improve, and we had the sea more or less behind us. It was when we entered on this second slant, about three minutes after the Fleet swung round, that, as though all men had thought it together, a word went round our forecastle – 'Missed!' After dinner, as they were smoking above the

spit-kids, the doctrine was amplified with suitable language by the
foc'sle experts, and it was explained to me with a great certainty
how the other side had out-manœuvred us 'by means of the 'ole
in the rules.' In other words, 'he had been overtook by 'is cruiser,'
precisely as the wiser heads had prophesied; and even at that early
stage of the game we had been sold. There was no way of finding
out anything for sure. A big scouting cruiser slipped off again a little
before dawn of the 10th, and six or seven hours later was reported
to be in sight with news of the enemy. At this point there came,
as we learned later, what you might call a hitch. Some unhappy
signalman, they assert, misplaced a flag of a signal whereby it was
caused to be believed that a cruiser had sighted the enemy where
there was no enemy. In that direction, then, the Fleet gave chase,
and though the thing was abortive, the run was a beautiful example
of what the new Navy can do at a pinch.

We Discovered Our Mistake

Then, I suppose, we discovered our mistake about the enemy,
and hurried all together for Blacksod Bay in the hope of cutting
him off. Arrived at the scattered Islands near the mouth, a cruiser
was sent inside to see if any one was at home, while the Flagship
bade the rest of us 'walk foreninst her while she considered on it.'
Meteorologically the weather was now glorious – a blazing sun,
and a light swell to which the cruisers rolled lazily, as hounds roll
on the grass at a check. Nautically there was a good deal of thunder
in the air. Everybody knew something had gone wrong, and when
the Flagship announced that she was not at all pleased with the
signalling throughout the Fleet it was no more than every one
expected.

Now the Flagship had some fifty or sixty signalmen, and a bridge
as broad as a houseboat and as clear as a ball-room. Our bridge was
perhaps four feet broad; the roar of a stoke-hold ventilating-fan,
placed apparently for that purpose, carefully sucked up two-thirds
of every shouted order; and between the bridge and the poop the
luckless signalman, for want of an overhead passage, had to run an
obstacle race along the crowded decks. We owned six signalmen.
After watching them for a week I was prepared to swear that each
had six arms and eight cinder-proof eyes; but the Flagship thought

otherwise. I heard what the signalmen thought later on; but that was by no means for publication.

High-Speed Scouting

Back came the cruiser with news that Blacksod Bay was empty. Meantime three other boats had been sent off to reinforce the racing cruiser whose constant business it was to keep touch with the enemy. That monster did most of our high-speed scouting, and several times at least saw something of the other side. We were not so lucky. With three second-class friends we were ordered to patrol at twelve knots an hour on a six mile beat thirteen miles to the North-east of Eagle Island, to fire a rocket if we saw anything of the enemy that night, and to stay out till we were recalled. When we reached our ground the sea was all empty save for one speck on the horizon that marked the next cruiser, also patrolling. A desolate and a naked shore, broken into barren Islands, turned purplish-grey in the sunset, and two lone lighthouses took up their duty. We tramped up and down through that marvellous transparent dusk, with more than the regularity of the Metropolitan Police. There was no lawful night, but a wine-coloured twilight cut in half by the moon-track on the still water. Unless the enemy poled in punts under the shadow of the shore and the faint mist that lay along it, he could not hope to creep round from the North unobserved. The signalmen blessed their gods – Marine ones – that they were away from the Flagship; the foc'sle and my friend the Marine assured the signalmen that they would be infallibly hanged at the yard-arm when we reached port; and we all talked things over forward as the steady tramp continued.

'I told you so! 'E's found an 'ole in the rules an' slipped through it,' was the burden of our song. We must have burned more coal than would ever be expedient in War, and we saw imaginary hulls with great zeal till the glorious sunrise, cut off from the battle, peering over the nettings, wet with dew, and just as ignorant of events around us as we shall be when the Real Thing begins.

[First published in the *Morning Post*, 5–11 November 1898, and then in book form by Macmillan in the same year.]

✠ ✠ ✠

CRUISERS

As our mother the Frigate, bepainted and fine,
Made play for her bully the Ship of the Line;
So we, her bold daughters by iron and fire,
Accost and decoy to our masters' desire.

Now, pray you, consider what toils we endure,
Night-walking wet sea-lanes, a guard and a lure;
Since half of our trade is that same pretty sort
As mettlesome wenches do practise in port.

For this is our office – to spy and make room,
As hiding yet guiding the foe to their doom;
Surrounding, confounding, we bait and betray
And tempt them to battle the sea's width away.

The pot-bellied merchant foreboding no wrong
With headlight and sidelight he lieth along,
Till, lightless and lightfoot and lurking, leap we
To force him discover his business by sea.

And when we have wakened the lust of a foe,
To draw him by flight toward our bullies we go,
Till, 'ware of strange smoke stealing nearer, he flies
Ere our bullies close in for to make him good prize.

So, when we have spied on the path of their host,
One flieth to carry that word to the coast;
And, lest by false doublings they turn and go free,
One lieth behind them to follow and see.

Anon we return, being gathered again,
Across the sad valleys all drabbled with rain –
Across the grey ridges all crisped and curled –
To join the long dance round the curve of the world.

The bitter salt spindrift, the sun-glare likewise,
The moon-track a-tremble, bewilders our eyes,
Where, linking and lifting, our sisters we hail
'Twixt wrench of cross-surges or plunge of head-gale.

As maidens awaiting the bride to come forth
Make play with light jestings and wit of no worth,
So, widdershins circling the bride-bed of death,
Each fleereth her neighbour and signeth and saith:–

'What see ye? Their signals, or levin afar?
What hear ye? God's thunder, or guns of our war?
What mark ye? Their smoke, or the cloud-rack outblown?
What chase ye? Their lights, or the Daystar low down?'

So, times past all number deceived by false shows,
Deceiving we cumber the road of our foes,
For this is our virtue: to track and betray;
Preparing great battles a sea's width away.

Now peace is at end and our peoples take heart,
For the laws are clean gone that restrained our art;
Up and down the near headlands and against the far wind
We are loosed (O be swift!) to the work of our kind!

[First published in the *Morning Post*, 14 August 1899, and then collected in *The Five Nations* (London: Methuen; New York: Doubleday, 1903).]

✠ ✠ ✠

THE DYKES

WE HAVE NO HEART for the fishing – we have no hand for the oar –
All that our fathers taught us of old pleases us no more.
All that our own hearts bid us believe we doubt where we do not
    deny –
There is nor proof in the bread we eat nor rest in the toil we ply.

Look you, our foreshore stretches far through sea-gate, dyke and
     groin –
Made land all, that our fathers made, where the flats and the
     fairway join.
They forced the sea a sea-league back. They died, and their work
     stood fast.
We were born to peace in the lee of the dykes, but the time of our
     peace is past.

Far off, the full tide clambers and slips, mouthing and resting all,
Nipping the flanks of the water-gates, baying along the wall;
Turning the shingle, returning the shingle, changing the set of the
     sand . . .
We are too far from the beach, men say, to know how the outwarks
     stand.

So we come down, uneasy, to look; uneasily pacing the beach.
These are the dykes our fathers made: we have never known a
     breach.
Time and again has the gale blown by and we were not afraid;
Now we come only to look at the dykes – at the dykes our fathers
     made.

O'er the marsh where the homesteads cower apart the harried
     sunlight flies,
Shifts and considers, wanes and recovers, scatters and sickness
     and dies –
An evil ember bedded in ash – a spark blown west by wind . . .
We are surrendered to night and the sea – the gale and the tide
     behind!

At the bridge of the lower saltings the cattle gather and blare,
Roused by the feet of running men, dazed by the lantern-glare.
Unbar and let them away for their lives – the levels drown as they
     stand,
Where the flood-wash forces the sluices aback and the ditches
     deliver inland.

Ninefold deep to the top of the dykes the galloping breakers
     stride,
And their overcarried spray is a sea – a sea of the landward side.

Coming, like stallions they paw with their hooves, going they
    snatch with their teeth,
Till the bents and the furze and the sand are dragged out, and the
    old-time hurdles are beneath.

Bid men gather fuel for fire, the tar, the oil and tow –
Flame we shall need, not smoke, in the dark if the riddled sea-
    banks go.
Bid the ringers watch in the tower (who know how the dawn shall
    prove?)
Each with his rope between his feet and the trembling bells above.

Now we can only wait till the day, wait and apportion our shame.
These are the dykes our fathers left, but we would not look to the
    same.
Time and again were we warned of the dykes, time and again we
    delayed.
Now, it may fall, we have slain our sons, as our fathers we have
    betrayed.

[Probably written in 1902; first published in *The Five Nations* (1903).]

SONG OF DIEGO VALDEZ

The God of Fair Beginnings
    Hath prospered here my hand –
The cargoes of my lading,
    And the keels of my command.
For out of many ventures
    That sailed with hope as high,
My own have made the better trade,
    And Admiral am I.

To me my King's much honour,
    To me my people's love –
To me the pride of Princes

And power all pride above;
To me the shouting cities,
　　To me the mob's refrain:–
'Who knows not noble Valdez
　　Hath never heard of Spain.'

But I remember comrades –
　　Old playmates on new seas –
When as we traded orpiment
　　Among the savages –
A thousand leagues to south'ard
　　And thirty years removed –
They knew not noble Valdez,
　　But me they knew and loved.

Then they that found good liquor,
　　They drank it not alone,
And they that found fair plunder,
　　They told us every one,
About our chosen islands
　　Or secret shoals between,
When, weary from far voyage,
　　We gathered to careen.

There burned our breaming-fagots
　　All pale along the shore:
There rose our worn pavilions –
　　A sail above an oar:
As flashed each yeaming anchor
　　Through mellow seas afire,
So swift our careless captains
　　Rowed each to his desire.

Where lay our loosened harness?
　　Where turned our naked feet?
Whose tavern 'mid the palm-trees?
　　What quenchings of what heat?
Oh, fountain in the desert!
　　Oh, cistern in the waste!
Oh, bread we ate in secret!
　　Oh, cup we spilled in haste!

The youth new-taught of longing,
    The widow curbed and wan,
The goodwife proud at season,
    And the maid aware of man –
All souls unslaked, consuming,
    Defrauded in delays,
Desire not more their quittance
    Than I those forfeit days!

I dreamed to wait my pleasure
    Unchanged my spring would bide:
Wherefore, to wait my pleasure,
    I put my spring aside
Till, first in face of Fortune,
    And last in mazed disdain,
I made Diego Valdez
    High Admiral of Spain.

Then walked no wind 'neath Heaven
    Nor surge that did not aid –
I dared extreme occasion,
    Nor ever one betrayed.
They wrought a deeper treason –
    (Led seas that served my needs!)
They sold Diego Valdez
    To bondage of great deeds.

The tempest flung me seaward,
    And pinned and bade me hold
The course I might not alter –
    And men esteemed me bold!
The calms embayed my quarry,
    The fog-wreath sealed his eyes;
The dawn-wind brought my topsails –
    And men esteemed me wise!

Yet, 'spite my tyrant triumphs,
    Bewildered, dispossessed –
My dream held I before me
    My vision of my rest;

But, crowned by Fleet and People,
    And bound by King and Pope –
Stands here Diego Valdez
    To rob me of my hope.

No prayer of mine shall move him.
    No word of his set free
The Lord of Sixty Pennants
    And the Steward of the Sea.
His will can loose ten thousand
    To seek their loves again –
But not Diego Valdez,
    High Admiral of Spain.

There walks no wind 'neath Heaven
    Nor wave that shall restore
The old careening riot
    And the clamorous, crowded shore –
The fountain in the desert,
    The cistern in the waste,
The bread we ate in secret,
    The cup we spilled in haste.

Now call I to my Captains –
    For council fly the sign –
Now leap their zealous galleys,
    Twelve-oared, across the brine.
To me the straiter prison,
    To me the heavier chain –
To me Diego Valdez,
    High Admiral of Spain!

[First published in full in *The Five Nations* (1903), although the third stanza was used as a chapter heading in *Kim* (London: Macmillan; New York: Doubleday Page, 1901).]

�֍   ✖   ✖

THE SEA AND THE HILLS

WHO HATH DESIRED THE Sea? – the sight of salt water
  unbounded –
The heave and the halt and the hurl and the crash of the comber
  wind-hounded?
The sleek-barrelled swell before storm, grey, foamless, enormous,
  and growing
Stark calm on the lap of the Line or the crazy-eyed hurricane
  blowing –
His Sea in no showing the same – his Sea and the same 'neath each
  showing:
His Sea as she slackens or thrills?
So and no otherwise – so and no otherwise – hillmen desire their
  Hills!

Who hath desired the Sea ? – the immense and contemptuous
  surges?
The shudder, the stumble, the swerve, as the star-stabbing
  bowsprit emerges?
The orderly clouds of the Trades, the ridged, roaring sapphire
  thereunder –
Unheralded cliff-haunting flaws and the headsail's low-volleying
  thunder –
His Sea in no wonder the same – his Sea and the same through
  each wonder:
His Sea as she rages or stills?
So and no otherwise – so and no otherwise – hillmen desire their
  Hills.

Who hath desired the Sea? Her menaces swift as her mercies?
The in-rolling walls of the fog and the silver-winged breeze that
  disperses?
The unstable mined berg going South and the calvings and groans
  that declare it –
White water half-guessed overside and the moon breaking timely
  to bare it –
His Sea as his fathers have dared – his Sea as his children shall
  dare it:
His Sea as she serves him or kills?

So and no otherwise – so and no otherwise – hillmen desire their
 Hills.

Who hath desired the Sea? Her excellent loneliness rather
Than forecourts of kings, and her outermost pits than the streets
 where men gather
Inland, among dust, under trees – inland where the slayer may
 slay him –
Inland, out of reach of her arms, and the bosom whereon he must
 lay him –
His Sea from the first that betrayed – at the last that shall never
 betray him:
His Sea that his being fulfils?
So and no otherwise – so and no otherwise – hillmen desire their
 Hills.

[First published in full in *The Five Nations* (1903), although the first verse
had appeared as the heading to Chapter XII of *Kim* (1901), and the second
verse as the heading to Chapter XIII.]

✖ ✖ ✖

THEIR LAWFUL OCCASIONS

'. . . And a security for such as pass on the seas upon their lawful
occasions.'

– Navy Prayer.

Part I

DISREGARDING THE INVENTIONS OF the Marine Captain, whose
other name is Gubbins, let a plain statement suffice.

H.M.S. *Caryatid* went to Portland to join Blue Fleet for manœuvres.
I travelled overland from London by way of Portsmouth, where I fell
among friends. When I reached Portland, H.M.S. *Caryatid*, whose
guest I was to have been, had, with Blue Fleet, already sailed for
some secret rendezvous off the west coast of Ireland, and Portland
breakwater was filled with Red Fleet, my official enemies and
joyous acquaintances, who received me with unstinted hospitality.

For example, Lieutenant-Commander A.L. Hignett, in charge of three destroyers, *Wraith*, *Stiletto*, and *Kobbold*, due to depart at 6 p.m. that evening, offered me a berth on his thirty-knot flagship, but I preferred my comforts, and so accepted sleeping-room in H.M.S. *Pedantic* (15,000 tons), leader of the second line. After dining aboard her I took boat to Weymouth to get my kit aboard, as the battleships would go to war at midnight. In transferring my allegiance from Blue to Red Fleet, whatever the Marine Captain may say, I did no wrong. I truly intended to return to the *Pedantic* and help to fight Blue Fleet. All I needed was a new toothbrush, which I bought from a chemist in a side street at 9.15 p.m. As I turned to go, one entered seeking alleviation of a gumboil. He was dressed in a checked ulster, a black silk hat three sizes too small, cord-breeches, boots, and pure brass spurs. These he managed painfully, stepping like a prisoner fresh from leg-irons. As he adjusted the pepper-plaster to the gum the light fell on his face, and I recognised Mr. Emanuel Pyecroft, late second-class petty officer of H.M.S. *Achimandrite*, an unforgettable man, met a year before under Tom Wessels' roof in Plymouth. It occurred to me that when a petty officer takes to spurs he may conceivably meditate desertion. For that reason I, though a taxpayer, made no sign. Indeed, it was Mr. Pyecroft, following me out of the shop, who said hollowly: 'What might you be doing here?'

'I'm going on manœuvres in the *Pedantic*,' I replied.

'Ho!' said Mr. Pyecroft. 'An' what manner o' manœuvres d'you expect to see in a blighted cathedral like the *Pedantic*? I know 'er. I knew her in Malta, when the *Vulcan* was her permanent tender, manœuvres! You won't see more than "Man an' arm watertight doors!" in your little woollen undervest.'

'I'm sorry for that.'

'Why?' He lurched heavily as his spurs caught and twanged like tuning-forks. 'War's declared at midnight. *Pedantic*s be sugared! Buy an 'am an' see life!'

For the moment I fancied Mr. Pyecroft, a fugitive from justice, purposed that we two should embrace a Robin Hood career in the uplands of Dorset. The spurs troubled me, and I made bold to say as much. 'Them!' he said, coming to an intricate halt. 'They're part of the *prima facie* evidence. But as for me – let me carry your bag – I'm second in command, leadin'-hand, cook, steward, an' lavatory man, with a few incidentals for sixpence a day extra, on No. 267 torpedo-boat.'

'They wear spurs there?'

'Well,' said Mr. Pyecroft, 'seein' that Two Six Seven belongs to Blue Fleet, which left the day before yesterday, disguises are imperative. It transpired thus. The Right Honourable Lord Gawd Almighty Admiral Master Frankie Frobisher, K.C.B., commandin' Blue Fleet, can't be bothered with one tin-torpedo-boat more or less; and what with lyin' in the Reserve four years, an' what with the new kind o' tiffy which cleans dynamos with brick-dust and oil (Blast these spurs! They won't render!), Two Six Seven's steam-gadgets was paralytic. Our Mr. Moorshed done his painstakin' best – it's his first command of a war-canoe, matoor age nineteen (down that alley-way, please!), but be that as it may, His Holiness Frankie is aware of us crabbin' ourselves round the breakwater at five knots, an' steerin' *pari passu*, as the French say. (Up this alley-way, please!) If he'd given Mr. Hinchcliffe, our chief engineer, a little time, it would never have transpired, for what Hinch can't drive he can coax; but the new port bein' a trifle cloudy, an' 'is joints tinglin' after a post-captain dinner, Frankie come on the upper bridge seekin' for a sacrifice. We, offerin' a broadside target, got it. He told us what 'is grandmamma, 'oo was a lady an' went to sea in stick-and-string bateaus, had told him about steam. He throwed in his own prayers for the 'ealth an' safety of all steam-packets an' their officers. Then he give us several distinct orders. The first few – I kept tally – was all about going to Hell; the next many was about not evolutin' in his company, when there; an' the last all was simply repeatin' the motions in quick time. Knowin' Frankie's groovin' to be badly eroded by age and lack of attention, I didn't much panic; but our Mr. Moorshed, 'e took it a little to heart. Me an' Mr. Hinchcliffe consoled 'im as well as service conditions permits of, an' we had a *résumé* supper at the back o' the camber – secluded an' lugubrious! Then one thing leadin' up to another, an' our orders, except about anchorin' where he's booked for, leavin' us a clear 'orizon, Number Two Six Seven is now – mind the edge of the wharf – here!'

By mysterious doublings he had brought me out on to the edge of a narrow strip of water crowded with coastwise shipping that runs far up into Weymouth town. A large foreign timber-brig lay at my feet, and under the round of her stern cowered, close to the wharf-edge, a slate-coloured, unkempt, two-funnelled craft of a type – but I am no expert – between the first-class torpedo-boat and the full-blooded destroyer. From her archaic torpedo-tubes at the stern, and quick-firers forward and amidships, she must have dated from the early 'nineties. Hammerings and clinkings, with spurts of steam and fumes of hot oil, arose from her inside, and a figure in a striped jersey squatted on the engine-room gratings.

'She ain't much of a war-canoe, but you'll see more life in her than on an whole squadron of bleedin' *Pedantics*.'

'But she's laid up here – and Blue Fleet have gone,' I protested.

'Pre-cisely. Only, in his comprehensive orders Frankie didn't put us out of action. Thus we're a non-neglectable fightin' factor which you mightn't think from this elevation; *an'* m'rover, Red Fleet don't know we're 'ere. Most of us' – he glanced proudly at his boots – 'didn't run to spurs, but we're disguised pretty devious, as you might say. Morgan, our signaliser, when last seen, was a Dawlish bathing-machine proprietor. Hinchcliffe was naturally a German waiter, and me you behold as a squire of low degree; while yonder Levantine dragoman on the hatch is our Mr. Moorshed. He was the second cutter's snotty – *my* snotty – on the *Archimandrite* – two years – Cape Station. Likewise on the West Coast, mangrove-swampin', an' gettin' the cutter stove in on small an' unlikely bars, an' manufacturin' lies to correspond. What I don't know about Mr. Moorshed is precisely the same gauge as what Mr. Moorshed don't know about me – half a millimetre, as you might say. He comes into awful opulence of his own when 'e's of age; an' judgin' from what passed between us when Frankie cursed 'im, I don't think 'e cares whether he's broke to-morrow or – the day after. Are you beginnin' to follow our tattics? They'll be worth followin'. Or *are* you goin' back to your nice little cabin on the *Pedantic* – which I lay they've just dismounted the third engineer out of – to eat four fat meals per diem, an' smoke in the casement?'

The figure in the jersey lifted its head and mumbled.

'Yes, Sir,' was Mr. Pyecroft's answer. 'I 'ave ascertained that *Stiletto*, *Wraith*, and *Kobbold* left at 6 p.m. with the first division o' Red Fleet's cruisers except *Devolution* and *Cryptic*, which are delayed by engine-room defects.' Then to me: 'Won't you go aboard? Mr. Moorshed 'ud like some one to talk to. You buy an 'am an' see life.'

At this he vanished; and the Demon of Pure Irresponsibility bade me lower myself from the edge of the wharf to the tea-tray plates of No. 267.

'What d'you want?' said the striped jersey.

'I want to join Blue Fleet if I can,' I replied. 'I've been left behind by – an accident.'

'Well?'

'Mr. Pyecroft told me to buy a ham and see life. About how big a ham do you need?'

'I don't want any ham, thank you. That's the way up the wharf. *Good*-night.'

'Good-night!' I retraced my steps, wandered in the dark till I found a shop, and there purchased, of sardines, canned tongue, lobster, and salmon, not less than half a hundredweight. A belated sausage-shop supplied me with a partially cut ham of pantomime tonnage. These things I, sweating, bore out to the edge of the wharf and set down in the shadow of a crane. It was a clear, dark summer night, and from time to time I laughed happily to myself. The adventure was preordained on the face of it. Pyecroft alone, spurred or barefoot, would have drawn me very far from the paths of circumspection. His advice to buy a ham and see life clinched it. Presently Mr. Pyecroft – I heard spurs clink – passed me. Then the jersey voice said: 'What the mischief's that?'

''Asn't the visitor come aboard, Sir? 'E told me he'd purposely abandoned the *Pedantic* for the pleasure of the trip with us. Told me he was official correspondent for the *Times*; an' I know he's jittery by the way 'e tries to talk Navy-talk. Haven't you seen 'im, Sir?'

Slowly and dispassionately the answer drawled long on the night; 'Pye, you are without exception the biggest liar in the Service!'

'Then what am I to do with the bag, Sir? It's marked with his name.' There was a pause till Mr. Moorshed said 'Oh!' in a tone which the listener might construe precisely as he pleased.

'*He* was the maniac who wanted to buy a ham and see life – was he? If he goes back to the *Pedantic*—'

'Pre-cisely, Sir. Gives us all away, Sir.'

'Then what possessed *you* to give it away to him, you owl?'

'I've got his bag. If 'e gives anything away, he'll have to go naked.'

At this point I thought it best to rattle my tins and step out of the shadow of the crane.

'I've bought the ham,' I called sweetly. 'Have you still any objection to my seeing life, Mr. Moorshed?'

'All right, if you're insured. Won't you come down?'

I descended; Pyecroft, by a silent flank movement, possessing himself of all the provisions, which he bore to some hole forward.

'Have you known Mr. Pyecroft long?' said my host.

'Met him once, a year ago, at Devonport. What do you think of him?'

'What do *you* think of him?'

'I've left the *Pedantic* – her boat will be waiting for me at ten o'clock, too – simply because I happened to meet him,' I replied.

'That's all right. If you'll come down below, we may get some grub.'

We descended a naked steel ladder to a steel-beamed tunnel, perhaps twelve feet long by six high. Leather-topped lockers ran along either side; a swinging table, with tray and lamp above, occupied the centre. Other furniture there was none.

'You can't shave here, of course. We don't wash, and, as a rule, we eat with our fingers when we're at sea. D'you mind?'

Mr. Moorshed, black-haired, black-browed, sallow-complexioned, looked me over from head to foot and grinned. He was not handsome in any way, but his smile drew the heart. 'You didn't happen to hear what Frankie told me from the flagship, did you? His last instructions, and I've logged 'em here in shorthand, were' – he opened a neat pocket-book – '*Get out of this and conduct your own damned manœuvres in your own damned tinker fashion! You're a disgrace to the Service, and your boat's offal.*'

'Awful?' I said.

'No – offal – tripes – swipes – ullage.' Mr. Pyecroft entered, in the costume of his calling, with the ham and an assortment of tin dishes, which he dealt out like cards.

'I shall take these as my orders,' said Mr. Moorshed. 'I'm chucking the Service at the end of the year, so it doesn't matter.'

We cut into the ham under the ill-trimmed lamp, washed it down with whisky, and then smoked. From the foreside of the bulkhead came an uninterrupted hammering and clinking, and now and then a hiss of steam.

'That's Mr. Hinchcliffe,' said Pyecroft. 'He's what is called a first-class engine-room artificer. If you hand 'im a drum of oil an' leave 'im alone, he can coax a stolen bicycle to do typewritin'.'

Very leisurely, at the end of his first pipe, Mr. Moorshed drew out a folded map, cut from a newspaper, of the area of manœuvres, with the rules that regulate these wonderful things, below.

'Well, I suppose I know as much as an average stick-and-string admiral,' he said, yawning. 'Is our petticoat ready yet, Mr. Pyecroft?'

As a preparation for naval manœuvres these councils seemed inadequate. I followed up the ladder into the gloom cast by the wharf edge and the big lumber-ship's side. As my eyes stretched to the darkness I saw that No. 267 had miraculously sprouted an extra pair of funnels – soft, for they gave as I touched them.

'More *prima facie* evidence. You runs a rope fore an' aft, an' you erects perpendick-u-arly two canvas tubes, which you distends with cane hoops, thus 'avin' as many funnels as a destroyer. At the word o' command, up they go like a pair of concertinas, an' consequently collapses equally 'andy when requisite. Comin' aft we shall doubtless overtake the Dawlish bathin'-machine proprietor fittin' on her bustle.'

Mr. Pyecroft whispered this in my ear as Moorshed moved toward a group at the stern.

'None of us who ain't built that way can be destroyers, but we can look as near it as we can. Let me explain to you, Sir, that the stern of a Thornycroft boat, which we are *not*, comes out in a pretty bulge, totally different from the Yarrow mark, which again we are not. But, on the other 'and, *Dirk, Stiletto, Goblin, Ghoul, Djinn,* and *A-frite* – Red Fleet dee-stroyers, with 'oom we hope to consort later on terms o' perfect equality – *are* Thornycrofts, an' carry that Grecian bend which we are now adjustin' to our *arrière-pensée* – as the French would put it – by means of painted canvas an' iron rods bent as requisite. Between you an' me an' Frankie, we are the *Gnome*, now in the Fleet Reserve at Pompey – Portsmouth, I should say.'

'The first sea will carry it all away,' said Moorshed, leaning gloomily outboard, 'but it will do for the present.'

'We've a lot of *prima facie* evidence about us,' Mr. Pyecroft went on. 'A first-class torpedo-boat sits lower in the water than a destroyer. Hence we artificially raise our sides with a black canvas wash-streak to represent extra freeboard; at the same time paddin' out the cover of the forward three-pounder like as if it was a twelve-pounder, an' variously fakin' up the bows of 'er. As you might say, we've took thought an' added a cubic to our stature. It's our len'th that sugars us. A 'undred an' forty feet, which is our len'th, into two 'undred and ten, which is about the *Gnome's*, leaves seventy feet over, which we haven't got.'

'Is this all your own notion, Mr. Pyecroft?' I asked.

'In spots, you might say – yes; though we all contributed to make up deficiencies. But Mr. Moorshed, not much carin' for further

Navy after what Frankie said, certainly threw himself into the part with avidity.'

'What the dickens are we going to do?'

'Speaking as a seaman gunner, I should say we'd wait till the sights came on, an' then fire. Speakin' as a torpedo-coxswain, L.T.O., T.I., M.D. etc., I presume we fall in – Number One in rear of the tube, etc., secure tube to ball or diaphragm, clear away securin'-bar, release safety-pin from lockin'-levers, an' pray Heaven to look down on us. As second in command o' 267, I say wait an' see!'

'What's happened? We're off,' I said. The timber-ship had slid away from us.

'We are. Stern first, an' broadside on! If we don't hit anything too hard, we'll do.'

'Come on the bridge,' said Mr. Moorshed. I saw no bridge, but fell over some sort of conning-tower forward, near which was a wheel. For the next few minutes I was more occupied with cursing my own folly than with the science of navigation. Therefore I cannot say how we got out of Weymouth Harbour, nor why it was necessary to turn sharp to the left and wallow in what appeared to be surf.

'Excuse me,' said Mr. Pyecroft behind us, 'I don't mind rammin' a bathin'-machine; but if only one of them week-end Weymouth blighters has thrown his empty baccy-tin into the sea here, we'll rip our plates open on it; 267 isn't the *Archimandrite*'s old cutter.'

'I am hugging the shore,' was the answer.

'There's no actual 'arm in huggin', but it can come expensive if pursooed.'

'Right O!' said Moorshed, putting down the wheel, and as we left those scant waters I felt 267 move more freely.

A thin cough ran up the speaking-tube.

'Well, what is it, Mr. Hinchcliffe ?' said Moorshed.

'I merely wished to report that she is still continuin' to go, Sir.'

'Right O! Can we whack her up to fifteen, d'you think?'

'I'll try, Sir; but we'd prefer to have the engine-room hatch open – at first, Sir.'

Whacked up then she was, and for half an hour we careered largely through the night, turning at last with a suddenness that slung us across the narrow deck.

'This,' said Mr. Pyecroft, who received me on his chest as a large rock receives a shadow, 'represents the *Gnome* arrivin' cautious from the direction o' Portsmouth, with Admiralty orders.'

He pointed through the darkness ahead, and after much staring my eyes opened to a dozen destroyers, in two lines, some few hundred yards away.

'Those are the Red Fleet destroyer flotilla, which is too frail to panic about among the full-blooded cruisers inside Portland breakwater, and several millimetres too excited over the approachin' war to keep a look-out inshore. Hence our tattics!'

We wailed through our siren – a long, malignant, hyena-like howl – and a voice hailed us as we went astern tumultuously.

'The *Gnome* – Carteret-Jones – from Portsmouth, with orders – mm – mm – *Stiletto*,' Moorshed answered through the megaphone in a high, whining voice, rather like a chaplain's.

'*Who?*' was the answer.

'Carter-et-Jones.'

'Oh Lord!'

There was a pause; a voice cried to some friend, 'It's Podgie, adrift on the high seas in charge of a whole dee-stroyer!'

Another voice echoed, 'Podgie!' and from its note I gathered that Mr. Carteret-Jones had a reputation, but not for independent command.

'Who's your sub?' said the first speaker, a shadow on the bridge of the *Dirk*.

'A gunner at present, Sir. The *Stiletto* – broken down – turns over to us.'

'When did the *Stiletto* break down?'

'Off the Start, Sir; two hours after – after she left here this evening, I believe! My orders are to report to you for the manœuvre signal-codes, and join Commander Hignett's flotilla, which is in attendance on *Stiletto*.'

A smothered chuckle greeted this last. Moorshed's voice was high and uneasy. Said Pyecroft, with a sigh: 'The amount o' trouble me an' my bright spurs 'ad fishin' out that information from torpedo-coxswains and similar blighters in pubs, all this afternoon, you would never believe.'

'But has the *Stiletto* broken down?' I asked weakly.

'How else are we to get Red Fleet's private signal-code? Anyway, if she 'asn't now, she will before manœuvres are ended. It's only executin' in anticipation.'

'Go astern and send your coxswain aboard for orders, Mr. Jones.' Water carries sound well, but I do not know whether we were intended to hear the next sentence: 'They must have given him *one* intelligent keeper.'

'That's me,' said Mr. Pyecroft, as a black and coal-stained dinghy – I did not foresee how well I should come to know her – was flung overside by three men. 'Havin' bought an 'am, we will now see life.' He stepped into the boat and was away.

'I say, Podgie!' – the speaker was in the last of the line of destroyers, as we thumped astern – 'aren't you lonely out there?'

'Oh, don't rag me!' said Moorshed. 'Do you suppose I'll have to manœuvre with your flo-tilla?'

'No, Podgie! I'm pretty sure our commander will see you sifting cinders in Tophet before you come with our flo-tilla.'

'Thank you! She steers rather wild at high speeds.'

Two men laughed together.

'By the way, who is Mr. Carteret-Jones when he's at home?' I whispered.

'I was with him in the *Britannia*. I didn't like him much, but I'm grateful to him now. I must tell him so some day.'

'They seemed to know him hereabouts.'

'He rammed the *Caryatid* twice with her own steam-pinnace.'

Presently, moved by long strokes, Mr. Pyecroft returned, skimming across the dark. The dinghy swung up behind him, even as his heel spurned it.

'Commander Fasset's compliments to Mr. L. Carteret-Jones, and the sooner he digs out in pursuance of Admiralty orders as received at Portsmouth, the better pleased Commander Fasset will be. But there's a lot more—'

'Whack her up, Mr. Hinchcliffe! Come on to the bridge. We can settle it as we go. Well?'

Mr. Pyecroft drew an important breath, and slid off his cap.

'Day an' night private signals of Red Fleet *complete*, Sir!' He handed a little paper to Moorshed. 'You see, Sir, the trouble was, that Mr. Carteret-Jones bein', so to say, a little new to his duties, 'ad forgot to give 'is gunner his Admiralty orders in writin', but, as I told Commander Fasset, Mr. Jones had been repeatin' 'em to me, nervous-like, most of the way from Portsmouth, so I knew 'em by heart – an' better. The Commander, recognisin' in me a man of agility, cautioned me to be a father an' mother to Mr. Carteret-Jones.'

'Didn't he know you?' I asked, thinking for the moment that there could be no duplicates of Emanuel Pyecroft in the Navy.

'What's a torpedo-gunner more or less to a full lootenant commandin' six thirty-knot destroyers for the first time? 'E seemed to cherish the 'ope that 'e might use the *Gnome* for 'is own 'orrible purposes; but what I told him about Mr. Jones's sad lack o' nerve comin' from Pompey, an' going dead slow on account of the dark, short-circuited *that* connection. "M'rover," I says to him, "our orders is explicit; *Stiletto*'s reported broke down somewhere off the Start, an' we've been tryin' to coil down a new stiff wire hawser all the evenin', so it looks like towin' 'er back, don't it?" I says. That more than ever jams his turrets, an' makes him keen to get rid of us. 'E even hinted that Mr. Carteret-Jones passin' hawsers an' assistin' the impotent in a sea-way might come pretty expensive on the taxpayer. I agreed in a disciplined way. I ain't proud. Gawd knows I ain't proud! But when I'm really diggin' out in the fancy line, I sometimes think that me in a copper punt, single-'anded, 'ud beat a cutter-full of De Rougemongs in a row round the fleet.'

At this point I reclined without shame on Mr. Pyecroft's bosom, supported by his quivering arm.

'Well?' said Moorshed, scowling into the darkness, as 267's bows snapped at the shore seas of the broader Channel, and we swayed together.

'"You'd better go on," says Commander Fasset, "an' do what you're told to do. I don't envy Hignett if he has to dry-nurse the *Gnome*'s commander. But what d'you want with signals?" 'e says. "It's criminal lunacy to trust Mr. Jones with anything that steams."'

'"May I make an observation, Sir?" I says. "Suppose," I says, "you was torpedo-gunner on the *Gnome*, an' Mr. Carteret-Jones was your commandin' officer, an' you had your reputation as a second in command for the first time," I says, well knowin' it was his first command of a flotilla, "what 'ud you do, Sir?" That gouged 'is unprotected ends open – clear back to the citadel.'

'What did he say?' Moorshed jerked over his shoulder.

'If you were Mr. Carteret-Jones, it might be disrespect for me to repeat it, Sir.'

'Go ahead,' I heard the boy chuckle.

'"Do?" 'e says. "I'd rub the young blighter's nose into it till I made a perishin' man of him, or a perspirin' pillow-case," 'e says, "which," he adds, "is forty per cent more than he is at present."'

'Whilst he's gettin' the private signals – they're rather particular ones – I went forrard to see the *Dirk*'s gunner about borrowin' a holdin'-down bolt for our twelve-pounder. My open ears, while I was rovin' over his packet, got the followin' authentic particulars.' I heard his voice change and his feet shifted. 'There's been a last council o' war of destroyer-captains at the flagship, an' a lot o' things 'as come out. To begin with, *Cryptic* and *Devolution*, Captain Panke and Captain Malan—'

'*Cryptic* and *Devolution*, first-class cruisers,' said Mr. Moorshed dreamily. 'Go on, Pyecroft.'

'—bein' delayed by minor defects in engine-room, did *not*, as we know, accompany Red Fleet's first division of scouting cruisers, whose rendezvous is unknown, but presumed to be somewhere off the Lizard. *Cryptic* an' *Devolution* left at 9.30 p.m. still reportin' copious minor defects in engine-room. Admiral's final instructions was they was to put in to Torbay, an' mend themselves there. If they can do it in twenty-four hours, they're to come on and join the Red battle squadron at the first rendezvous, down Channel somewhere. (I couldn't get that, Sir.) If they can't, he'll think about sendin' them some destroyers for escort. But his present intention is to go 'ammer and tongs down Channel, usin' 'is destroyers for all they're worth, an' thus keepin' Blue Fleet too busy off the Irish coast to sniff into any eshtuaries.'

'But if those cruisers are crocks, why does the Admiral let 'em out of Weymouth at all?' I asked.

'The taxpayer,' said Mr. Moorshed.

'An' newspapers,' added Mr. Pyecroft. 'In Torbay they'll look as they was muckin' about for strategical purposes – hammerin' like blazes in the engine-room all the weary day, an' the skipper droppin' questions down the engine-room hatch every two or three minutes. *I've* been there. Now, Sir?' I saw the white of his eye turn broad on Mr. Moorshed.

The boy dropped his chin over the speaking-tube.

'Mr. Hinchcliffe, what's her extreme economical radius?'

'Three hundred and forty knots, down to swept bunkers.'

'Can do,' said Moorshed. 'By the way, have her revolutions any bearing on her speed, Mr. Hinchcliffe?'

'None that I can make out yet, Sir.'

'Then slow to eight knots. We'll jog down to forty-nine, forty-five, or four about, and three east. That puts us say forty miles from Torbay by nine o'clock to-morrow morning. We'll have to muck about till dusk before we run in and try our luck with the cruisers.'

'Yes, Sir. Their picket boats will be panickin' round them all night. It's considered good for the young gentlemen.'

'Hallo! War's declared! They're off!' said Moorshed.

He swung 267's head round to get a better view. A few miles to our right the low horizon was spangled with small balls of fire, while nearer ran a procession of tiny cigar-ends.

'Red hot! Set 'em alight,' said Mr. Pyecroft. 'That's the second destroyer flotilla diggin' out for Commander Fasset's reputation.'

The smaller lights disappeared; the glare of the destroyers' funnels dwindled even as we watched.

'They're going down Channel with lights out, thus showin' their zeal an' drivin' all watch-officers crazy. Now, if you'll excuse me, I think I'll get you your pyjamas, an' you'll turn in,' said Pyecroft.

He piloted me to the steel tunnel, where the ham still swung majestically over the swaying table, and dragged out trousers and a coat with a monk's hood, all hewn from one hairy inch-thick board.

'If you fall over in these you'll be drowned. They're lammies. I'll chock you off with a pillow; but sleepin' in a torpedo-boat's what you might call an acquired habit.'

I coiled down on an iron-hard horse-hair pillow next the quivering steel wall to acquire that habit. The sea, sliding over 267's skin, worried me with importunate, half-caught confidences. It drummed tackily to gather my attention, coughed, spat, cleared its throat, and, on the eve of that portentous communication, retired up stage as a multitude whispering. Anon, I caught the tramp of armies afoot, the hum of crowded cities awaiting the event, the single sob of a woman, and dry roaring of wild beasts. A dropped shovel clanging on the stokehold floor was, naturally enough, the unbarring of arena gates; our sucking uplift across the crest of some little swell, nothing less than the haling forth of new worlds; our half-turning descent into the hollow of its mate, the abysmal plunge of God-forgotten planets. Through all these phenomena and more – though I ran with wild horses over illimitable plains of rustling grass; though I crouched belly-flat under appalling fires of musketry; though I was Livingstone, painless and incurious in the grip of his lion – my shut eyes saw the lamp swinging in its gimbals, the irregularly gliding patch of light on the steel ladder, and every elastic shadow in the corners of the frail angle-irons; while my body strove to accommodate itself to the infernal vibration of the machine. At the last I rolled limply on the floor, and woke to real life with a bruised nose and a great call to go on deck at once.

'It's all right,' said a voice in my booming ears. 'Morgan and Laughton are worse than you!'

I was gripping a rail. Mr. Pyecroft pointed with his foot to two bundles beside a torpedo-tube, which at Weymouth had been a signaller and a most able seaman. 'She'd do better in a bigger sea,' said Mr. Pyecroft. 'This lop is what fetches it up.'

The sky behind us whitened as I laboured, and the first dawn drove down the Channel, tipping the wave-tops with a chill glare. To me that round wind which runs before the true day has ever been fortunate and of good omen. It cleared the trouble from my body, and set my soul dancing to 267's heel and toe across the northerly set of the waves – such waves as I had often watched contemptuously from the deck of a ten-thousand-ton liner. They shouldered our little hull sideways and passed, scalloped, and splayed out, toward the coast, carrying our white wake in loops along their hollow backs. In succession we looked down a lead-gray cutting of water for half a clear mile, were flung up on its ridge, beheld the Channel traffic – full-sailed to that fair breeze – all about us, and swung slantwise, light as a bladder, elastic as a basket, into the next furrow. Then the sun found us, struck the wet gray bows to living, leaping opal, the colourless deep to hard sapphire, the many sails to pearl, and the little steam-plume of our escape to an inconstant rainbow.

'A fair day and a fair wind for all, thank God!' said Emanuel Pyecroft, throwing back the cowl-like hood of his blanket coat. His face was pitted with coal-dust and grime, pallid for lack of sleep; but his eyes shone like a gull's.

'I told you you'd see life. Think o' the *Pedantic* now. Think o' her Number One chasin' the mobilised gobbies round the lower deck flats. Think o' the pore little snotties now bein' washed, fed, and taught, an' the yeoman o' signals with a pink eye waken' bright an' brisk to another perishin' day of five-flag hoists. Whereas *we* shall caulk an' smoke cigarettes, same as the Spanish destroyers did for three weeks after war was declared.' He dropped into the wardroom singing:

'If you're going to marry me, marry me, Bill,
It's no use muckin' about!'

The man at the wheel, uniformed in what had once been a tam-o'-shanter, a pair of very worn R.M.L.I. trousers rolled up to the knee, and a black sweater, was smoking a cigarette. Moorshed, in a gray Balaclava and a brown mackintosh with a flapping cape, hauled at our supplementary funnel guys, and a thing like a waiter from a Soho restaurant sat at the head of the engine-room ladder exhorting the unseen below. The following wind beat down our smoke and covered all things with an inch-thick layer of stokers, so that eyelids, teeth, and feet gritted in their motions. I began to see that my previous experiences among battleships and cruisers had been altogether beside the mark.

[First published in two parts in October 1903 in *Collier's Magazine*; it was collected in *Traffics and Discoveries* (1904).]

✠   ✠   ✠

Once settled at Bateman's in Sussex, Kipling enjoyed another period of considering the sea in Britain's history. The fruit of his ruminations was particularly evident in his Puck stories and accompanying verses. It was also found in the poems which accompanied his *A School History of England* (written with C.R.L. Fletcher).

CHINA-GOING P.&O.'S

CHINA-GOING P.&O.'s
Pass Pau Amma's playground close,
And his Pusat Tasek lies
Near the track of most B.I.'s.
N.Y.K. and N.D.L.
Know Pau Amma's home as well
As the Fisher of the Sea knows
'Bens,' M.M.'s and Rubattinos.
But (and this is rather queer)
A.T.L.'s can not come here;
O. and O. and D.O.A.
Must go round another way.
Orient, Anchor, Bibby, Hall,

Never go that way at all.
U.C.S. would have a fit
If it found itself on it.
And if 'Beavers' took their cargoes
To Penang instead of Lagos,
Or a fat Shaw-Savill bore
Passengers to Singapore,
Or a White Star were to try a
Little trip to Sourabaya,
Or a B.S.A. went on
Past Natal to Cheribon,
Then great Mr. Lloyds would come
With a wire and drag them home
You'll know what my riddle means
When you've eaten mangosteens.

[First published in *Just So Stories for Little Children* (London: Macmillan; New York: Doubleday, Page, 1902).]

✠ ✠ ✠

I'VE NEVER SAILED THE AMAZON

I'VE NEVER SAILED THE Amazon,
I've never reached Brazil;
But the Don and Magdalena,
They can go there when they will!

Yes, weekly from Southampton,
Great steamers, white and gold,
Go rolling down to Rio
(Roll down – roll down to Rio!)
And I'd like to roll to Rio
Some day before I'm old!

I've never seen a Jaguar,
Nor yet an Armadill
O dilloing in his armour,
And I s'pose I never will,

Unless I go to Rio
These wonders to behold
Roll down – roll down to Rio
Roll really down to Rio!
Oh, I'd love to roll to Rio
Some day before I'm old!

[First published in *Just So Stories for Little Children* (1902).]

SONG OF THE RED WAR-BOAT

SHOVE OFF FROM THE wharf-edge! Steady!
Watch for a smooth! Give way!
If she feels the lop already
She'll stand on her head in the bay.
It's ebb – it's dusk – it's blowing –
The shoals are a mile of white,
But (snatch her along!) we're going
To find our master to-night.

For we hold that in all disaster
Of shipwreck, storm, or sword,
A Man must stand by his Master
When once he has pledged his word.

Raging seas have we rowed in
But we seldom saw them thus,
Our master is angry with Odin –
Odin is angry with us!
Heavy odds have we taken,
But never before such odds.
The Gods know they are forsaken.
We must risk the wrath of the Gods!

Over the crest she flies from,
Into its hollow she drops,

Cringes and clears her eyes from
The wind-torn breaker-tops,
Ere out on the shrieking shoulder
Of a hill-high surge she drives.
Meet her! Meet her and hold her!
Pull for your scoundrel lives!

The thunder below and clamor
The harm that they mean to do!
There goes Thor's own Hammer
Cracking the dark in two!
Close! But the blow has missed her,
Here comes the wind of the blow!
Row or the squall'll twist her
Broadside on to it! – Row!

Heark'ee, Thor of the Thunder!
We are not here for a jest –
For wager, warfare, or plunder,
Or to put your power to test.
This work is none of our wishing –
We would house at home if we might –
But our master is wrecked out fishing.
We go to find him to-night.

For we hold that in all disaster –
As the Gods Themselves have said –
A Man must stand by his Master
Till one of the two is dead.

That is our way of thinking,
Now you can do as you will,
While we try to save her from sinking
And hold her head to it still.
Bale her and keep her moving,
Or she'll break her back in the trough . . .
Who said the weather's improving,
Or the swells are taking off?

Sodden, and chafed and aching,
Gone in the loins and knees –
No matter – the day is breaking,
And there's far less weight to the seas!
Up mast, and finish baling –
In oar, and out with mead –
The rest will be two-reef sailing . . .
That was a night indeed!

But we hold it in all disaster
(And faith, we have found it true!)
If only you stand by your Master,
The Gods will stand by you!

[First published in *Rewards and Fairies* (London: Macmillan; New York: Doubleday, Page, 1910), where it is linked to the story 'The Conversion of St Wilfrid'.]

✠　✠　✠

SPEECH GIVEN AT A NAVAL CLUB, OCTOBER 1908: THE SPIRIT OF THE NAVY

NONE COULD FORETELL WHAT would be required of the men or the ships in that hour; but both were so tempered that, when their hour came, it was seen to be no more than one of their hours.

At a Naval Club: October 1908

It occurs to me that the reputation to which your Chairman alludes was achieved not by doing anything in particular, but by writing stories – telling tales if you like – about things which other men have done. They say in the Navy, I believe, that a man is often influenced throughout the whole of his career by the events of his first commission. The circumstances of my early training happened to throw me among disciplined men of action – men who belonged to one or other of the Indian Services – men who were therefore accustomed to act under orders, and to live under authority, as the good of their Service required.

My business being to write, I wrote about them and their lives. I did not realise, then, what I realised later, that the men who belong to the Services – disciplined men of action, living under authority – constitute a very small portion of our world, and do not attract much of its attention or its interest. I did not realise then that where men of all ranks work together for aims and objects which are not for their own personal advantage, there arises among them a spirit, a tradition, and an unwritten law, which it is not very easy for the world at large to understand, or to sympathise with.

For instance, I belonged then to a Service where the unwritten law was that if you gave a man twice as much work to do in a day as he could do, he would do it; but if you only gave him as much as he could do, he wouldn't do half of it. This in itself made me sympathise with the tradition of other Services who have the same unwritten law, and with the spirit which underlies every service on land and sea – specially on the Sea.

But as you yourselves know well, Gentlemen, the spirit of the Navy is too old, too varied, and too subtle, to be adequately interpreted by any outsider, no matter how keen his interest, or how deep his affection. He may paint a more or less truthful picture of externals; he may utter faithfully all that has been given him to say, but the essential soul of the machine – the spirit that makes the Service – will, and must, always elude him. How can it well be otherwise? The life out of which this spirit is born has always been a life more lonely, more apart than any life there is. The forces that mould that life have been forces beyond man's control; the men who live that life do not, as a rule, discuss the risks that they face every day in the execution of their duty, any more than they talk of that immense and final risk which they are preparing themselves to face at the Day of Armageddon. Even if they did, the world would not believe – would not understand.

So the Navy has been as a rule both inarticulate and unfashionable. Till very recently – till just the other day in fact – when a fleet disappeared under the skyline, it went out into empty space – absolute isolation – with no means visible or invisible of communicating with the shore. It is of course different since Marconi came in, but the tradition of the Navy's aloofness and separation from the tax-payer world at large still remains.

It is not altogether a bad tradition, d'you think? The Navy represents the man at the wheel in our ship of state, and speaking as a tax-payer, the less the passengers, that is the tax-payers, talk to or about the man at the wheel, the better it will be for all aboard the ship.

Isn't it possible that the very thoroughness with which the Navy has protected the nation in the past may constitute a source of weakness both for the Navy and the nation? We have been safe for so long, and during all these generations have been so free to follow our own devices, that we tax-payers as a body to-day are utterly ignorant of the facts and the forces on which England depends for her existence. But instead of leaving the Navy alone, as our ancestors did, some of us are now trying to think. And thinking is a highly dangerous performance for amateurs. Some of us are like the monkeys in Brazil. We have sat so long upon the branch that we honestly think we can saw it off and still sit where we were. Some of us think that the Navy does not much matter one way or the other; some of us honestly regard it as a brutal and bloodthirsty anachronism, which if it can't be openly abolished, ought to be secretly crippled as soon as possible. Such views are not shocking or surprising. After four generations of peace and party politics they are inevitable; but the passengers holding these views need not be encouraged to talk too much to the man at the wheel.

There remain now a few – comparatively very few – of us tax-payers who take an interest in the Navy; but here again our immense ignorance, our utter divorce from the actualities of the Navy or any other Service, handicaps us. Some of us honestly think that navies depend altogether on guns, armour, and machinery, and if we have these better or worse than anyone else, we are mathematically better or worse than anyone else. The battle of Tsu-shima – in the Sea of Japan – has rather upset the calculations; but you know how they are worked out. Multiply the calibre of a ship's primary armament by the thickness of her average plating in millimetres; add the indicated horse-power of the forward bilge-pumps, and divide it by the temperature of the cordite magazines. Then reduce the result to decimals and point out that what the country needs is more *Incredibles* or *Insupportables*, or whatever the latest fancy pattern of war-canoe happens to be. Now nobody wants to undervalue machinery, but surely, Gentlemen, guns and machinery and armour are only ironmongery after all. They may be the best ironmongery in the world, and we must have them, but if talking, and arguing, and recriminating, and taking sides about them is going to react unfavourably on the men who have to handle the guns and sleep behind the armour, and run the machinery, why then, the less talk we have on Service matters outside the Service, the better all round. Silence is what we want.

Isn't the morale of a Service a thousandfold more important than its material? Can't we scratch up a fleet of *Impossibles* or *Undockables* in a few years for a few millions; but hasn't it taken thirty generations to develop the spirit of the Navy? And is anything except that spirit going to save the nation in the dark days ahead of us?

I don't know what has happened since the days of Trafalgar to make us think otherwise. The Navy may bulk larger on paper – or in the papers – than it did in Nelson's time, but it is more separated from the life of the nation than it was then – for the simple reason that it is more specialised and scientific. In peace it exists under conditions which it takes years of training to understand; in war it will be subjected to mental and physical strains three days of which would make the mere sea-fight of Trafalgar a pleasant change and rest. We have no data to guide us for the future, but in judging by our thousand-year-old past, we can believe, and thank God for it, that whatever man may do, or neglect to do, the spirit of the Navy, which is man-made, but which no body of men can kill, will rise to meet and overcome every burden and every disability that may be imposed upon it – from without or within.

[Collected (with thirty other speeches) in *A Book of Words* (London: Macmillan, 1928).]

✠ ✠ ✠

In the Edwardian years leading up to the First World War, Kipling travelled regularly by sea to South Africa, Canada and across the Mediterranean to Egypt, a journey he evoked in *Egypt of the Magicians*.

EGYPT OF THE MAGICIANS

Sea Travel

I HAD LEFT EUROPE for no reason except to discover the Sun, and there were rumours that he was to be found in Egypt.

But I had not realised what more I should find there.

A P.&O. boat carried us out of Marseilles. A serang of lascars, with whistle, chain, shawl, and fluttering blue clothes, was at work on the baggage-hatch. Somebody bungled at the winch. The serang called him a name unlovely in itself but awakening delightful memories in the hearer.

'O Serang, is that man a fool?'

'Very foolish, sahib. He comes from Surat. He only comes for his food's sake.'

The serang grinned; the Surtee man grinned; the winch began again, and the voices that called: 'Lower away! Stop her!' were as familiar as the friendly whiff from the lascars' galley or the slap of bare feet along the deck. But for the passage of a few impertinent years, I should have gone without hesitation to share their rice. Serangs used to be very kind to little white children below the age of caste. Most familiar of all was the ship itself. It had slipped my memory, nor was there anything in the rates charged to remind me, that single-screws still lingered in the gilt-edged passenger trade.

Some North Atlantic passengers accustomed to real ships made the discovery, and were as pleased about it as American tourists at Stratford-on-Avon.

'Oh, come and see!' they cried. 'She has *one* screw – only one screw! Hear her thump! And *have* you seen their old barn of a saloon? *And* the officers' library? It's open for two half-hours a day week-days and one on Sundays. You pay a dollar and a quarter deposit on each book. We wouldn't have missed this trip for anything. It's like sailing with Columbus.'

They wandered about – voluble, amazed, and happy, for they were getting off at Port Said.

I explored, too. From the rough-ironed table-linen, the thick tooth-glasses for the drinks, the slummocky set-out of victuals at meals, to the unaccommodating regulations in the curtainless cabin, where they had not yet arrived at bunk-edge trays for morning tea, time and progress had stood still with the P.&O. To be just, there were electric-fan fittings in the cabins, but the fans were charged extra; and there was a rumour, unverified, that one could eat on deck or in one's cabin without a medical certificate from the doctor. All the rest was under the old motto: '*Quis separabit*' – 'This is quite separate from other lines.'

'After all,' said an Anglo-Indian, whom I was telling about civilised ocean travel, 'they don't want you Egyptian trippers. They're sure of *us*, because—' and he gave me many strong reasons connected with leave, finance, the absence of competition, and the ownership of the Bombay foreshore.

'But it's absurd,' I insisted. 'The whole concern is out of date. There's a notice on my deck forbidding smoking and the use of naked lights, and there's a lascar messing about the hold-hatch outside my cabin with a candle in a lantern.'

Meantime, our one-screw tub thumped gingerly toward Port Said, because we had no mails aboard, and the Mediterranean, exhausted after severe February hysterics, lay out like oil.

* * *

I had some talk with a Scotch quartermaster who complained that lascars are not what they used to be, owing to their habit (but it has existed since the beginning) of signing on as a clan or family – all sorts together.

The serang said that, for *his* part, he had noticed no difference in twenty years. 'Men are always of many kinds, sahib. And that is because God makes men this and that. Not all one pattern – not by any means all one pattern.' He told me, too, that wages were rising, but the price of ghee, rice, and curry-stuffs was up, too, which was bad for wives and families at Porbandar. 'And that also is thus, and no talk makes it otherwise.' After Suez he would have blossomed into thin clothes and long talks, but the bitter spring chill nipped him, as the thought of partings just accomplished and work just ahead chilled the Anglo-Indian contingent.

But no stories could divert one long from the peculiarities of that amazing line which exists strictly for itself. There was a bathroom (occupied) at the windy end of an open alleyway. In due time the bather came out.

Said the steward, as he swabbed out the tub for his successor: 'That was the Chief Engineer. 'E's been some time. Must 'ave 'ad a mucky job below, this mornin'.'

I have a great admiration for Chief Engineers. They are men in authority, needing all the comforts and aids that can possibly be given them – such as bathrooms of their own close to their own cabins, where they can clean off at leisure.

It is not fair to mix them up with the ruck of passengers, nor is it done on real ships. Nor, when a passenger wants a bath in the evening, do the stewards of real ships roll their eyes like vergers in a cathedral and say, 'We'll see if it can be managed.' They double down the alleyway and shout, 'Matcham' or 'Ponting' or 'Guttman,' and in fifteen seconds one of those swift three has the taps going and the towels out. Real ships are not annexes of Westminster Abbey or Borstal Reformatory. They supply decent accommodation in return for good money, and I imagine that their directors instruct their staffs to look pleased while at work.

Some generations back there must have been an idea that the P.&O. was vastly superior to all lines afloat – a sort of semipontifical show not to be criticised. How much of the notion was due to its own excellence and how much to its passenger-traffic monopoly does not matter. To-day, it neither feeds nor tends its passengers, nor keeps its ships well enough to put on any airs at all.

For which reason, human nature being what it is, it surrounds itself with an ungracious atmosphere of absurd ritual to cover grudged and inadequate performance.

What it really needs is to be dropped into a March North Atlantic, without any lascars, and made to swim for its life between a C.P.R. boat and a North German Lloyd – till it learns to smile.

[Seven letters first appeared under the title 'Egypt of the Magicians' in *Nash's Magazine* and *Cosmopolitan Magazine* during the summer and autumn of 1914. They were subsequently collected in *Letters of Travel, 1892–1913* (London: Macmillan; New York: Doubleday, 1920).]

❇ ❇ ❇

During the First World War Kipling became involved in propaganda work, both for the army and navy. Perhaps since his own son John was killed while serving with the Welsh Guards at the Battle of Loos in September 1915, Kipling seems to have preferred dealing with the navy, which led to a number of poems and journalistic articles which were later collected in books.

THE FRINGES OF THE FLEET

In Lowestoft a boat was laid,
　Mark well what I do say!
And she was built for the herring-trade,
　But she has gone a-rovin', a-rovin', a-rovin',
　The Lord knows where!

They gave her Government coal to burn,
And a Q.F. gun at bow and stern,
And sent her out a-rovin', etc.

Her skipper was mate of a bucko ship
Which always killed one man per trip,
So he is used to rovin', etc.

Her mate was skipper of a chapel in Wales,
And so he fights in topper and tails –
Religi-ous tho' rovin', etc.

Her engineer is fifty-eight,
So he's prepared to meet his fate,
Which ain't unlikely rovin', etc.

Her leading-stoker's seventeen,
So he don't know what the Judgments mean,
Unless he cops 'em rovin', etc.

Her cook was chef in the Lost Dogs' Home,
　Mark well what I do say!
And I'm sorry for Fritz when they all come
　A-rovin', a-rovin', a-roarin' and a-rovin',
　Round the North Sea rovin',
　The Lord knows where!

The Auxiliaries

I

The Navy is very old and very wise. Much of her wisdom is on record and available for reference; but more of it works in the unconscious blood of those who serve her. She has a thousand years of experience, and can find precedent or parallel for any situation that the force of the weather or the malice of the King's enemies may bring about.

The main principles of sea-warfare hold good throughout all ages and, so far as the Navy has been allowed to put out her strength, these principles have been applied over all the seas of the world. For matters of detail the Navy, to whom all days are alike, has simply returned to the practice and resurrected the spirit of old days.

In the late French wars, a merchant sailing out of a Channel port might in a few hours find himself laid by the heels and under way for a French prison. His Majesty's ships of the Line – and even the big frigates, took little part in policing the waters for him, unless he were in convoy. The sloops, cutters, gun-brigs, and local craft of all kinds were supposed to look after that, while the Line was busy else-where. So the merchants passed resolutions against the inadequate protection afforded to the trade, and the narrow seas were full of single-ship actions; mail-packets, West Country brigs, and fat East Indiamen fighting for their own hulls and cargo anything that the watchful French ports sent against them; the sloops and cutters bear-ing a hand if they happened to be within reach.

The Oldest Navy

It was a brutal age, ministered to by hard-fisted men, and we had put it a hundred decent years behind us when – it all comes back again! To-day there are no prisons for the crews of merchantmen, but they can go to the bottom by mine and torpedo even more quickly than their ancestors were run into Le Havre. The submarine takes the place of the privateer; the Line, as in the old wars, is occupied, bombarding and blockading, elsewhere, but the sea-borne traffic must continue, and that is being looked after by the lineal descendants of the crews of the long extinct cutters and sloops and gun-brigs. The hour struck, and they reappeared, to the tune of fifty thousand odd men in more than two thousand ships, of which I have seen a few hundred. Words of command may have changed a little, the tools are certainly more complex, but the spirit of the new crews who come to the old job is utterly unchanged. It is the same fierce, hard-living, heavy-handed, very cunning service out of which the Navy as we know it to-day was born. It is called indifferently the Trawler and Auxiliary Fleet. It is chiefly composed of fishermen, but it takes in every one who may have maritime tastes – from retired admirals to the son of the sea-cook. It exists for the benefit of the traffic and the annoyance of the enemy. Its doings are recorded by flags stuck into charts; its casualties are buried in obscure corners of the newspapers. The Grand Fleet knows it slightly; the restless light cruisers who chaperon it from the background are more intimate; the destroyers working off unlighted coasts over unmarked shoals come, as you might say, in direct contact with it; the submarine alternately praises and – since one periscope is very like another – curses its activities; but the steady procession of traffic in home waters, liner and tramp, six every sixty minutes, blesses it altogether.

Since this most Christian war includes laying mines in the fairways of traffic, and since these mines may be laid at any time by German submarines especially built for the work, or by neutral ships, all fairways must be swept continuously day and night. When a nest of mines is reported, traffic must be hung up or deviated till it is cleared out. When traffic comes up Channel it must be examined for contraband and other things; and the examining tugs lie out in a blaze of lights to remind ships of this. Months ago, when the war was young, the tugs did not know what to look for specially. Now they do. All this mine-searching and reporting and sweeping, *plus* the direction and examination of the traffic, *plus* the laying of our own ever-shifting mine-fields, is part of the Trawler Fleet's work, because the Navy-as-we-knew-it is busy elsewhere. And there is always the enemy submarine with a price on her head, whom the Trawler fleet hunts and traps with zeal and joy. Add to this, that there are boats, fishing for real fish, to be protected in their work at sea or chased off dangerous areas where, because they are strictly forbidden to go, they naturally repair, and you will begin to get some idea of what the Trawler and Auxiliary Fleet does.

[. . .]

Farewell and adieu to you, Greenwich ladies,
Farewell and adieu to you, ladies ashore!
For we've received orders to work to the eastward
Where we hope in a short time to strafe 'em some more.

We'll duck and we'll dive like little tin turtles,
We'll duck and we'll dive underneath the North Seas,
Until we strike something that doesn't expect us,
From here to Cuxhaven it's go as you please!

The first thing we did was to dock in a mine-field,
Which isn't a place where repairs should be done;
And there we lay doggo in twelve-fathom water
With tri-nitro-toluol hogging our run.

The next thing we did, we rose under a Zeppelin,
With his shiny big belly half blocking the sky.
But what in the – Heavens can you do with six-pounders?
So we fired what we had and we bade him good-bye.

Submarines

I

The chief business of the Trawler fleet is to attend to the traffic. The submarine in her sphere attends to the enemy. Like the destroyer, the submarine has created its own type of officer and man – with a language and traditions apart from the rest of the Service, and yet at heart unchangingly of the Service. Their business is to run monstrous risks from earth, air, and water, in what, to be of any use, must be the coldest of cold blood.

The commander's is more a one-man job, as the crew's is more team work, than any other employment afloat. That is why the relations between submarine officers and men are what they are. They play hourly for each other's lives with Death the Umpire always at their elbow on tiptoe to give them 'Out.'

There is a stretch of water, once dear to amateur yachtsmen, now given over to scouts, submarines, destroyers, and, of course, contingents of trawlers. We were waiting the return of some boats which were due to report. A couple surged up the still harbour in the afternoon light and tied up beside their sisters. There climbed out of them three or four high-booted, sunken-eyed pirates clad in sweaters, under jackets that a stoker of the last generation would have disowned. This was their first chance to compare notes at close hand. Together they lamented the loss of a Zeppelin – 'a perfect mug of a Zepp,' who had come down very low and offered one of them a sitting shot. 'But what *can* you do with our guns? I gave him what I had, and then he started bombing.'

'I know he did,' another said. 'I heard him. That's what brought me down to you. I thought he had you that last time.'

'No, I was forty foot under when he hove out the big 'un. What happened to *you*?'

'My steering-gear jammed just after I went down, and I had to go round in circles till I got it straightened out. But *wasn't* he a mug!'

'Was he the brute with the patch on his port side?' a sister-boat demanded.

'No! This fellow had just been hatched. He was almost sitting on the water, heaving bombs over.'

'And my blasted steering-gear went and chose *then* to go wrong,' the other commander mourned.

'I thought his last little egg was going to get me!'

Half an hour later I was formally introduced to three or four quite strange, quite immaculate officers, freshly shaved, and a little tired about the eyes, whom I thought I had met before.

Labour and Refreshment

Meantime (it was on the hour of evening drinks) one of the boats was still unaccounted for. No one talked of her. They rather discussed motor-cars and Admiralty constructors, but – it felt like that queer twilight watch at the front when the homing aeroplanes drop in. Presently a signaller entered: '*V.42* outside, sir; wants to know which channel she shall use.' 'Oh, thank you. Tell her to take so-and-so.' . . . Mine, I remember, was vermouth and bitters, and later on *V.42* himself found a soft chair and joined the committee of instruction. Those next for duty, as well as those in training, wished to hear what was going on, and who had shifted what to where, and how certain arrangements had worked. They were told in language not to be found in any printable book. Questions and answers were alike Hebrew to one listener, but he gathered that every boat carried a second in command – a strong, persevering youth, who seemed responsible for every thing that went wrong, from a motor cylinder to a torpedo. Then somebody touched on the mercantile marine and its habits.

Said one philosopher: 'They can't be expected to take any more risks than they do. I wouldn't, if I was a skipper. I'd loose off at any blessed periscope I saw.'

'That's all very fine. You wait till you've had a patriotic tramp trying to strafe you at your own back-door,' said another.

Some one told a tale of a man with a voice, notable even in a Service where men are not trained to whisper. He was coming back, empty-handed, dirty, tired, and best left alone. From the peace of the German side he had entered our hectic home-waters, where the usual tramp shelled, and by miraculous luck, crumpled his periscope. Another man might have dived, but Boanerges kept on rising. Majestic and wrathful he rose personally through his main hatch, and at 2,000 yards (have I said it was a still day?) addressed the tramp. Even at that distance she gathered it was a Naval officer with a grievance, and by the time he ran alongside she was in a state of coma, but managed to stammer: 'Well, sir, at least you'll admit that our shooting was pretty good.'

'And that,' said my informant, 'put the lid on!' Boanerges went down lest he should be tempted to murder, and the tramp affirms she heard him rumbling beneath her, like an inverted thunderstorm, for fifteen minutes.

'All those tramps ought to be disarmed, and we ought to have all their guns,' said a voice out of a corner.

'What? Still worrying over your "mug"?' some one replied.

'He was a mug!' went on the man of one idea. 'If I'd had a couple of twelves even, I could have strafed him proper. I don't know whether I shall mutiny, or desert, or write to the First Sea Lord about it.'

'Strafe all Admiralty constructors to begin with. I could build a better boat with a 4-inch lathe and a sardine-tin than—,' the speaker named her by letter and number.

'That's pure jealousy,' her commander explained to the company. 'Ever since I installed – ahem! – my patent electric wash-basin he's been intriguin' to get her. Why? We know he doesn't wash. He'd only use the basin to keep beer in.'

Underwater Works

However often one meets it, as in this war one meets it at every turn, one never gets used to the Holy Spirit of Man at his job. The 'common sweeper,' growling over his mug of tea that there was 'nothing in sweepin',' and these idly chaffing men, new shaved and attired, from the gates of Death which had let them through for the fiftieth time, were all of the same fabric – incomprehensible, I should imagine, to the enemy. And the stuff held good throughout all the world – from the Dardanelles to the Baltic, where only a little while ago another batch of submarines had slipped in and begun to be busy. I had spent some of the afternoon in looking through reports of submarine work in the Sea of Marmora. They read like the diary of energetic weasels in an overcrowded chicken-run, and the results for each boat were tabulated something like a cricket score. There were no maiden overs. One came across jewels of price set in the flat official phraseology. For example, one man who was describing some steps he was taking to remedy certain defects, interjected casually: 'At this point I had to go under for a little, as a man in a boat was trying to grab my periscope with his hand.' No reference before or after to the said man or his fate. Again: 'Came across a dhow with a Turkish skipper. He seemed so miserable that I let him go.' And elsewhere in those waters, a submarine overhauled a steamer full of Turkish passengers, some of whom, arguing on their allies' lines, promptly leaped overboard. Our boat fished them out and returned them, for she was not killing civilians. In another affair, which included several ships (now at the bottom) and one submarine, the commander relaxes enough to note that: 'The men behaved very well under direct and flanking fire from rifles at about fifteen yards.' This was *not* I believe, the submarine that fought the Turkish cavalry on the beach. And in addition to matters much more marvellous than any I have hinted at, the reports deal with repairs and shifts and contrivances carried through in the face of dangers that read like the last delirium of romance. One boat went down the Straits and found herself rather canted over to one side. A mine and chain had jammed under her forward diving-plane. So far as I made out, she shook it off by standing on her head and jerking backwards; or it may have been, for the thing has occurred more than once, she merely rose as much as she could when she could, and then 'released it by hand,' as the official phrase goes.

Four Nightmares

And who, a few months ago, could have invented, or having invented, would have dared to print such a nightmare as this: There was a boat in the North Sea who ran into a net and was caught by the nose. She rose, still entangled, meaning to cut the thing away on the surface. But a Zeppelin in waiting saw and bombed her, and she had to go down again at once – but not too wildly or she would get herself more wrapped up than ever. She went down, and by slow working and weaving and wriggling, guided only by guesses at the meaning of each scrape and grind of the net on her blind forehead, at last she drew clear. Then she sat on the bottom and thought. The question was whether she should go back at once and warn her confederates against the trap, or wait till the destroyers which she knew the Zeppelin would have signalled for, should come out to finish her still entangled, as they would suppose, in the net? It was a simple calculation of comparative speeds and positions, and when it was worked out she decided to try for the double event. Within a few minutes of the time she had allowed for them, she heard the twitter of four destroyers' screws quartering above her; rose; got her shot in; saw one destroyer crumple; hung round till another took the wreck in tow; said good-bye to the spare brace (she was at the end of her supplies), and reached the rendezvous in time to turn her friends.

And since we are dealing in nightmares, here are two more – one genuine, the other, mercifully, false. There was a boat not only at, but *in* the mouth of a river – well home in German territory. She was spotted, and went under, her commander perfectly aware that there was not more than five feet of water over her conning-tower so that even a torpedo-boat, let alone a destroyer, would hit it if she came over. But nothing hit anything. The search was conducted on scientific principles while they sat on the silt and suffered. Then the commander heard the rasp of a wire trawl sweeping over his hull. It was not a nice sound, but there happened to be a couple of gramophones aboard, and he turned them both on to drown it. And in due time that boat got home with everybody's hair of just the same colour as when they had started!

The other nightmare arose out of silence and imagination. A boat had gone to bed on the bottom in a spot where she might reasonably expect to be looked for, but it was a convenient jumping off, or up, place for the work in hand. About the bad hour of 2.30 a.m. the commander was waked by one of his men, who whispered to him: 'They've got the chains on us, sir!' Whether it was pure nightmare, an hallucination of long wakefulness, something relaxing and releasing in that packed box of machinery, or the disgustful reality, the commander could not tell, but it had all the makings of panic in it. So the Lord and long training put it into his head to reply! 'Have they? Well, we shan't be coming up till nine o'clock this morning. We'll see about it then. Turn out that light, please.'

He did not sleep, but the dreamer and the others did; and when morning came and he gave the order to rise, and she rose unhampered, and he saw the grey smeared seas from above once again, he said it was a very refreshing sight.

Lastly, which is on all fours with the gamble of the chase, a man was coming home rather bored after an uneventful trip. It was necessary for him to sit on the bottom for a while, and there he played patience. Of a sudden it struck him, as a vow and an omen, that if he worked out the next game correctly he would go up and strafe something. The cards fell all in order. He went up at once and found himself alongside a German, whom, as he had promised and prophesied to himself, he destroyed. She was a mine-layer, and needed only a jar to dissipate like a cracked electriclight bulb. He was somewhat impressed by the contrast between the single-handed game fifty feet below, the ascent, the attack, the amazing result, and when he descended again, his cards just as he had left them.

[First published in the *Daily Telegraph* in the UK and in the *New York American* and other Hearst newspapers in the United States on 20, 23, 25, 27 and 30 November and on 2 December 1915, and then collected in *The Fringes of the Fleet* (1915) and later, with other naval stories, in *Sea Warfare* (1916).]

✖ ✖ ✖

TALES OF 'THE TRADE'

THEY BEAR, IN PLACE of classic names,
Letters and numbers on their skin.
They play their grisly blindfold games

In little boxes made of tin.
Sometimes they stalk the Zeppelin,
Sometimes they learn where mines are laid
Or where the Baltic ice is thin.
That is the custom of 'The Trade.'

Few prize-courts sit upon their claims.
They seldom tow their targets in.
They follow certain secret aims
Down under, far from strife or din.
When they are ready to begin
No flag is flown, no fuss is made
More than the shearing of a pin.
That is the custom of 'The Trade.'

The Scout's quadruple funnel flames
A mark from Sweden to the Swin,
The Cruiser's thundrous screw proclaims
Her comings out and goings in:
But only whiffs of paraffin
Or creamy rings that fizz and fade
Show where the one-eyed Death has been.
That is the custom of 'The Trade.'

Their feats, their fortunes and their fames
Are hidden from their nearest kin;
No eager public backs or blames,
No journal prints the yarns they spin
(The Censor would not let it in!)
When they return from run or raid.
Unheard they work, unseen they win.
That is the custom of 'The Trade.'

Some Work in the Baltic

No one knows how the title of 'The Trade' came to be applied to the Submarine Service. Some say that the cruisers invented it because they pretend that submarine officers look like unwashed chauffeurs. Others think it sprang forth by itself, which means that it was coined by the Lower Deck, where they always have the proper names for things. Whatever the truth, the Submarine Service is now 'the trade'; and if you ask them why, they will answer: 'What else could you call it? The Trade's "the trade," of course.'

It is a close corporation; yet it recruits its men and officers from every class that uses the sea and engines, as well as from many classes that never expected to deal with either. It takes them; they disappear for a while and return changed to their very souls, for the Trade lives in a world without precedents, of which no generation has had any previous experience – a world still being made and enlarged daily. It creates and settles its own problems as it goes along, and if it cannot help itself no one else can. So the Trade lives in the dark and thinks out inconceivable and impossible things which it afterwards puts into practice.

It keeps books, too, as honest traders should. They are almost as bald as ledgers, and are written up, hour by hour, on a little sliding table that pulls out from beneath the commander's bunk. In due time they go to my Lords of the Admiralty, who presently circulate a few carefully watered extracts for the confidential information of the junior officers of the Trade, that these may see what things are done and how. The juniors read but laugh. They have heard the stories, with all the flaming detail and much of the language, either from a chief actor while they perched deferentially on the edge of a mess-room fender, or from his subordinate, in which case they were not so deferential, or from some returned member of the crew present on the occasion, who, between half-shut teeth at the wheel, jerks out what really happened. There is very little going on in the Trade that the Trade does not know within a reasonable time. But the outside world must wait until my Lords of the Admiralty release the records. Some of them have been released now.

Submarine and Ice-Breaker

Let us take, almost at random, an episode in the life of H.M. Submarine E9. It is true that she was commanded by Comander Max Horton, but the utter impersonality of the tale makes it as though the boat herself spoke. (Also, never having met or seen any of the gentlemen concerned in the matter, the writer can be impersonal too.) Some time ago, E9 was in the Baltic, in the deeps of winter, where she used to be taken to her hunting grounds by an ice-breaker. Obviously a submarine cannot use her sensitive nose to smash heavy ice with, so the broad-beamed pushing chaperone comes along to see her clear of the thick harbour and shore ice. In the open sea apparently she is left to her own devices. In company of the ice-breaker, then, E9 'proceeded' (neither in the Senior nor the Junior Service does any one officially 'go' anywhere) to a 'certain position.'

Here – it is not stated in the book, but the Trade knows every aching, single detail of what is left out – she spent a certain time in testing arrangements and apparatus, which may or may not work properly when immersed in a mixture of block-ice and dirty ice-cream in a temperature well towards zero. This is a pleasant job, made the more delightful by the knowledge that if you slip off the superstructure the deadly Baltic chill will stop your heart long before even your heavy clothes can drown you. Hence (and this is not in the book either) the remark of the highly trained sailor-man in these latitudes who, on being told by his superior officer in the execution of his duty to go to Hell, did insubordinately and enviously reply: 'D'you think I'd be here if I could?' Whereby he caused the entire personnel, beginning with the Commander to say 'Amen,' or words to that effect. E9 evidently made things work.

Next day she reports: 'As circumstances were favourable decided to attempt to bag a destroyer.' Her 'certain position' must have been near a well-used destroyer-run, for shortly afterwards she sees three of them, but too far off to attack, and later, as the light is failing, a fourth destroyer towards which she manœuvres. 'Depth-keeping,' she notes, 'very difficult owing to heavy swell.' An observation balloon on a gusty day is almost as stable as a submarine 'pumping' in a heavy swell, and since the Baltic is shallow, the submarine runs the chance of being let down with a whack on the bottom. None the less, E9 works her way to within 600 yards of the quarry; fires and waits just long enough to be sure that her torpedo is running straight, and that the destroyer is holding her course. Then she 'dips to avoid detection.' The rest is deadly simple: 'At the correct moment after firing, 45 to 50 seconds, heard the unmistakable noise of torpedo detonating.' Four minutes later she rose and 'found destroyer had disappeared.' Then, for reasons probably connected with other destroyers, who, too, may have heard that unmistakable sound, she goes to bed below in the chill dark till it is time to turn homewards. When she rose she met storm from the north and logged it accordingly. 'Spray froze as it struck, and bridge became a mass of ice. Experienced considerable difficulty in keeping the conning-tower hatch free from ice. Found it necessary to keep a man continuously employed on this work. Bridge screen immovable, ice six inches thick on it. Telegraphs frozen.' In this state she forges ahead till midnight, and any one who pleases can imagine the thoughts of the continuous employee scraping and hammering round the hatch, as well as the delight of his friends below when the ice-slush spattered down the conning-tower. At last she considered it 'advisable to free the boat of ice, so went below.'

'As Requisite'

In the Senior Service the two words 'as requisite' cover everything that need not be talked about. E9 next day 'proceeded as requisite' through a series of snowstorms and recurring deposits of ice on the bridge till she got in touch with her friend the ice-breaker; and in her company ploughed and rooted her way back to the work we know. There is nothing to show that it was a near thing for E9, but somehow one has the idea that the ice-breaker did not arrive any too soon for E9's comfort and progress. (But what happens in the Baltic when the ice-breaker does not arrive?)

That was in winter. In summer quite the other way, E9 had to go to bed by day very often under the long-lasting northern light when the Baltic is as smooth as a carpet, and one cannot get within a mile and a half of anything with eyes in its head without being put down. There was one time when E9, evidently on information received, took up 'a certain position' and reported the sea 'glassy.' She had to suffer in silence, while three heavily laden German ships went by, for an attack would have given away her position. Her reward came next day, when she sighted (the words run like Marryat's) 'enemy squadron coming up fast from eastward, proceeding inshore of us.' They were two heavy battleships with an escort of destroyers, and E9 turned to attack. She does not say how she crept up in that smooth sea within a quarter of a mile of the leading ship, 'a three-funnel ship, of either the Deutschland or Braunschweig class,' but she managed it, and fired both bow torpedoes at her.

'No. 1 torpedo was seen and heard to strike her just before foremost funnel: smoke and *débris* appeared to go as high as masthead.' That much E9 saw before one of the guardian destroyers ran at her. 'So,' says she, 'observing her I took my periscope off the battleship.' This was excusable, as the destroyer was coming up with intent to kill and E9 had to flood her tanks and get down quickly. Even so, the destroyer only just missed her, and she truck bottom in 43 feet. 'But,' says E9, who, if she could not see, kept her ears open, 'at the correct interval (the 45 or 50 seconds mentioned in the previous case) the second torpedo was heard to explode, though not actually seen.' E9 came up twenty minutes later to make sure. The destroyer was waiting for her a couple of hundred yards away, and again E9 dipped for the life, but 'just had time to see one large vessel approximately four or five miles away.'

Putting courage aside, think for a moment of the mere drill of it all – that last dive for that attack on the chosen battleship; the eye at the periscope watching 'No. 1 torpedo' get home; the rush of the vengeful destroyer; the instant orders for flooding everything; the swift descent which had to be arranged for with full knowledge of the shallow sea-floors waiting below, and a guess at the course that might be taken by the seeking bows above, for assuming a destroyer to draw 10 feet and a submarine on the bottom to stand 25 feet to the top of her conning-tower, there is not much clearance in 43 feet salt water, specially if the boat jumps when she touches bottom. And through all these and half a hundred other simultaneous considerations, imagine the trained minds below, counting, as only torpedo-men can count, the run of the merciless seconds that should tell when that second shot arrived. Then 'at the correct interval' as laid down in the table of distances, the boom and the jar of No. 2 torpedo, the relief, the exhaled breath and untightened lips; the impatient waiting for a second peep, and when that had been taken and the eye at the periscope had reported *one* little nigger-boy in place of two on the waters, perhaps cigarettes, &c., while the destroyer sickle about at a venture overhead.

Certainly they give men rewards for doing such things, but what reward can there be in any gift of Kings or peoples to match the enduring satisfaction of having done them, not alone, but with and through and by trusty and proven companions?

Defeated by Darkness

E1, also a Baltic boat, her Commander F.N. Laurence, had her experiences too. She went out one summer day and late – too late – in the evening sighted three transports. The first she hit. While she was arranging for the second, the third inconsiderately tried to ram her before her sights were on. So it was necessary to go down at once and waste whole minutes of the precious scanting light. When she rose, the stricken ship was sinking and shortly afterwards blew up. The other two were patrolling near by. It would have been a fair chance in daylight, but the darkness defeated her and she had to give up the attack.

It was E1 who during thick weather came across a squadron of battle-cruisers and got in on a flanking ship – probably the *Moltke*. The destroyers were very much on the alert, and she had to dive at once to avoid one who only missed her by a few feet. Then the fog shut down and stopped further developments. Thus do time and chance come to every man.

The Trade has many stories, too, of watching patrols when a boat must see chance after chance go by under her nose and write – merely write – what she has seen. Naturally they do not appear in any accessible records. Nor, which is a pity, do the authorities release the records of glorious failures, when everything goes wrong; when torpedoes break surface and squatter like ducks; or arrive full square with a clang and burst of white water and – fail to explode; when the devil is in charge of all the motors, and clutches develop play that would scare a shore-going mechanic bald; when batteries begin to give off death instead of power, and atop of all, ice or wreckage of the strewn seas racks and wrenches the hull till the whole leaking bag of tricks limps home on six missing cylinders and one ditto propeller, *plus* the indomitable will of the red-eyed husky scarecrows in charge.

There might be worse things in this world for decent people to read than such records.

[First published in *The Times*, 21, 23 and 28 June 1916, then published in a limited (twenty-five copies) privately produced edition in London, 1916, before being collected in *Sea Warfare* (1916).]

🕱 🕱 🕱

THE DESTROYERS AT JUTLAND

'HAVE YOU NEWS OF my boy Jack?'
    Not this tide.
'When d'you think that he'll come back?'
    Not with this wind blowing, and this tide.

'Has any one else had word of him?'
    Not this tide.
For what is sunk will hardly swim,
    Not with this wind blowing, and this tide.

'Oh, dear, what comfort can I find?'
    None this tide,
    Nor any tide,
Except he did not shame his kind –
    Not even with that wind blowing, and that tide.

Then hold your head up all the more,
    This tide,
    And every tide;
Because he was the son you bore,
    And gave to that wind blowing and that tide!

Stories of the Battle

CRIPPLE AND PARALYTIC

There was much destroyer-work in the Battle of Jutland. The actual battle field may not have been more than twenty thousand square miles, but the incidental patrols, from first to last, must have covered many times that area. Doubtless the next generation will comb out every detail of it. All we need remember is there were many squadrons of battleships and cruisers engaged over the face of the North Sea, and that they were accompanied in their dread comings and goings by multitudes of destroyers, who attacked the enemy both by day and by night from the afternoon of May 31 to the morning of June 1, 1916. We are too close to the gigantic canvas to take in the meaning of the picture; our children stepping backward through the years may get the true perspective and proportions.

To recapitulate what every one knows.

The German fleet came out of its North Sea ports, scouting ships ahead; then destroyers, cruisers, battle-cruisers, and, last, the main battle-fleet in the rear. It moved north, parallel with the coast of stolen Schleswig-Holstein and Jutland. Our fleets were already out; the main battle-fleet (Admiral Jellicoe) sweeping down from the north, and our battle-cruiser fleet (Admiral Beatty) feeling for the enemy. Our scouts came in contact with the enemy on the afternoon of May 31 about 100 miles off the Jutland coast, steering north-west. They satisfied themselves he was in strength, and reported accordingly to our battle-cruiser fleet, which engaged the enemy's battle-cruisers at about half-past three o'clock. The enemy steered south-east to rejoin their own fleet, which was coming up from that quarter. We fought him on a parallel course as he ran for more than an hour.

Then his battle-fleet came in sight, and Beatty's fleet went about and steered north-west in order to retire on our battle-fleet, which was hurrying down from the north. We returned fighting very much over the same waters as we had used in our slant south. The enemy up till now had lain to the eastward of us, whereby he had the advantage in that thick weather of seeing our hulls clear against the afternoon light, while he himself worked in the mists. We then steered a little to the north-west bearing him off towards the east till at six o'clock Beatty had headed the enemy's leading ships and our main battle-fleet came in sight from the north. The enemy broke back in a loop, first eastward, then south, then south-west as our fleet edged him off from the land, and our main battle-fleet, coming up behind them, followed in their wake. Thus for a while we had the enemy to westward of us, where he made a better mark; but the day was closing and the weather thickened, and the enemy wanted to get away. At a quarter past eight the enemy, still heading south-west, was covered by his destroyers in a great screen of grey smoke, and he got away.

NIGHT AND MORNING

As darkness fell, our fleets lay between the enemy and his home ports. During the night our heavy ships, keeping well clear of possible mine-fields, swept down south to south and west of the Horns Reef, so that they might pick him up in the morning. When morning came our main fleet could find no trace of the enemy to the southward, but our destroyer-flotillas further north had been very busy with enemy ships, apparently running for the Horns Reef Channel. It looks, then, as if when we lost sight of the enemy in the smoke screen and the darkness he had changed course and broken for home astern our main fleets. And whether that was a sound manœuvre or otherwise, he and the still flows of the North Sea alone can tell.

But how is a layman to give any coherent account of an affair where a whole country's coast-line was background to battle covering geographical degrees? The records give an impression of illimitable grey waters, nicked on their uncertain horizons with the smudge and blur of ships sparkling with fury against ships hidden under the curve of the world. One sees these distances maddeningly obscured by walking mists and weak fogs, or wiped out by layers of funnel and gun smoke, and realises how, at the pace the ships were going, anything might be stumbled upon in the haze or charge out of it when it lifted. One comprehends, too, how the far-off glare of a great vessel afire might be reported as a local fire on a near-by enemy, or *vice versa*; how a silhouette caught, for an instant, in a shaft of pale light let down from the low sky might be fatally difficult to identify till too late. But add to all these inevitable confusions and misreckonings of time, shape, and distance, charges at every angle of squadrons through and across other squadrons; sudden shifts of the centres of the fights, and even swifter restorations; wheelings, sweepings, and regroupments such as accompany the passage across space of colliding universes. Then blanket the whole inferno with the darkness of night at full speed, and – see what you can make of it.

Three Destroyers

A little time after the action began to heat up between our battle-cruisers and the enemy's, eight or ten of our destroyers opened the ball for their branch of the service by breaking up the attack of an enemy light cruiser and fifteen destroyers. Of these they accounted for at least two destroyers – some think more – and drove the others back on their battle-cruisers. This scattered that fight a good deal over the sea. Three of our destroyers held on for the enemy's battle-fleet, who came down on them at ranges which eventually grew less than 3000 yards. Our people ought to have been lifted off the seas bodily, but they managed to fire a couple of torpedoes apiece while the range was diminishing. They had no illusions. Says one of the three, speaking of her second shot, which she loosed at fairly close range, 'This torpedo was fired because it was considered very unlikely that the ship would escape disablement before another opportunity offered.' But still they lived – three destroyers against all a battle-cruiser fleet's quick-firers, as well as the fire of a batch of enemy destroyers at 600 yards. And they were thankful for small mercies. 'The position being favourable,' a third torpedo was fired from each while they yet floated.

At 2500 yards, one destroyer was hit somewhere in the vitals and swerved badly across her next astern, who 'was obliged to alter course to avoid a collision, thereby failing to fire a fourth torpedo.' Then that next astern 'observed signal for destroyers' recall,' and went back to report to her flotilla captain – alone. Of her two companions, one was 'badly hit and remained stopped between the lines.' The other 'remained stopped, but was afloat when last seen'. Ships that 'remain stopped' are liable to be rammed or sunk by methodical gun-fire. That was, perhaps, fifty minutes' work put in before there was any really vicious 'edge' to the action, and it did not steady the nerves of the enemy battle-cruisers any more than another attack made by another detachment of ours.

'What does one do when one passes a ship that "remains stopped"?' asked of a youth who had had experience.

'Nothing special. They cheer, and you cheer back. One doesn't think about it till afterwards. You see, it may be your luck in another minute.'

LUCK

There were many other torpedo attacks in all parts of the battle that misty afternoon, including a quaint episode of an enemy light cruiser who 'looked as if she were trying' to torpedo one of our battle-cruisers while the latter was particularly engaged. A destroyer of ours, returning from a special job which required delicacy, was picking her way back at 30 knots through batches of enemy battle-cruisers and light cruisers with the idea of attaching herself to the nearest destroyer-flotilla and making herself useful. It occurred to her that as she 'was in a most advantageous position for repelling enemy's destroyers endeavouring to attack, she could not do better than to remain on the "engaged bow" of our battle-cruiser.' So she remained and considered things.

There was an enemy battle-cruiser squadron in the offing; with several enemy light cruisers ahead of that squadron, and the weather was thickish and deceptive. She sighted the enemy light cruiser, 'class uncertain,' only a few thousand yards away, and 'decided to attack her in order to frustrate her firing torpedoes at our Battle Fleet.' (This in case the authorities should think that light cruiser, wished to buy rubber.) So she fell upon the light cruiser with every gun she had, at between two and four thousand yards, and secured a number of hits, just the same as at target practice. While thus occupied she sighted out of the mist a squadron of enemy battle-cruisers that had worried her earlier in the afternoon. Leaving the light cruiser, she closed to what she considered a reasonable distance of the newcomers, and let them have, as she thought, both her torpedoes. She possessed an active Acting Sub-Lieutenant, who, though officers of that rank think otherwise, is not very far removed from an ordinary midshipman of the type one sees in tow of relatives at the Army and Navy Stores. He sat astride one of the tubes to make quite sure things were in order, and fired when the sights came on.

But, at that very moment, a big shell hit the destroyer on the side and there was a tremendous escape of steam. Believing – since she had seen one torpedo leave the tube before the smash came – believing that both her tubes had been fired, the destroyer turned away 'at greatly reduced speed' (the shell reduced it), and passed, quite reasonably close, the light cruiser whom she had been hammering so faithfully till the larger game appeared. Meantime, the Sub-Lieutenant was exploring what damage had been done by the big shell. He discovered that only *one* of the two torpedoes had left the tubes, and 'observing enemy light cruiser beam on and apparently temporarily stopped,' he fired the providential remainder at her, and it hit her below the conning-tower and well and truly exploded, as was witnessed by the Sub-Lieutenant himself, the Commander, a leading signalman, and several other ratings. Luck continued to hold! The Acting Sub-Lieutenant further reported that 'we still had three torpedoes left' and at the same time drew my attention to enemy's line of battleships.' They rather looked as if they were coming down with intent to assault. So the Sub-Lieutenant fired the rest of the torpedoes, which at least started off correctly from the shell-shaken tubes, and must have crossed the enemy's line. When torpedoes turn up among a squadron, they upset the steering and distract the attention of all concerned. Then the destroyer judged it time to take stock of her injuries. Among other minor defects she could neither steam, steer, nor signal.

TOWING UNDER DIFFICULTIES

Mark how virtue is rewarded! Another of our destroyers an hour or so previously had been knocked clean out of action, before she had done anything, by a big shell which gutted a boiler-room and started an oil fire. (That is the drawback to oil.) She crawled out between the battleships till she 'reached an area of comparative calm' and repaired damage. She says: 'The fire having been dealt with it was found a mat kept the stokehold dry. My only trouble now being lack of speed, I looked round for useful employment, and saw a destroyer in great difficulties, so closed her.' That destroyer was our paralytic friend of the intermittent torpedo-tubes, and a grateful ship she was when her crippled sister (but still good for a few knots) offered her a tow, 'under very trying conditions with large enemy ships approaching.' So the two set off together, Cripple and Paralytic, with heavy shells falling round them, as sociable as a couple of lame hounds. Cripple worked up to 12 knots, and the weather grew vile, and the tow parted. Paralytic, by this time, had raised steam in a boiler or two, and made shift to get along slowly on her own, Cripple hirpling beside her, till Paralytic could not make any more headway in that rising sea, and Cripple had to tow her once more. Once more the tow parted. So they tied Paralytic up rudely and effectively with a cable round her after bollards and gun (presumably because of strained forward bulkheads) and hauled her stern-first, through heavy seas, at continually reduced speeds, doubtful of their position, unable to sound because of the seas, and much pestered by a wind which backed without warning, till, at last, they made land, and turned into the hospital appointed for brave wounded ships. Everybody speaks well of Cripple. Her name crops up in several reports, with such compliments as the men of the sea use when they see good work. She herself speaks well of her Lieutenant, who, as executive officer, 'took charge of the fire and towing arrangements in a very creditable manner,' and also of Tom Battye and Thomas Kerr, engine-room artificer and stoker petty officer, who 'were in the stokehold at the time of the shell striking, and performed cool and prompt decisive action, although both suffering from shock and slight injuries.'

USEFUL EMPLOYMENT

Have you ever noticed that men who do Homeric deeds often describe them in Homeric language? The sentence 'I looked round for useful employment' is worthy of Ulysses when 'there was an evil sound at the ships of men who perished and of the ships themselves broken at the same time.'

Roughly, very roughly, speaking, our destroyers enjoyed three phases of 'prompt decisive action' – the first, a period of daylight attacks (from to 4 to 6 P.M.) such as the one I have just described, while the battle was young and the light fairly good on the afternoon of May 31; the second, towards dark, when the light had lessened and the enemy were more uneasy, and, I think, in more scattered formation; the third, when darkness had fallen, and the destroyers had been strung out astern with orders to help the enemy home, which they did all night as opportunity offered. One cannot say whether the day or the night work was the more desperate. From private advices, the young gentlemen concerned seem to have functioned with efficiency either way. As one of them said: 'After a bit, you see, we were all pretty much on our own, and you could really find out what your ship could do.'

I will tell you later of a piece of night work not without merit.

[First published in the *Daily Telegraph* and *New York Times* on 19, 23, 26 and 31 October 1916, and then collected in *Sea Warfare* (1916).]

✠ ✠ ✠

SPEECH TO SOME JUNIOR NAVAL OFFICERS OF AN EAST COAST PATROL, 1918: THE FIRST SAILOR

Home came the ships bearing message by sulphur and smoke
   of the battle.
Home came the tide to the beach and kissed the inviolate sands.

ADMIRALS, VICE-ADMIRALS AND REAR-ADMIRALS of the future – I am sorry for you. When you are at sea you are exposed to the exigencies of the Service, the harsh reprimands of your superiors, the malice of the King's enemies, and the Act of God. When you come ashore you endure, as you will this evening, the assaults of the civil population teaching you your own job. For instance, my lecture deals with the origin, evolution, and development from the earliest ages, of that packet of assorted miseries which we call a Ship. With my lecture will be included a succinct but accurate history of late Able Seaman, Leading Hand *and* Commander, Clarke, founder of the Royal Navy and the Mercantile Marine.

The late Commander Clarke flourished between fifteen and twenty thousand years ago, on a marshy island on the south side of a tidal estuary that faced East. Barring that he did not use patent medicines, daily papers, and similar modern excrescences, he was very like yourselves, though in a different rig. His wife, Mrs. Clarke, wove baskets out of reeds, and made eel-traps out of willows and osiers.

Neither of them knew that the river in front of them would be called the Thames, or that the island they inhabited would be called Sheer Necessity. But they knew what sheer necessity meant. It was sheer necessity for them to swim, spear salmon with flint-headed spears; knock seals on the head with wooden clubs; catch and trap fish; dig for cockles with a flattened piece of wood like a paddle; cure and dress skins; and, above all, keep the home-fires burning in their mud and wood hut. This was easy, because the river brought down any amount of unrationed drift-wood from the great forests in the interior of England, and laid it almost at Nobby's door. He had only to swim out, get astride of a log, and paddle it ashore with the paddle he used for digging his cockles.

But he noticed that the logs nearly always turned over with him, and tipped him into the water. He didn't mind the duckings. What annoyed him was being ducked however well he balanced himself. He did not understand logs behaving as if they were alive. You see, for aught Nobby knew, logs might be alive. According to his religion, everything else was alive. The Winds were alive. The Tides were alive. He saw them being driven up and down the river by a God who lived in the Moon. The Sun was alive too. Nobby could see the exact place where he came out of his House under the Sea. The Sun lived at the End of the World which, as everybody in his world knew, was East of Margate Sands. If the God of the Ebb Tide caught you fishing too far out from the bank of the river, he carried you out to the End of the World, and you never came back again, because you were burned up alive in the Sun's House. That was both Fact and Religion. But the logs and driftwood used to pass out of Thames mouth with the ebb, in long processions to the End of the World; and Nobby noticed that many of those very same logs would come back again with the flood, not even charred! This proved to him that the logs knew some sort of magic which he didn't – otherwise how could they get back from the House where the Sun rose without being burned up? That was Logic. At last he spoke about it to the High Priest of his tribe, and asked him whether a man could go and come as the logs did. The High Priest laughed and quoted an ancient saying of the Tribe when young men boasted or children wanted something they couldn't get. 'Wait a bit!' he said. 'As soon as the Stick marries the Basket, you'll get to the World's End and back – won't you?' That is a silly saying isn't it? It's almost as silly as the old music-hall chorus that used to be sung in London ever so long ago:

> When the Pigs begin to fly
> Oh, won't the pork be high?
> And we'll send old maids to Parliament –
> When? –
> When the Pigs begin to fly.

Now, you may have noticed, gentlemen, that the Pig, as represented by the Hun, has begun to fly. At the same time, the vote is being given to the ladies, whom we shall see at Westminster anon; and I need not draw the attention of any gun-room officer to the present scandalous price of tinned sausages. This shows that, though many a prophecy turns out to be a joke, some jokes – specially in the Service – become prophecies.

So it was in Nobby's case. He didn't know what you and I know about the Doctrine of Evolution. *He* didn't know that the Stick, which the High Priest talked about, represented the single log which is the Father of all dug-out makee-paddloes, such as West African canoes, and the whole breed of rafts, praus, catamarans, and outriggers from Dakar to Malaysia; or that the Basket is the Mother of all built-up shipping that has a keel and ribs – from the kayak, junk, and dhow, dromond, bus, caravel, carrack, and Seventy-Four, to the modern transatlantic liner, now on convoy-duty, the overworked and under-gunned sloop, the meritorious but damp destroyer and *sea-sick omnes*, throughout all the oceans. Such considerations did not weigh with him. Being a simple soul, he was merely annoyed with those logs that turned over beneath him; and he was puzzled over the logs that went to the End of the World and back again.

One day when he was retrieving his firewood as usual, he saw a log drift past that took his fancy. He swam out and straddled it, making ready to balance if it turned over. But it didn't. For the first time in the history of mankind, Nobby felt the gentle roll and recover of a ballasted keel beneath him. He leaned to port and starboard to make sure. *Still* the log didn't turn over. Why? Because it had been a small stunted tree growing on a sou'-western exposure which had bent it over to the north-east, thus giving the trunk a pleasing sheer at the bows. To steady itself against prevailing winds, the tree had wrapped its roots round a big boulder. Then a gale had torn it out of the bank it grew on, hundreds of miles up the river, and it had drifted down to the sea, rubbing and scraping on gravel and sandbars till there was hardly any trace left of its branches. But the tough old roots were still firmly wrapped round the boulder, and the log, therefore, floated more or less plumb.

As far as we can make out, the earliest steps of invention, like those of promotion, are mostly due to accident taken advantage of by the observant mind. Accident, Providence, or Joss had presented the observant Nobby with the Mothermodel, so to speak, of all the ships that would be built hereafter. But all that Nobby knew was that, at last, he had found a log which didn't roll over, and he meant to keep it. Therefore he made his wife put raw-hide lashings over the boulder among the roots so that the boulder should not drop out or shift. They greased the lashings, of course, the same way as they greased themselves with seal-oil when they went swimming, because grease keeps out wet. For the same reason they greased the whole log except along the top where they wanted to take hold of it. As they rubbed the stuff in, they scraped smooth, with shell and flint scrapers, all knots and bumps where the branches had been. Later on – it may have been weeks, it may have been months or years – it occurred to Nobby to hollow out the log so as he could sit *in* it comfortably, instead of *on* it. So he and his wife put red-hot ashes on the top, surrounded them with a little mud, and scraped away the wood as it charred. Bit by bit, they burned and scraped out as much of the inside of the log as they wanted. Nobby didn't know where the buoyancy of a boat ought to be, but he liked to stretch his legs out in the well.

Then, he and his wife went out paddling very cautiously up and down the marshes behind them, or very close to the bank of the big river. Naturally, they were afraid of the God of the Tide carrying them off to the End of the World and burning them alive in the Sun's House. All the same Nobby's eyes used to flicker sometimes towards the End of the World in the direction of Margate Sands where the Sun lived and where the logs went.

One moonlight night in April or May, B.C. fourteen thousand nine hundred odd, Nobby showed the High Priest how Mrs. Clarke had woven a sort of basket-work back-rest in and out of what was left of the roots at the stern of the log, and how he had covered it with seal-skin to keep water from slopping down his back. As a matter of fact, it was the first dim idea of a poop and sternworks that the mind of man had conceived. Nobby had made it for his own comfort – the way most inventions are made.

The High Priest looked at it. 'Ah!' he said. 'It strikes *me* that the Stick is beginning to marry the Basket.'

'In that case,' said Nobby very quickly, 'what about me going to the End of the World?'

'Officially,' said the High Priest, 'I can't countenance any such action, because you would be officially burned up by the Sun when he got out of bed, and I should have to damn your soul officially afterwards. Unofficially, of course, if *I* were your age I'd have a shot at it.'

I merely mention this conversation to show you that general instructions throwing the entire responsibility of the accident on the Watch Officer, while leaving the Post Captain without a stain on his character at the ensuing Court of Enquiry, were not unknown even in that remote age.

Then Nobby went home, where his wife was putting the children to bed, with a long lie about having to look after an eel-trap down the river. Mrs. Clarke said: 'So the High Priest has talked you into it, has he? Let me tuck the babies up and I'll come too.'

So they pushed off about midnight, paddling in the slack water. They hugged the shore all along the Columbine, past Nayland Rock to Longnose Ridge – one fool-man and one devoted woman on a twenty-five-foot long log, forty-two inches extreme beam, and ten inches freeboard, bound, as they thought, for the End of the World

– and back, if they weren't burned up alive by the God of the Sun *en route*. The ebb took them, at dawn, three or four miles beyond the North Foreland. There was a bit of a swell from the east, and when their log topped the long smooth ridges they saw the red-hot glare of the Sun God coming up out of his House. That panicked them! By great good luck, however, he rose two miles ahead of them. If they had paddled a little harder during the night, they would have been right on top of him. But he got up at a safe distance, and began climbing the sky as usual, and left those terrific rolling waters emptier than ever. Then they wanted to go home. They had lost the North Foreland in the morning haze; they had lost their heads; they would have lost their paddles if those hadn't been lashed. They had lost everything except the instinct that told them to keep the Sun at their backs and dig out. They dug out till they dripped – the first human beings who had ever come back from the End of the World. At last they reached Garrison Point again, white with the salt that had dried on them, their backs and shoulders aching like toothache, their eyes a foot deep in their heads, and the flesh on their bones ribbed and sodden with the wet. Can you imagine such feelings? When Nobby limped up the beach, Mrs. Nobby said: '*Now* I hope you are satisfied!'

Being a married man, Nobby told her he would never do it again. *But*, being the father of all sailormen, he was down on the beach next day, studying how to tune up his boat for her next cruise. Never forget that, as far back as we can trace it, the mind of primitive man was much the same as yours or mine. He knew he lived under a law of cause and effect. But, since a good many of the causes of things were unknown to him, he was rather astonished at some of the effects. So was Nobby a day or two later. While they were overhauling the canoe after its desperate voyage, it occurred to them it might be a good notion to lace a covering over the well to keep the water out. First they cleared everything out of the well, and in doing so lashed the spare paddle to the left-hand side of the poop, where it hung down like a dagger with its broad blade in the water. Then they fetched out a three-cornered skin of scraped sealgut, sewn together with sinew, which Mrs. Nobby had meant to make into slickers for family use. Nobby sat down aft, holding one corner of the skin, while Mrs. Nobby went forward to about midships, put her foot on another corner of the skin to steady it, and held the third corner up to the full stretch of her arm above her head. While they were thus measuring the triangle of shining water-tight, wind-tight stuff, all puffed out by the breeze that was blowing from their left side, the canoe began to heel and slide. Nobby grabbed the head of the spare paddle on the left side of the boat, to steady himself, and drew it towards him. The canoe ran on across the wind to the full length of her mooring-thong, and fetched up with a jerk. Now this was a reversal of every law Nobby had ever worked under, because it was axiomatic that the God of the Wind only pushed one way. If you stood on two logs lashed together, and held out your cloak with both arms, and set your feet on the lower ends of it, the God of whichever Wind was blowing at the time, would push you straight in front of him. Nothing else was possible or conceivable. Yet here was his boat moving across the path of the sou'-west breeze! There couldn't be any mistake, because Nobby pointed it off on his fingers. He didn't know that the natural opening between the first and second fingers of a man's hand is eleven and one-quarter degrees; but he *did* know that if you pointed your first finger, holding your third and fourth fingers down with your thumb, into the eye of anything, and watched where your second finger pointed, and began again at that point with your first finger, and so on round the horizon (which was just thirty-two jabs) you could measure off the distance in finger-points between your first mark and where you were going. In this case, there were about seven of his fingerpoints between the Sou'-West wind's eye and the canoe's track. To make quite sure, he unmoored, carefully repeated the motions, got Mrs. Nobby to hold the skin again, pulled the head of the paddle towards him when the wind puffed; and the boat slid off for almost a quarter of a mile at right angles to the wind.

Nobby paddled back, more scared than when he had gone to the World's End, and went to see the High Priest about it. The High Priest explained like a book. He said that Nobby finding a log which didn't turn over with him; and his getting to the World's End and back on it, without being burned up by the Sun; *and* this last miracle of the Wind, coming on top of the other two, proved that Nobby was beloved by all the Gods of Tide, Sun, and Wind, *and* the Log that carried him.

'I hope that's the case,' said Nobby, who was modest by nature. 'But the next time I go foreign I shall hoist that skin on a stick and have both hands free for miracles in case the Gods spring any more.' Accordingly, he stuck a stick in a hole that he had burned out in the log a little forward of midships, and on the principle that you can't have too much of a good thing, he hung up another three-cornered sail in front of the first, and fastened one of its corners down to the nose of the boat. But as the free corner flapped about too much, Nobby got Mrs. Nobby to sew a thong to it, and led the thong aft to the well, so that he could stop the flapping by pulling on it. Then, the miracles began in earnest! For months and months Nobby never knew when he hoisted those two triangular skins – the first fore-and-aft sails in the world – what the log and the Gods of the Wind, and the paddle, and the strings of the sails, were going to do next. And when the God of the Tide took a hand in the circus, Nobby's hair stood on end. One day, everything would go beautifully. The God of the Tide on his leebow would make the old log look up almost within six finger-points of the wind; and Nobby would skim along at the rate of knots, thinking he'd found out all about it at last. Next day, with a lee-going tide, he would find the canoe bumping broadside on to every shoal he'd ever guessed at, and dozens that he hadn't. Sails, wind, tide, steering – everything – was an incomprehensible wonder, which generally ended in an upset. He had nothing but his own experience to guide him, *plus* the certainty of something happening every time that he took liberties with the Gods. And he didn't know when he *had* taken a liberty till he was tipped out of the boat. But he stuck to his job, and in time he trained his eldest son to help him, till, after years and years of every sort of accident and weather, and hard work and hard thinking and wet lying, he mastered the second of the Two Greatest Mysteries in the world – he understood the Way of a Ship on the Sea.

One fine day in autumn, with a north-west wind and good visibility, the High Priest came to him and said: 'I wish you'd slip up the hill with me for a minute, and give me your opinion of the view'. Nobby came at once, and when they got to Pigtail Corner, the Priest pointed to a square sail off the tail of the Mouse Shoal, some few miles away, and said: 'What do you make of *that*?'

Nobby looked hard; then he said: 'That's not a *ship*. It's one of those dam' barbarians from Harwich. They scull about there in any sort of coffin.' The Priest said: 'What are you going to do about it?'

'I'm going to have a look at him presently,' said Nobby, screwing up his eyes. 'Meantime, it's slack water and he's crossing the Knob Channel before the wind, because he don't know how to navigate otherwise. But in a little while, the God of the Ebb will carry him out towards the End of the World. Then he'll panic, same as I did; and he'll dig out pretty hard to close the land. But it's *my* impression the God of the Ebb Tide will defeat him, and he'll spend most of the night between the land and the World's End, paddling like a duck with the cramps. If he's lucky, he'll be brought back again by the God of the Flood Tide. But *then*, if this Nor'west wind holds, he'll find the God of the Wind fighting the God of the Flood every foot of the way; and he'll be put to it to keep his end up in that lop. If he isn't drowned, he'll be rather fatigued. I ought to pick him up when the Sun gets out of bed to-morrow, somewhere between Margate Sands and the End of the World – probably off the South Shingles.'

'That's very interesting,' said the High Priest, 'but what does it mean exactly?'

'Well,' said Nobby, 'it means exactly that I've got to beat to wind-ward most of this night on a lee-going tide, which, with all respect to the Gods, is the most sanguinary awkward combination *I* know; and if I don't hit mud more than a dozen times between, here and the South Shingles, I shall think myself lucky. But don't let that spoil your sleep, old man.'

'No, I won't,' said the High Priest. 'Go and keep your ceaseless vigil in your lean grey hull and – and – I'll pray for you.'

Nobby didn't even say 'Thank you'. He went down to the beach where his eldest son was waiting with the boat.

'Bite loose the behind-end string,' says Nobby, signifying in his language: 'Let go the stern-fast'.

'Very good, Sir,' says the boy, gnashing his teeth. 'Where are we going, Dad?'

'The Gods only know,' says Nobby. 'But I know that if we aren't off the South Shingles when the Sun gets out of bed to-morrow, *your* leave's stopped, for one.'

By these arbitrary and unfeeling means was discipline and initiative originally inculcated in the Senior Service.

That cruise was all that Nobby had told the High Priest it would be, and a good deal more. As long as the light lasted he moved along fairly well, but after dark he was doing business alone with the Gods of the Wind and the Tide, and the sails and the strings (which naturally fouled), in an unbuoyed, unlighted estuary, chockful of shoals and flats and rips and knocks and wedges and currents and overfalls; also densely populated with floating trees and logs carrying no lights, adrift at every angle. *Can* you imagine anything like it, gentlemen, in all your experience? When they had collided with their fifth floating oak, Nobby calls forward to ask his son whether he was enjoying pleasant dreams, or what else.

'But I can't *see* 'em,' says the child, wiping his nose with the back of his hand.

'See 'em!' says Nobby. 'Who the Hell expects you to see 'em on a night like this? You've got to *smell* 'em, my son.'

Thus early, gentlemen, was the prehistoric and perishing Watch Officer inducted into the mysteries of his unpleasing trade.

So Nobby threshed along as he best could, praying to every God he knew not to set him too far to leeward when the Sun rose. And the object he was sweating his soul and carcass out for, was the one object that all his legitimate and illegitimate descendants on the seas have sweated for ever since – to get to windward of the enemy. When day broke, he found himself a couple of miles or so south-east of the South Shingles, with Margate Sands somewhere on his right, and the End of the World ahead of him glowing redder and redder as the Sun rose. He couldn't have explained how he got there, any more than he could have explained what made him lie just there, waiting for his Harwich friend, and thumping and hammering in the bubble of the wind against the tide.

In due course, the flood brought up a big ship – fifteen foot by eight if she was an inch – made of wickerwork covered with skins. She sat low with two men trying to paddle her, and two more trying to bale. Nobby came down wind, and rammed her at the unheard-of velocity of four point two knots. She heeled over, and while the boy, who was a destructive young devil, stabbed at her skin-plating with his spear, Nobby drove his porpoise-harpoon, with line attached, in among the crew, and through her bilge. Next minute, his canoe was riding head to wind, moored by his harpoon-line to the rim of the basket flush with the water, just as the big skin square-sail floated out of her, neatly blanketing seventy-five per cent of her personnel. A minute later, the boy had hit one surviving head in the water, Nobby had cut his line, and – the first naval engagement in English history was finished, and the first English Commander was moaning over loss of stores expended in action. (Because Nobby knew he'd have to account for that harpoon and line at home.) Then he got the God of the Wind on his right side, hit land somewhere between Margate Sands and Westgate-on-Sea, and came along the shore under easy paddle to Garrison Point; the boy talking very hard and excited.

There not being any newspapers in those days, he told the High Priest exactly what he had done, and drew battle-charts in the mud with a stick, giving his courses, which were roughly North-East; then South-East; and Westerly homeward after the action.

'Well,' said the High Priest, 'I don't pretend to understand navigation, but N.E.S.E.W. means No Enemy Sails English Waters. *That's* as plain as print. It looks to me, though, as if you've started a bigger game than you've any idea of. Do I understand that you followed your enemy to the End of the World and drowned him there?'

'Yes; but that wasn't *my* fault,' said Nobby. 'He went there first. He hadn't any business in my water.'

'Quite so,' said the High Priest, 'but that's only the beginning of it.'

'Well,' said Nobby, 'what's going to be the end of it? What'll happen to *me*, for instance?'

'I'll tell you,' said the High Priest, and he began to prophesy in the irritating way that civilians do. 'You'll have a hard wet life and your sons after you. When you aren't being worried by the sea or your enemies, you'll be worried by your own tribe, teaching you your own job.'

'*That's* nothing new,' said Nobby. 'Carry on!'

'You'll win the world without anyone *caring* how you did it: you'll keep the world without anyone *knowing* how you did it: and you'll carry the world on your backs without anyone *seeing* how you did it. But neither you nor your sons will get anything out of that little job except Four Gifts – one for the Sea, one for the Wind, one for the Sun, and one for the Ship that carries you.'

'Well, I'm glad there will be some advantages connected with the Service. I haven't discovered 'em yet,' said Nobby.

'Yes,' said the Priest. 'You and your sons after you will be long in the head, slow in the tongue, heavy in the hand, *and* – as you were yesterday at the World's End – always a little bit to windward. That you can count on for ever and ever and ever.'

'That'll come in handy for the boy,' said Nobby. 'He didn't do so badly in our little affair yesterday. But what about this Stick-and-Basket pidgin you're always hinting at?'

'There's no end to what happens when the Stick marries the Basket,' said the High Priest. 'There will only be another beginning and a fresh start. Your logs will grow as high as hills and as long as villages, and as wide as rivers. And when they are at their highest and longest and widest, they'll all get up in the air and fly.'

'That's a bad look-out for the boy,' said Nobby. 'I've only brought him up to the sea-trade.'

'Live easy and die easy as far as that is concerned,' said the High Priest. 'For, winning the world, and keeping the world, and carrying the world on their backs – on land, or on sea, or in the air – your sons will always have the Four Gifts. Long-headed and slow-spoken and heavy – damned heavy – in the hand, will they be; and always and always a little bit to windward of every enemy – that they may be a safeguard to all who pass on the seas on their lawful occasions.'

[Collected (with thirty other speeches) in *A Book of Words* (London: Macmillan, 1928).]

❊   ❊   ❊

It took Kipling almost a decade to recover from the shock of losing his son. Gradually he began to venture abroad – to France, to Spain, to Algeria and to the West Indies. In 1927 he paid his first visit south of the Equator for almost twenty years. Accompanied by his wife, he chose to go to Brazil, which clearly held a place in his imagination, as he had written in *Just So Stories*: 'I'd love to roll to Rio, some day before I'm old.' His articles on this journey were published in the *Morning Post* later that year, and collected in his book *Brazilian Sketches*.

BRAZILIAN SKETCHES

The Journey Out

A TRIP SOUTH

ONCE IN A CHILD'S dream, I wandered into a Fifth Quarter of the world, and found everything different from all previous knowledge; as only children or old folk desire it to be. Now, the dream has come true.

The South American boats are a world to themselves, more intimate and specialised than any other. Inquiries begin to be

answered in Portuguese or Spanish, while we lie at Southampton docks; the ship's notices stand in both tongues; and the passengers do not in the least concern themselves with anything or anybody, or any motive or policy that, till then, one had held to be important. Before our steamer began to shift the sun, all known centres of gravity had shifted, and were spinning on new bearings.
[. . .]

THE CLERKS OF 'PERNAM'

Then, one early morn, our ship stopped, and by consequence all the little draughts and breezes that run up and down her stopped too; and heat – the genuine heat of lands that have not 'weather' – beat friendlily on the back. It was Pernambuco, opening another jewelled day, with boats alongside where men sold golden and pink mangoes, and green parrakeets, every patch and flash of colour definite as enamelwork; the whole backed by the concrete of new piers, oil-tanks and warehouses. Behind these, low coast with veritable palms and bananas, quite unchanged since last seen, and hints of villas on a wooded cape that ran out into the turquoise.

Overside, dim shapes of shovel-nosed sharks who are respectable harbour-scavengers and need not be fished for. And as one stared, there unrolled itself a length of well-known film – a shore-boat with a man in white kit that had been often washed. He came aboard and introduced himself to a very young man in quite new London 'whites,' with the creases still down the front of the trousers, who turned to his companions and bade them farewell. It was just a Pernambuco Bank taking over a new clerk. When the pair were gone – the young figure looking all ways at once – and I had finished estimating the number of shore-boats of different makes, in different ports, at that hour, with allowance for change of time, convoying just the same suit of whites – I asked a man, 'What do you think he'll make of it?'

'He'll like it no end, and he'll talk about his first commission at Pernam, as long as he lives. They all do. I know I did. It's a dear little place.' Which must be good news to some mother, the far side of the sea.

And further, this beach gave me this tale for the instruction of psychologists. Not long since, a couple of Bank clerks of Pernambuco went out (men take liberties with these waters) three miles in a Canadian canoe, which upset. After due consideration, the one who could swim best pushed off for the shore to get help. It took him hours and hours; but what he resented most, at the last despairing lap, was the sight of his lit club house on the shore, where he knew his friends were all drinking happily. However, he survived, gave the news, and a launch hurried out and rescued the other man after some sixteen hours soaking. He, the tale ended, was all right; but the swimmer went 'absolutely off' gin and bitters for weeks. He said they, somehow, reminded him of the taste of salt water.

Coastwise Traffic

There is a fascinating and old-established life behind the green of the shores – with adventure and fun today, and unbroken tradition from Elizabeth's time, and in the background, a world almost untouched. We had entered a stream of its society – people going up and down the coast on little excursions, all apparently rich, all pleasantly at ease, all well acquainted with each other, or each other's acquaintances. It snapped whatever last link there had been with the rest of the world. These places belonged to another Power, and had risen on foundations utterly alien to ours.

An old Portuguese fort beside some new harbour-works hinted as much. A Dutch cut on the sterns of the sailing barges added another hint (the Dutch and the Portuguese had it out together, here, a couple of centuries since), and the easy-moving, easy-spoken passengers filled in the rest. They were going, on their own concerns, to Bahia, 300 – or Rio, a thousand – or Buenos Aires, 2,000 odd – miles down the road. That boat yonder with the banded funnels was a Brazilian Lloyd. She would run 1,200 miles north, and then up the Amazon for another thousand or two. Letters for Europe could be posted at Pernambuco, because the Dutch or the Italian or the French mail would be up to-morrow to take them on. So learning, we brushed along the green, resounding empty coasts till a vast bay opened, and we lay off Bahia, where, again, everyone coming aboard knew everyone, and the impression of age and solidity deepened in the face of ancient churches and serene old houses.

One felt, without telling, that Bahia was the Mother City – the hearth of all that flaming energy when Brazil was being born. Here, too, the Church had ruled, very completely, and here had come the slaves in their thousands, unaware that their children should be citizens of a Republic where the Colour question is not. Here you find the dishes and meats of the old regime – wonderful confections that derive from 'palm-oil chop' at its highest; the fruits and the fruit-juice drinks; the rampant colours, greens, reds, and yellows, as of a negress's head-dress; the glare and blaze that takes possession, but does not hurt; and the orderly alternation of the land and sea breezes. Everything that really civilised men can need; and, just because of these advantages, they prefer to talk about their docks and wharves, which, after all, come by nature and public loans to any decent seaboard town.

So we went on past a certain Cape where the air and water are always chilly for a few hours, while a Brazilian told me tales of the old time explorers and Captains and the Priests who came after them, in the years when fiery Portugal was raking half the world into her lap. They had as little fear, reason, or what is called common-sense, as any of our sea-workers of the same date, otherwise they would have left the proposition alone. For, he pointed out, from Bahia south to Rio runs a ridge of mountain some two or three thousand feet high within a few miles of the coast, and to get anywhere at all they had first to deal with the tribes in the low ground, and then to work themselves up to the ledge that gives on to the real country. 'You'll see it better when you are at Rio or Santos,' said he. 'That ledge has held us back fifty years. In the old days, one rode it on mule-back – as my father did. Everything came down in packages – coffee and all. That was why we had to have slaves. People don't keep slaves for fun. It's a question of transport. Nothing kills slavery but roads.'

And while he was explaining, the heat, past Cape Frio, sucked in again, the mountains lifted themselves more loftily and fantastically into hammer-heads and tusks of rock, velveted, up to any slope short of vertical, with matted, solid fighting green forest-growth, and there was a general stir and possessiveness along the decks. Most of our Southampton passengers were almost home again.

[First published in the *Morning Post*, 29 November to 20 December 1927 and then collected in a book published in New York by Doubleday, 1940.]

✠ ✠ ✠

The postwar years were another prolific period for Kipling's writing about the sea, a distillation of his life's work. His *Epitaphs of the War* in 1919 included several with a nautical theme. He also wrote some of his most interesting sailing stories, such as 'The Manner of Men'. Other works included poems like 'The King and the Sea', written to celebrate King George V's Silver Jubilee in 1935, and speeches at events which celebrated seamanship of one kind or another. In 1927 he was, to his great delight, made an honorary Master Mariner, attached to Trinity House. He also enjoyed the friendship of two leading businessmen, Sir Donald Currie and Sir Percy Bates, who were the heads of the Union Castle and of the Cunard Lines, both of whom became his correspondents. His letters to Bates about the naming of the *Queen Mary* are included below.

EPITAPHS OF THE WAR

A Drifter Off Tarentum

HE FROM THE WIND-BITTEN north with ship and companions descended.
Searching for eggs of death spawned by invisible hulls.
Many he found and drew forth. Of a sudden the fishery ended
In flame and a clamorous breath not new to the eye-pecking gulls.

Destroyers in Collision

For Fog and Fate no charm is found
To lighten or amend.
I, hurrying to my bride, was drowned –
Cut down by my best friend.

Convoy Escort

I was a shepherd to fools
Causelessly bold or afraid.
They would not abide by my rules.
Yet they escaped. For I stayed.

[First published in *The Years Between* (London: Methuen, 1919).]

✠ ✠ ✠

THE MANNER OF MEN

'If after the manner of men I have fought with beasts.'
– I COR. XV. 32.

HER CINNABAR-TINTED TOPSAIL, NICKING the hot blue horizon, showed she was a Spanish wheat-boat hours before she reached Marseilles mole. There, her mainsail brailed itself, a spritsail broke out forward, and a handy driver aft; and she threaded her way through the shipping to her berth at the quay as quietly as a veiled woman slips through a bazaar.

The blare of her horns told her name to the port. An elderly hook-nosed Inspector came aboard to see if her cargo had suffered in the run from the South, and the senior ship-cat purred round her captain's legs as the after-hatch was opened.

'If the rest is like this –' the Inspector sniffed – 'you had better run out again to the mole and dump it.'

'That's nothing,' the captain replied. 'All Spanish wheat heats a little. They reap it very dry.'

"Pity you don't keep it so, then. What would you call that – crop or pasture?'

The Inspector pointed downwards. The grain was in bulk, and deck-leakage, combined with warm weather, had sprouted it here and there in sickly green films.

'So much the better,' said the captain brazenly. 'That makes it waterproof. Pare off the top two inches, and the rest is as sweet as a nut.'

'I told that lie, too, when I was your age. And how does she happen to be loaded?'

The young Spaniard flushed, but kept his temper.

'She happens to be ballasted, under my eye, on lead-pigs and bagged copper-ores.'

'I don't know that they much care for verdigris in their dole-bread at Rome. But – you were saying?'

'I was trying to tell you that the bins happen to be grain-tight, two-inch chestnut, floored and sided with hides.'

'Meaning dressed African leathers on your private account?'

'What has that got to do with you? We discharge at Port of Rome, not here.'

'So your papers show. And what might you have stowed in the wings of her?'

'Oh, apes! Circumcised apes – just like you!'

'Young monkey! Well, if you are not above taking an old ape's advice, next time you happen to top off with wool and screw in more bales than are good for her, get your ship undergirt before you sail. I know it doesn't look smart coming into Port of Rome, but it'll save your decks from lifting worse than they are.'

There was no denying that the planking and waterways round the after-hatch had lifted a little. The captain lost his temper.

'I know your breed!' he stormed. 'You promenade the quays all summer at Caesar's expense, jamming your Jew-bow into everybody's business; and when the norther blows, you squat over your brazier and let us skippers hang in the wind for a week!'

'You have it! Just that sort of a man am I now,' the other answered. 'That'll do, the quarter-hatch!'

As he lifted his hand the falling sleeve showed the broad gold armlet with the triple vertical gouges which is only worn by master mariners who have used all three seas – Middle, Western, and Eastern.

'Gods!' the captain saluted. 'I thought you were—'

'A Jew, of course. Haven't you used Eastern ports long enough to know a Red Sidonian when you see one?'

'Mine the fault – yours be the pardon, my father!' said the Spaniard impetuously. 'Her topsides are a trifle strained. There was a three days' blow coming up. I meant to have had her undergirt off the Islands, but hawsers slow a ship so – and one hates to spoil a good run.'

'To whom do you say it?' The Inspector looked the young man over between horny sun and salt creased eyelids like a brooding pelican. 'But if you care to get up your girt-hawsers tomorrow, I can find men to put 'em overside. It's no work for open sea. Now! Main-hatch, there! . . . I thought so. She'll need another girt abaft the foremast.' He motioned to one of his staff, who hurried up the quay to where the port Guard-boat basked at her mooring-ring. She was a stoutly-built, single-banker, eleven a side, with a short punching ram; her duty being to stop riots in harbour and piracy along the coast.

'Who commands her?' the captain asked.

'An old shipmate of mine, Sulinus – a River man. We'll get his opinion.'

In the Mediterranean (Nile keeping always her name) there is but one river – that shifty-mouthed Danube, where she works through her deltas into the Black Sea. Up went the young man's eyebrows.

'Is he any kin to a Sulinor of Tomi, who used to be in the flesh-traffic – and a Free Trader? My uncle has told me of him. He calls him Mango.'

'That man. He was my second in the wheat-trade my last five voyages, after the Euxine grew too hot to hold him. But he's in the Fleet now . . . You know your ship best. Where do you think the after-girts ought to come?'

The captain was explaining, when a huge dishfaced Dacian, in short naval cuirass, rolled up the gangplank, carefully saluting the bust of Caesar on the poop, and asked the captain's name.

'Baeticus, for choice,' was the answer.

They all laughed, for the sea, which Rome mans with foreigners, washes out many shore-names.

'My trouble is this,' Baeticus began, and they went into com-mittee, which lasted a full hour. At the end, he led them to the poop, where an awning had been stretched, and wines set out with fruits and sweet shore water.

They drank to the Gods of the Sea, Trade, and Good Fortune, spilling those small cups overside, and then settled at ease.

'Girting's an all-day job, if it's done properly,' said the Inspector. 'Can you spare a real working-party by dawn tomorrow, Mango?'

'But surely – for you, Red.'

'I'm thinking of the wheat,' said Quabil curtly. He did not like nicknames so early.

'Full meals and drinks,' the Spanish captain put in.

'Good! Don't return 'em too full. By the way'– Sulinor lifted a level cup – 'where do you get this liquor, Spaniard?'

'From our Islands (the Balearics). Is it to your taste?'

'It is.' The big man unclasped his gorget in solemn preparation.

Their talk ran professionally, for though each end of the Medi-terranean scoffs at the other, both unite to mock landward, wooden-headed Rome and her stiff-jointed officials.

Sulinor told a tale of taking the Prefect of the Port, on a breezy day, to Forum Julii, to see a lady, and of his lamentable condition when landed.

'Yes,' Quabil sneered. 'Rome's mistress of the world – as far as the foreshore.'

'If Caesar ever came on patrol with me,' said Sulinor, 'he might understand there was such a thing as the Fleet.'

'Then he'd officer it with well-born young Romans,' said Quabil. 'Be grateful you are left alone. You are the last man in the world to want to see Caesar.'

'Except one,' said Sulinor, and he and Quabil laughed.

'What's the joke?' the Spaniard asked. Sulinor explained.

'We had a passenger, our last trip together, who wanted to see Caesar. It cost us our ship and freight. That's all.'

'Was he a warlock – a wind-raiser?'

'Only a Jew philosopher. But he had to see Caesar. He said he had; and he piled up the *Eirene* on his way.'

'Be fair,' said Quabil. 'I don't like the Jews – they lie too close to my own hold – but it was Caesar lost me my ship.' He turned to Baeticus. 'There was a proclamation, our end of the world, two seasons back, that Caesar wished the Eastern wheat-boats to run through the winter, and he'd guarantee all loss. Did you get it, youngster?'

'No. Our stuff is all in by September. I wager Caesar never paid you! How late did you start?'

'I left Alexandria across the bows of the Equinox – well down in the pickle, with Egyptian wheat – half pigeon's dung – and the usual load of Greek sutlers and their women. The second day out the sou'-wester caught me. I made across it north for the Lycian coast, and slipped into Myra till the wind should let me get back into the regular grain-track again.'

Sailor-fashion, Quabil began to illustrate his voyage with date and olive stones from the table.

'The wind went into the north, as I knew it would, and I got under way. You remember, Mango? My anchors were apeak when a Lycian patrol threshed in with Rome's order to us to wait on a Sidon packet with prisoners and officers. Mother of Carthage, I cursed him!'

"Shouldn't swear at Rome's Fleet. 'Weatherly craft, those Lycian racers! Fast, too. I've been hunted by them! 'Never thought I'd command one,' said Sulinor, half aloud.

'And now I'm coming to the leak in my decks, young man,' Quabil eyed Baeticus sternly. 'Our slant north had strained her, and

I should have undergirt her at Myra. Gods know why I didn't! I set up the chain-staples in the cable-tier for the prisoners. I even had the girt-hawsers on deck – which saved time later; but the thing I should have done, that I did not.'

'Luck of the Gods!' Sulinor laughed. 'It was because our little philosopher wanted to see Caesar in his own way at our expense.'

'Why did he want to see him?' said Baeticus.

'As far as I ever made out from him and the centurion, he wanted to argue with Caesar – about philosophy.'

'He was a prisoner, then?'

'A political suspect – with a Jew's taste for going to law,' Quabil interrupted. 'No orders for irons. Oh, a little shrimp of a man, but – but he seemed to take it for granted that he led everywhere. He messed with us.'

'And he was worth talking to, Red,' said Sulinor.

'You thought so; but he had the woman's trick of taking the tone and colour of whoever he talked to. Now – as I was saying . . .'

There followed another illustrated lecture on the difficulties that beset them after leaving Myra. There was always too much west in the autumn winds, and the *Eirene* tacked against it as far as Cnidus. Then there came a northerly slant, on which she ran through the Aegean Islands, for the tail of Crete; rounded that, and began tacking up the south coast.

'Just darning the water again, as we had done from Myra to Cnidus,' said Quabil ruefully. 'I daren't stand out. There was the bone-yard of all the Gulf of Africa under my lee. But at last we worked into Fairhaven – by that cork yonder. Late as it was, I should have taken her on, but I had to call a ship-council as to lying up for the winter. That Rhodian law may have suited open boats and cock-crow coasters, but it's childish for ocean-traffic.'

'I never allow it in any command of mine,' Baeticus spoke quietly. 'The cowards give the order, and the captain bears the blame.'

Quabil looked at him keenly. Sulinor took advantage of the pause.

'We were in harbour, you see. So our Greeks tumbled out and voted to stay where we were. It was my business to show them that the place was open to many winds, and that if it came on to blow we should drive ashore.'

'Then I,' broke in Quabil, with a large and formidable smile, 'advised pushing on to Phenike, round the cape, only forty miles across the bay. My mind was that, if I could get her undergirt there, I might later – er – coax them out again on a fair wind, and hit Sicily. But the undergirting came first. She was beginning to talk too much – like me now.'

Sulinor chafed a wrist with his hand.

'She was a hard-mouthed old water-bruiser in any sea,' he murmured.

'She could lie within six points of any wind,' Quabil retorted, and hurried on. 'What made Paul vote with those Greeks? He said we'd be sorry if we left harbour.'

'Every passenger says that, if a bucketful comes aboard,' Baeticus observed.

Sulinor refilled his cup, and looked at them over the brim, under brows as candid as a child's, ere he set it down.

'Not Paul. He did not know fear. He gave me a dose of my own medicine once. It was a morning watch coming down through the Islands. We had been talking about the cut of our topsail – he was right – it held too much lee wind – and then he went to wash before he prayed. I said to him: "You seem to have both ends and the bight of most things coiled down in your little head, Paul. If it's a fair question, what is your trade ashore?" And he said: "I've been a man-hunter – Gods forgive me; and now that I think The God has forgiven me, I am man-hunting again." Then he pulled his shirt over his head, and I saw his back. Did you ever see his back, Quabil?'

'I expect I did – that last morning, when we all stripped; but I don't remember.'

'I shan't forget it! There was good, sound lictor's work and criss-cross Jew scourgings like gratings; and a stab or two; and, besides those, old dry bites – when they get good hold and rugg you. That showed he must have dealt with the Beasts. So, whatever he'd done, he'd paid for. I was just wondering what he had done, when he said: "No; not your sort of man-hunting." "It's your own affair," I said: "but I shouldn't care to see Caesar with a back like that. I should hear the Beasts asking for me." "I may that, too, some day," he said, and began sluicing himself, and – then – What's brought the girls out so early? Oh, I remember!'

There was music up the quay, and a wreathed shore-boat put forth full of Arlesian women. A long-snouted three-banker was hauling from a slip till her trumpets warned the benches to take hold. As they gave way, the hrmph-hrmph of the oars in the oar-ports reminded Sulinor, he said, of an elephant choosing his man in the Circus.

'She has been here re-masting. They've no good rough-tree at Forum Julii,' Quabil explained to Baeticus. 'The girls are singing her out.'

The shallop ranged alongside her, and the banks held water, while a girl's voice came across the clock-calm harbour-face,

> 'Ah, would swift ships had never been about the seas to rove!
> For then these eyes had never seen nor ever wept their love.
> Over the ocean-rim he came – beyond that verge he passed.
> And I who never knew his name must mourn him to the last!'

'And you'd think they meant it,' said Baeticus, half to himself.

'That's a pretty stick,' was Quabil's comment as the man-of-war opened the island athwart the harbour. 'But she's overmasted by ten foot. A trireme's only a bird-cage.'

"Luck of the Gods I'm not singing in one now,' Sulinor muttered. They heard the yelp of a bank being speeded up to the short sea-stroke.

'I wish there was some way to save mainmasts from racking.' Baeticus looked up at his own, bangled with copper wire.

'The more reason to undergirt, my son,' said Quabil. 'I was going to undergirt that morning at Fairhaven. You remember, Sulinor? I'd given orders to overhaul the hawsers the night before. My fault! Never say "To-morrow." The Gods hear you. And then the wind came out of the south, mild as milk. All we had to do was to slip round the headland to Phenike – and be safe.'

Baeticus made some small motion, which Quabil noticed, for he stopped.

'My father,' the young man spread apologetic palms, 'is not that lying wind the indraught of Mount Ida? It comes up with the sun, but later—'

'You need not tell me! We rounded the cape, our decks like a fair (it was only half a day's sail), and then, out of Ida's bosom the full north-easter stamped on us! Run? What else? I needed a lee to clean up in. Clauda was a few miles down wind; but whether the old lady would bear up when she got there, I was not so sure.'

'She did.' Sulinor rubbed his wrists again. 'We were towing our longboat half-full. I steered somewhat that day.'

'What sail were you showing?' Baeticus demanded.

'Nothing – and twice too much at that. But she came round when Sulinor asked her, and we kept her jogging in the lee of the island. I said, didn't I, that my girt-hawsers were on deck?'

Baeticus nodded. Quabil plunged into his campaign at long and large, telling every shift and device he had employed. 'It was scanting daylight,' he wound up, 'but I daren't slur the job. Then we streamed our boat alongside, baled her, sweated her up, and secured. You ought to have seen our decks!'

''Panic?' said Baeticus.

'A little. But the whips were out early. The centurion – Julius – lent us his soldiers.'

'How did your prisoners behave?' the young man went on.

Sulinor answered him. 'Even when a man is being shipped to the Beasts, he does not like drowning in irons. They tried to rive the chain-staples out of her timbers.'

'I got the main-yard on deck'– this was Quabil. 'That eased her a little. They stopped yelling after a while, didn't they?'

'They did,' Sulinor replied. 'Paul went down and told them there was no danger. And they believed him! Those scoundrels believed him! He asked me for the keys of the leg-bars to make them easier. "I've been through this sort of thing before," he said, "but they are new to it down below. Give me the keys." I told him there was no order for him to have any keys; and I recommended him to line his hold for a week in advance, because we were in the hands of the Gods. "And when are we ever out of them?" he asked. He looked at me like an old gull lounging just astern of one's taffrail in a full gale. You know that eye, Spaniard?'

'Well do I!'

'By that time'– Quabil took the story again – 'we had drifted out of the lee of Clauda, and our one hope was to run for it and pray we weren't pooped. None the less, I could have made Sicily with luck. As a gale I have known worse, but the wind never shifted a point, d'ye see? We were flogged along like a tired ox.'

'Any sights?' Baeticus asked.

'For ten days not a blink.'

'Nearer two weeks,' Sulinor corrected. 'We cleared the decks of everything except our groundtackle, and put six hands at the tillers. She seemed to answer her helm – sometimes. Well, it kept me warm for one.'

'How did your philosopher take it?'

'Like the gull I spoke of. He was there, but outside it all. You never got on with him, Quabil?'

'Confessed! I came to be afraid at last. It was not my office to show fear, but I was. He was fearless, although I knew that he knew the peril as well as I. When he saw that trying to – er – cheer me made me angry, he dropped it. 'Like a woman, again. You saw more of him, Mango?'

'Much. When I was at the rudders he would hop up to the steerage, with the lower-deck ladders lifting and lunging a foot at a time, and the timbers groaning like men beneath the Beasts. We used to talk, hanging on till the roll jerked us into the scuppers. Then we'd begin again. What about? Oh! Kings and Cities and Gods and Caesar. He was sure he'd see Caesar. I told him I had noticed that people who worried Those Up Above' – Sulinor jerked his thumb towards the awning – 'were mostly sent for in a hurry.'

'Hadn't you wit to see he never wanted you for yourself, but to get something out of you?' Quabil snapped.

'Most Jews are like that – and all Sidonians!' Sulinor grinned. 'But what could he have hoped to get from anyone? We were doomed men all. You said it, Red.'

'Only when I was at my emptiest. Otherwise I knew that with any luck I could have fetched Sicily! But I broke – we broke. Yes, we got ready – you too – for the Wet Prayer.'

'How does that run with you?' Baeticus asked, for all men are curious concerning the bride-bed of Death.

'With us of the River,' Sulinor volunteered, 'we say: "I sleep; presently I row again."'

'Ah! At our end of the world we cry: "Gods, judge me not as a God, but a man whom the Ocean has broken."' Baeticus looked at Quabil, who answered, raising his cup: 'We Sidonians say, "Mother of Carthage, I return my oar!" But it all comes to the one in the end.' He wiped his beard, which gave Sulinor his chance to cut in.

'Yes, we were on the edge of the Prayer when – do you remember, Quabil? – he clawed his way up the ladders and said: "No need to call on what isn't there. My God sends me sure word that I shall see Caesar. And he has pledged me all your lives to boot. Listen! No man will be lost." And Quabil said: "But what about my ship?"' Sulinor grinned again.

'That's true. I had forgotten the cursed passengers,' Quabil confirmed. 'But he spoke as though my *Eirene* were a fig-basket. "Oh, she's bound to go ashore, somewhere," he said, "but not a life will be lost. Take this from me, the Servant of the One God." Mad! Mad as a magician on market-day!'

'No,' said Sulinor. 'Madmen see smooth harbours and full meals. I have had to – soothe that sort.'

'After all,' said Quabil, 'he was only saying what had been in my head for a long time. I had no way to judge our drift, but we likely might hit something somewhere. Then he went away to spread his cook-house yarn among the crew. It did no harm, or I should have stopped him.'

Sulinor coughed, and drawled:

'I don't see anyone stopping Paul from what he fancied he ought to do. But it was curious that, on the change of watch, I—'

'No – I!' said Quabil.

'Make it so, then, Red. Between us, at any rate, we felt that the sea had changed. There was a trip and a kick to her dance. You know, Spaniard. And then – I will say that, for a man half-dead, Quabil here did well.'

'I'm a bosun-captain, and not ashamed of it. I went to get a cast of the lead. (Black dark and raining marlinspikes!) The first cast warned me, and I told Sulinor to clear all aft for anchoring by the stern. The next – shoaling like a slip-way – sent me back with all hands, and we dropped both bowers and spare and the stream.'

'He'd have taken the kedge as well, but I stopped him,' said Sulinor.

'I had to stop her! They nearly jerked her stern out, but they held. And everywhere I could peer or hear were breakers, or the noise of tall seas against cliffs. We were trapped! But our people had been starved, soaked, and half-stunned for ten days, and now they were close to a beach. That was enough! They must land on the instant; and was I going to let them drown within reach of safety? Was there panic? I spoke to Julius, and his soldiers (give Rome her due!) schooled them till I could hear my orders again. But on the kiss-of-dawn some of the crew said that Sulinor had told them to lay out the kedge in the long-boat.'

'I let 'em swing her out,' Sulinor confessed.

'I wanted 'em for warnings. But Paul told me his God had promised their lives to him along with ours, and any private sacrifice would spoil the luck. So, as soon as she touched water, I cut the rope before a man could get in. She was ashore – stove – in ten minutes.'

'Could you make out where you were by then?' Baeticus asked Quabil.

'As soon as I saw the people on the beach – yes. They are my sort – a little removed. Phoenicians by blood. It was Malta – one day's run from Syracuse, where I would have been safe! Yes, Malta and my wheat gruel. Good port-of-discharge, eh?'

They smiled, for Melita may mean 'mash' as well as 'Malta.'

'It puddled the sea all round us, while I was trying to get my bearings. But my lids were salt-gummed, and I hiccoughed like a drunkard.'

'And drunk you most gloriously were, Red, half an hour later!'

'Praise the Gods – and for once your pet Paul! That little man came to me on the fore-bitts, puffed like a pigeon, and pulled out a breastful of bread, and salt fish, and the wine – the good new wine. "Eat," he said, "and make all your people eat, too. Nothing will come to them except another wetting. They won't notice that, after they're full. Don't worry about your work either," he said. "You can't go wrong today. You are promised to me." And then he went off to Sulinor.'

'He did. He came to me with bread and wine and bacon – good they were! But first he said words over them, and then rubbed his hands with his wet sleeves. I asked him if he were a magician. "Gods forbid!" he said. "I am so poor a soul that I flinch from touching dead pig." As a Jew, he wouldn't like pork, naturally. Was that before or after our people broke into the store-room, Red?'

'Had I time to wait on them?' Quabil snorted. 'I know they gutted my stores full-hand, and a double blessing of wine atop. But we all took that – deep. Now this is how we lay.' Quabil smeared a ragged loop on the table with a wine-wet finger. 'Reefs – see, my son – and overfalls to leeward here; something that loomed like a point of land on our right there; and, ahead, the blind gut of a bay with a Cyclops surf hammering it. How we had got in was a miracle. Beaching was our only chance, and meantime she was settling like a tired camel. Every foot I could lighten her meant that she'd take ground closer in at the last. I told Julius. He understood. "I'll keep order," he said. "Get the passengers to shift the wheat as long as you judge it's safe."'

'Did those Alexandrian achators really work?' said Baeticus.

'I've never seen cargo discharged quicker. It was time. The wind was taking off in gusts, and the rain was putting down the swells. I made out a patch of beach that looked less like death than the rest of the arena, and I decided to drive in on a gust under the spitfire-sprit – and, if she answered her helm before she died on us, to humour her a shade to starboard, where the water looked better. I stayed the foremast; set the spritsail fore and aft, as though we were boarding; told Sulinor to have the rudders down directly he cut the cables; waited till a gust came; squared away the sprit, and drove.'

Sulinor carried on promptly:–

'I had two hands with axes on each cable, and one on each rudder-lift; and, believe me, when Quabil's pipe went, both blades were down and turned before the cable-ends had fizzed under! She jumped like a stung cow! She drove. She sheared. I think the swell lifted her, and overran. She came down, and struck aft. Her stern broke off under my toes, and all the guts of her at that end slid out like a man's paunched by a lion. I jumped forward, and told Quabil there was nothing but small kindlings abaft the quarter-hatch, and he shouted: "Never mind! Look how beautifully I've laid her!"'

'I had. What I took for a point of land to starboard, y'see, turned out to be almost a bridge-islet, with a swell of sea 'twixt it and the main. And that meeting-swill, d'you see, surging in as she drove, gave her four or five foot more to cushion on. I'd hit the exact instant.'

'Luck of the Gods, I think! Then we began to bustle our people over the bows before she went to pieces. You'll admit Paul was a help there, Red?'

'I dare say he herded the old judies well enough; but he should have lined up with his own gang.'

'He did that, too,' said Sulinor. 'Some fool of an under-officer had discovered that prisoners must be killed if they look like escaping; and he chose that time and place to put it to Julius – sword drawn. Think of hunting a hundred prisoners to death on those decks! It would have been worse than the Beasts!'

'But Julius saw – Julius saw it,' Quabil spoke testily. 'I heard him tell the man not to be a fool. They couldn't escape further than the beach.'

'And how did your philosopher take that?' said Baeticus.

'As usual,' said Sulinor. 'But, you see, we two had dipped our hands in the same dish for weeks; and, on the River, that makes an obligation between man and man.'

'In my country also,' said Baeticus, rather stiffly.

'So I cleared my dirk – in case I had to argue. Iron always draws iron with me. But he said, "Put it back. They are a little scared." I said, "Aren't you?" "What?" he said; "of being killed, you mean? No. Nothing can touch me till I've seen Caesar." Then he carried on steadying the ironed men (some were slavering mad) till it was time to unshackle them by fives, and give 'em their chance. The natives made a chain through the surf, and snatched them out breast-high.'

'Not a life lost! 'Like stepping off a jetty,' Quabil proclaimed.

'Not quite. But he had promised no one should drown.'

'How could they – the way I had laid her – gust and swell and swill together?'

'And was there any salvage?'

'Neither stick nor string, my son. We had time to look, too. We stayed on the island till the first spring ship sailed for Port of Rome. They hadn't finished Ostia breakwater that year.'

'And, of course, Caesar paid you for your ship?'

'I made no claim. I saw it would be hopeless; and Julius, who knew Rome, was against any appeal to the authorities. He said that was the mistake Paul was making. And, I suppose, because I did not trouble them, and knew a little about the sea, they offered me the Port Inspectorship here. There's no money in it – if I were a poor man. Marseilles will never be a port again. Narbo has ruined her for good.'

'But Marseilles is far from under-Lebanon,' Baeticus suggested.

'The further the better. I lost my boy three years ago in Foul Bay, off Berenice, with the Eastern Fleet. He was rather like you about the eyes, too. You and your circumcised apes!'

'But – honoured one! My master! Admiral! – Father mine – how could I have guessed?'

The young man leaned forward to the other's knee in act to kiss it. Quabil made as though to cuff him, but his hand came to rest lightly on the bowed head.

'Nah! Sit, lad! Sit back. It's just the thing the Boy would have said himself. You didn't hear it, Sulinor?'

'I guessed it had something to do with the likeness as soon as I set eyes on him. You don't so often go out of your way to help lame ducks.'

'You can see for yourself she needs undergirting, Mango!'

'So did that Tyrian tub last month. And you told her she might bear up for Narbo or bilge for all of you! But he shall have his working-party tomorrow, Red.'

Baeticus renewed his thanks. The River man cut him short.

'Luck of the Gods,' he said. 'Five – four – years ago I might have been waiting for you anywhere in the Long Puddle with fifty River men – and no moon.'

Baeticus lifted a moist eye to the slip-hooks on his yardarm, that could hoist and drop weights at a sign.

'You might have had a pig or two of ballast through your benches coming alongside,' he said dreamily.

'And where would my overhead-nettings have been?' the other chuckled.

'Blazing – at fifty yards. What are firearrows for?'

'To fizzle and stink on my wet sea-weed blindages. Try again.'

They were shooting their fingers at each other, like the little boys gambling for olive-stones on the quay beside them.

'Go on – go on, my son! Don't let that pirate board,' cried Quabil.

Baeticus twirled his right hand very loosely at the wrist.

'In that case,' he countered, 'I should have fallen back on my foster-kin – my father's island horsemen.'

Sulinor threw up an open palm.

'Take the nuts,' he said. 'Tell me, is it true that those infernal Balearic slingers of yours can turn a bull by hitting him on the horns?'

'On either horn you choose. My father farms near New Carthage. They come over to us for the summer to work. There are ten in my crew now.'

Sulinor hiccoughed and folded his hands magisterially over his stomach.

'Quite proper. Piracy must be put down! Rome says so. I do so,' said he.

'I see,' the younger man smiled. 'But tell me, why did you leave the slave – the Euxine trade, O Strategos?'

'That sea is too like a wine-skin. 'Only one neck. It made mine ache. So I went into the Egyptian run with Quabil here.'

'But why take service in the Fleet? Surely the Wheat pays better?'

'I intended to. But I had dysentery at Malta that winter, and Paul looked after me.'

'Too much muttering and laying-on of hands for me,' said Quabil; himself muttering about some Thessalian jugglery with a snake on the island.

'You weren't sick, Quabil. When I was getting better, and Paul was washing me off once, he asked if my citizenship were in order. He was a citizen himself. Well, it was and it was not. As second of a wheat-ship I was ex officio Roman citizen – for signing bills and so forth. But on the beach, my ship perished, he said I reverted to my original shtay – status – of an extra-provinshal Dacian by a Sich – Sish – Scythian – I think she was – mother. Awkward – what? All the Middle Sea echoes like a public bath if a man is wanted.'

Sulinor reached out again and filled. The wine had touched his huge bulk at last.

'But, as I was saying, once in the Fleet nowadays one is a Roman with authority – no waiting twenty years for your papers. And Paul said to me: 'Serve Caesar. You are not canvas I can cut to advantage at present. But if you serve Caesar you will be obeying at least some sort of law.' He talked as though I were a barbarian. Weak as I was, I could have snapped his back with my bare hands. I told him so. 'I don't doubt it,' he said. 'But that is neither here nor there. If you take refuge under Caesar at sea, you may have time to think. Then I may meet you again, and we can go on with our talks. But that is as The God wills. What concerns you now is that, by taking service, you will be free from the fear that has ridden you all your life.'

'Was he right?' asked Baeticus after a silence.

'He was. I had never spoken to him of it, but he knew it. He knew! Fire – sword – the sea – torture even – one does not think of them too often. But not the Beasts! Aie! Not the Beasts! I fought two dog-wolves for the life on a sand-bar when I was a youngster. Look!'

Sulinor showed his neck and chest.

'They set the sheep-dogs on Paul at some place or other once – because of his philosophy. And he was going to see Caesar – going to see Caesar! And he – he had washed me clean after dysentery!'

'Mother of Carthage, you never told me that!' said Quabil.

'Nor should I now, had the wine been weaker.'

[First published in the *London Magazine* in September 1930, and collected
in *Limits and Renewals* (London: Macmillan, 1932).]

✠ ✠ ✠

LETTERS

To Sir Percy Bates, 15 August 1929
[Bateman's] 15 Aug 29

Dear Bates,

Ever so many thanks for all the suggestions. Smith I have and I
am sending at once for Lyndsay. I shall have to be quite sure about
pumps before I commit myself. Didn't think they were used at that
time of the world?

As to lading, I am cutting out as much as I can of direct reference
to St Paul's ship from Mysia. The tale is told by her Captain, after he
had lost his job and had got a billet as Port Inspector at Marseilles
where he inspects cargoes of wheat from Spain – Malaga way. He
tells his tale to the skipper of a Spanish boat (108' between perps,
35' beam; and, say 16' hold. What would that tonnage be?) She
is ballasted on Spanish pigs stitched into hide, and concentrated
copper ores, bagged in hide-bags. (Hides can be sold full value at
Port of Rome, remember.) The grain is in bulk in grain-tight bins of
inch and a half Spanish chestnut and live oak planking (all saleable
at Ostia) and each of the two holds is practically bulkheaded as the
planking is spiked against the big X-pieces that stiffen her laterally.
They have topped off the loose grain with several layers of bagged
wheat – hides again. Now comes the question of dunnage at the
sides. What do you think? The bins would be clear of her sides
by more than usual allowance, to permit of the wheat swelling.
Would the bins be like ore-bins? And would it be good stevedoring
to put say horns and horn tips for side-stuff. The point of all this
fuss, is to have a row between the Port Inspector and the skipper
on account of alleged 'dunnage' (Captain's private venture) which
the Inspector insists ought to come in as low freight. From that
argument the tale of the loss of the *Eirene* (St Paul's ship) begins.
The only reference to her cargo is one about 'filthy Egyptian wheat
– half mud and no wonder seeing how they pull it up by the roots

and where they thresh it'. All the interest appears to be thrown on the big competent Spanish skipper with his natural contempt for a man who has lost his ship. The ex-master is merely a worried and perturbed man who has run up against yet another new God on the seas.

Your notion of wheat in the ear as cargo is fascinating but I won't venture on it till I know a heap more. Clay amphorae are obviously impossible. Tell me what you can about bagged wheat (100lb bags) and hides. Spain produced both. I allow a four foot square bale-hole in each hold. One at the foot of the main mast and one in the eyes of her almost at the foot of the artimon. Also one aft. She is trimmed by the stern. Her hatches are small. She carries her proper compliment of cats and previous to loading has bean smoked out 'tween decks with raw cinnabar over lamps – to destroy the rats. Further information and advice will be thankfully received by

Yours ever,

R.K.

PS Cabins are knocked down as the passenger trade warrants. They'd be under the half-decks for the saloon and under the break of the foc'sle for deck passenger; but there they would be merely sparred off. Overhanging galleries as often as not fastened by rope. A good deal of the ship's working takes place in the galleries. The steering oars come up under the break of the poop.

To Sir Percy Bates, 5 December 1930

As to my new ship, with the proper stern, her name will be the *Magnalia* which being translated literally, means 'mighty works' – as see Cotton's Magnalia Christi. You would like to call her the *Imperia,* but as the Empire is now out of commission, that will not be any good.

She will not, as your Board will suggest, be called *Magnolia* by the foolish public because every Englishman knows something about magna meaning 'great' (and it comes before Charta) and it is a fine, full and sonorous title without any of the arrogance that caused the Gods to open up the *Titanic.* Also it can't be twisted into Yiddish, like the *Levi Nathan.* I will not travel on her because nothing this side Gehenna would make me go to New York, but

I will give her my blessing, and, if I live so long, I will try to come down to her launch. Incidentally, if you want to break new ground, put up a bronze memorial in the yard, when she's finished, to the men who died during her construction. They're doing it on some of the sections of the Hudson Bay Lines just now, and it pleases the men no end. You see, it's practically war-service.

Some of the Cunarders asked me down to a lunch I should have tremendously enjoyed at S'hampton but, naturally I haven't been able to get away at all since the wife went down. She is better now but – rheumatism is the devil at coming back.

All our love to you and yours,

Ever,

R.K.

Bateman's, Burwash, Sussex, July 29, 35

Dear Percy

'Got both your notes – typed and written. I see the point-of-view about Royal heads. Well, this leaves us a clear obverse for the relief of the Q.M. with an inscription (above it for choice) at which no one can kick. ME REGINA COMMISIT PELAGO. Then, below the relief, the year of Her Husband's reign in which the ship was launched. With that space to come and go on, the artist can pile up the bulk and the shouldering of the Q.M. as high as he pleases. (I take this opportunity of apologizing to the Company for my unjust aspersions on her funnels.) It will need the most delicate work to give, in a few twiddles, the impression, of the heated haze, rather than smoke, above the said funnels.

For the reverse of the medal, I think you will find maps scratchy in effect and they are too like travel-folders.

I suggest, however, that your man goes to the Director of the Naval Museum at Greenwich and digs out what old sea-medals we may have there. There may be some model that could be used. Otherwise, France is our mistress in medal-work and he could slip over to Paris and see what they have done.

But – seeing that the Medal is history – why not chuck all design on the reverse and have an exquisitely lettered, beautifully-spaced inscription, giving her tonnage, length, breadth, building-yard and speed? That will remain through the centuries. My own idea is that Baker or Lutyens know about as much about lettering as need be known. They have done a lot in that line on our War Grave memorials.

For enrichment (I was looking at an old medal only yesterday) the medal might be rimmed with the bound laurel-wreath – as I have tried to indicate in the two sketches sent herewith. They are done to half-crown scale which, I take it, are the dimensions of the ordinary medal as they will be sold.

I worked out the notion of the map and the Atlantic route and it made the backside of the medal look like a bust foot-ball.

I think that all this is going to be great fun. The attitude of the 'Palace' is distinctly 'cheek.' They may be many things but they aren't judges of English Art. We are not in the least likely to make the interiors of our Liners look like Belgian Whore-shops; but I don't expect you have a formula for putting that decently.

Ever

Ruddy

[The National Maritime Museum]

✠ ✠ ✠

THE KING AND THE SEA

(17th July 1935)

AFTER HIS REALMS AND States were moved
To bare their hearts to the King they loved,
Tendering themselves in homage and devotion,
The Tide Wave up the Channel spoke
To all those eager, exultant folk:–
'Hear now what Man was given you by the Ocean!

'There was no thought of Orb or Crown
When the single wooden chest went down
To the steering-flat, and the careless Gunroom haled him
To learn by ancient and bitter use,
How neither Favour nor Excuse,

Nor aught save his sheer self henceforth availed him

'There was no talk of birth or rank
By the slung hammock or scrubbed plank
In the steel-grated prisons where I cast him;
But niggard hours and a narrow space
For rest – and the naked light on his face –
While the ship's traffic flowed, unceasing, past him.

'Thus I schooled him to go and come –
To speak at the word – at a sign be dumb;
To stand to his task, not seeking others to aid him;
To share in honour what praise might fall
For the task accomplished, and – over all –
To swallow rebuke in silence. Thus I made him.

'I loosened every mood of the deep
On him, a child and sick for sleep,
Through the long watches that no time can measure,
When I drove him, deafened and choked and blind,
At the wave-tops cut and spun by the wind;
Lashing him, face and eyes, with my displeasure.

'I opened him all the guile of the seas –
Their sullen, swift-sprung treacheries,
To be fought, or forestalled, or dared, or dismissed with
    laughter.
I showed him Worth by Folly concealed,
And the flaw in the soul that a chance revealed
(Lessons remembered – to bear fruit thereafter).

'I dealt him Power beneath his hand,
For trial and proof, with his first Command –
Himself alone, and no man to gainsay him.
On him the End, the Means, and the Word,
And the harsher judgment if he erred,
And – outboard – Ocean waiting to betray him.

'Wherefore, when he came to be crowned,
Strength in Duty held him bound,

So that not Power misled nor ease ensnared him
Who had spared himself no more than his seas had spared
   him!'

- - -

After His Lieges, in all His Lands,
Had laid their hands between His hands,
And His ships thundered service and devotion,
The Tide Wave, ranging the Planet, spoke
On all Our foreshores as it broke:–
'Know now what Man I gave you – I, the Ocean!'

[First published in *The Times* and other papers on 17 July 1935 and
collected in *The Definitive Edition of Rudyard Kipling's Verse* (New York:
Doubleday, 1940).]